Lizards Hold the Sun

Dani Trujillo

Sin Verguenzas

Copyright © 2023 by Dani Trujillo

All rights reserved.

No portion of this book may be reproduced in any form without written permission from the publisher or author, except as permitted by U.S. copyright law. For permission requests, contact Sin Verguenzas LLC.

The story, all names, characters, and incidents portrayed in this production are fictitious. No identification with actual persons (living or deceased), places, buildings, and products is intended or should be inferred.

Book Cover by Marcus Trujillo

Illustrations by Dani Trujillo & Joe Tafolla

1st edition 2023

Also by Dani Trujillo
When Stars Have Teeth (2024)

Included On
Never Whistle at Night (9/2023)

Contents

	Chapter	1
1.	Chapter 1	3
2.	Chapter 2	15
3.	Chapter 3	25
4.	Chapter 4	45
5.	Chapter 5	53
6.	Chapter 6	69
7.	Chapter 7	77
8.	Chapter 8	91
9.	Chapter 9	101
10.	Chapter 10	109
11.	Chapter 11	131
12.	Chapter 12	139
13.	Chapter 13	147
14.	Chapter 14	159
15.	Chapter 15	179
16.	Chapter 16	189
17.	Chapter 17	203
18.	Chapter 18	215
19.	Chapter 19	221

20.	Chapter 20	231
21.	Chapter 21	249
22.	Spain	251
	EPILOGUE	253
	Acknowledgments	256
	When Stars Have Teeth	258
	About the Author	263

For all of us.

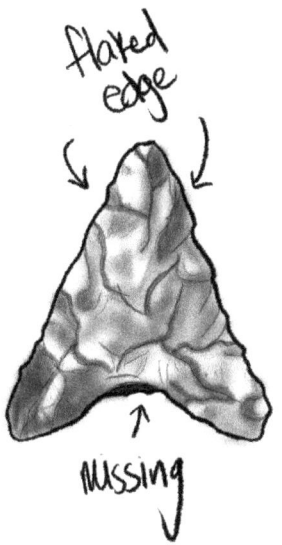

CHAPTER 1

Xiomara's nails tapped an unconscious rhythm into her thigh. How much farther could it be? It hadn't looked like this on the map. The trees were never-ending, and she hadn't seen the horizon in hours. White water sprayed against the side of the boat, the scent of salt curling around her nose with her loose hair. The group was silent, save for the swish of windbreakers brushing against each other, only three other passengers along for the ride. She said a prayer that the incoming summer would be warmer than this.

Xiomara clenched her hands around Anubis and his fuzzy sweater, the air bitingly cool as they slid through the water. Xiomara rescued Anubis when he wandered onto their dig site in Jalisco as a skinny puppy. He spent the first eight months of his life with her camping on that same site. Xiomara had brought him to work every day since.

Docking along a wide, wooden platform, Xiomara found her name written on a piece of cardboard between the hands of a tall blue-haired woman wearing a wide smile. She waved to the woman, dragging her suitcase across the rocky mud to the idling car. Anubis was strapped to a leash around Xiomara's hips, his nose sniffing everything he could reach. His mohawk stood completely upright from the salted wind, as if he had been electrocuted.

"Hi!" a voice squealed. "You're finally here." The woman wrapped their hands together, pulling them into her chest, then pressing them back into Xiomara's chest. Breath shared between them, and she opened the car door, saving them from the whipping cold wind.

"I'm Rosebud." Tucking her short blue curls behind her ear, Rosebud navigate them out of the dirt parking lot. "I'm who you've been emailing during this whole process." She scratched Anubis, fluffing his mohawk with her long nails.

"Oh!" Xiomara eased. The woman in the emails had been extremely kind and helpful. "I'm sorry I didn't recognize your name. I don't think I've slept since I left Mexico."

"No worries. I am sorry your cabin isn't ready yet. Sometimes the boys forget to lock the doors, and the bears rose a bit early this year." She rolled her eyes. "You're going to have a great time staying with my wife and me! She's a fantastic cook."

"That sounds amazing." Xiomara's stomach grumbled at the mention of a meal.

"Are you hungry now?"

Damn, was her stomach that loud?

"Let's get something at the café, and then I'll bring you to the house so you can settle in and get some rest." Rosebud told Xiomara how they were having an early spring, the air far warmer than typical this time of year.

"Is it always this humid?" Xiomara asked, taking a deep breath in the recycled air of the cab. Outside, the air was thick, as though she was underwater.

"Oh no." Rosebud laughed as they pulled onto a smooth dirt road framed by trees on both sides. "Our winters can be pretty dry."

"Does it snow a lot?" Xiomara leaned with the car as they went around a curve, the earth dropping straight to the sea below. Her fingers gripped the edge of her seat, looping through Anubis' leash to keep him close.

"Well, we usually only get a few snowfalls, but it can be up to a meter or more at a time." Rosebud shook her head. "It's beautiful, though… the trees covered in white, lakes frozen enough for skating, fish hungry enough to go for a lure."

"Can't wait." Xiomara grimaced. She hated the cold and had next to no experience with snow. She had been to New York City in the dead of winter once. That was the extent of her snow experience—piles of dirty, gray snow and icy crosswalks.

The trees were budding, colorful flowers peeking from their green shells. Noisy. It was noisy here. Birds sang to each other, and the air whistled while the sea ebbed at the shore. The casino rose out of the trees like an amethyst. A banner hung on the construction fence, *Welcome to Bunchberry Nation*. Their tribal seal was a petite yellow hummingbird, its wings spread wide as it soared the sky.

The car ambled over a narrow bridge, passing a weathered wooden building with the words *This Is Indian Land* spray-painted in red on the side.

"Town begins right about here." Rosebud quirked her chin forward, where the dirt road turned to asphalt. "Main Street is pretty much all we have."

The Trading Post. Good Morning Cafe. Gas N' Go. City Hall.

That was it. The entire main street. Xiomara could see the asphalt turn to dirt just past the buildings. There was nothing visible beyond that, save for trees and bushes. This place really was remote.

"This is City Hall, where we work." Rosebud bumped Xiomara with her elbow as though they had already developed an inside joke.

"Will I have my own cabin still?" Xiomara glanced at Anubis. He was a smaller, hairless dog, so he didn't irritate people's allergies. She hoped they wouldn't take up too much space and overstay their welcome before excavation began.

"You do...there was a slight bear situation." She grimaced. "It should be ready soon."

"Bear situation?" Xiomara controlled the expression on her face, but she wasn't interested in seeing a bear while living here.

"We're pretty remote up here. Sometimes bears pass through town." Rosebud waved a hand in a sweeping motion, showing the insignificance of the *bear situation*. "It's no big deal. The house comes with a rifle."

A rifle? *Great*.

"Up for lunch?" Rosebud pointed across the street.

"That sounds amazing." Xiomara's stomach grumbled at the mention of a meal.

Rosebud guided them across the street to the *Good Morning Cafe*. Assuring her that Anubis was allowed inside, they sat at the bar for quickest service. Anubis tucked himself between Xiomara's ankles, big brown eyes hopeful she would drop a few scraps.

Sitting side by side at the bar, Xiomara ordered a mutton sandwich on a bannock bun. It was the size of a small pizza. She eyed it, suspicious of her ability to finish it.

"Do you want to share?" Rosebud offered her green chile chicken soup to Xiomara. The intoxicating scent of the cilantro packed soup made Xiomara's mouth water.

She nodded. "Absolutely." Rosebud asked the waiter for another bowl while Xiomara put half her sandwich on Rosebud's plate. "Where do you guys get hatch green chiles out here anyway?"

"The chef is Navajo." Rosebud smiled. "Ashley is our Chief's cousin. She moved up here from Shiprock to take over the cafe a few years ago. She gets like four huge shipments every summer to last the entire year. She's got the whole province addicted. People will drive over an hour just to try the hatch chiles."

"I understand their dedication." Xiomara smiled. "My mom makes this delicious salsa with tomatillos and hatch green chiles." Xiomara scooped a spoonful of the soup into her salivating mouth. "You'd love it."

"That sounds delicious. I'll ask Ashley for some chiles, so you can make it." Rosebud smiled as though it would be that simple, but Xiomara wasn't convinced she could find tomatillos all the way up here.

A brunette woman joined them at the bar top, wiping her hands on a towel made from Blue Bird Flour sacks. "They told me there was another desert person out here." She pushed her lips forward at the soup. "What do you think?"

"It's fantastic." Xiomara smiled at Ashley, enjoying another mouthful of the spicy broth, green chunks of chiles, red corn, and shredded chicken. The soup had arrived with fresh limes and cilantro with raw white onion. It tasted like home. Like the heat of the desert and the sand in her shoes and the way spices sleep in the air. Spices had a way of sinking into her skin, making themselves at home and reminding her of where she belonged, even when home was miles away.

She devoured the soup while Rosebud and Ashley discussed the very intense procurement of chiles and customs clearances necessary to import them to this tiny island. Xiomara listened with half an ear, her attention stolen by the gentle hands of fresh roasted cumin. She could smell her mother's tamales and hear the sheep braying outside. Closing her eyes, she made a promise to return, as always. No matter how far she strayed, Chihuahua always called her home.

But for now, she was *here*.

"Here it is!" Rosebud's chubby-cheeked smile eclipsed her eyes, infecting Xiomara with the same wide grin. The cottage was painted pale pink with black doors and trim. Everything about this place offered a glimpse into Rosebud's mind. The woman exuded the gothic happiness her house portrayed.

They gathered Xiomara's bags together and headed in through the side door. Anubis entered at Xiomara's side, staying close to her in this unfamiliar place. Rosebud's home was small but meticulously decorated. A small white and blue kitchen with an eat-in dining table opened to a pink and orange living room with enough crochet to fool a 70's era time traveler.

"It's not much, but I think it turned out pretty cute." Rosebud stuck two pink glasses under the faucet while Xiomara wandered to the big picture window off the living room. "Kate and I renovated the whole place ourselves."

"I love the colors; it's so joyous." Xiomara complimented.

"It's especially cold in here during winter because of this window." She handed Xiomara a glass of water. "But the view is worth it."

Rosebud's window featured an unobstructed view east, straight across the woodlands. The land before Xiomara was strikingly green, the grasses growing rapidly in chase of the warming sun. With a lush tree line to the left and the sharp cliff's edge straight ahead, the expansive blue lake stretched before her.

"It's stunning."

"Have you been to Canada before?" Rosebud asked.

"Yes." Xiomara thought about it. "I think not too far from here, actually. I did my college field school in Michigan, but we crossed the border all the time."

"Oh, no way. That is so cool." Rosebud sighed. "I've always wanted to travel. I went on a school trip to Mesa Verde once, some donation from an oil organization or something." Rosebud rolled her eyes. "It was incredible, though. Have you been there?"

"I have." Xiomara nodded. "Mesa Verde is incredible. We have some amazing archaeology down south, too."

"Oh my gosh, I would loooooove to go to Mexico-o-o." Rosebud lilted.

"Why haven't you?" Xiomara watched Anubis settle in the sunspot on the floor.

"You'd be surprised how sticky this place is." Rosebud's smile was forlorn. "It's like being a piece of gum on the bottom of the shoe. You can kiss the cement and the sand and the dirt, but you always come back to the shoe. You belong to the shoe. Irrevocably."

"I know what you mean." Homesickness built a house of guilt in Xiomara's gut.

"Come on, let me show you the room. I'm sure you're exhausted. It takes forever to get here." Rosebud guided Xiomara down the hall. "That's our room at the end." She pointed to a black door. "This is the guest bathroom." A jewel toned blue door. "And this is your room." The door was bright yellow. Like sunshine.

A simple wooden bed frame housed a queen-size mattress covered in a white duvet with a crocheted blanket at the foot. Brown, red, rust orange, yellow... The 70's era time traveler had made it to this room, too. The walls were cream and adorned with a retro stripe pattern of yellow, orange, and teal going across the entirety of the room, even the doors and frames of the closet and bathroom. It was... bright.

"I know it's a little bare, but you shouldn't be here long, I promise." Rosebud held her breath for a beat. "We don't get a lot of guests all the way up here, so I hope I haven't forgotten anything."

"It's perfect." Xiomara set her purse on the bed beside the matching yellow towels. The colors were overwhelming, but she could handle it for a few days.

"Well, I will let you get settled. You have a big day tomorrow. Kate usually serves dinner at eight." Rosebud had the door half closed when Anubis ran into the room. "He's welcome to sleep in the bed." The door clicked shut.

Xiomara sighed and flopped onto the mattress next to Anubis. Her body wound tighter than a spool, so tense her muscles refused to relax. Tomorrow was a big day, certainly. More than a year in the making, it was finally time to start the complete excavation of the B0102 settlement and full museum curation with the recovered artifacts. It was a huge project that could take more than a year to complete. The weight of responsibility settled on her shoulders.

Emptying her chest of breath, she stretched her arms above her head before wrestling her phone from the wrappings of her shoulder bag.

She opened WhatsApp to her mom's name.

Estoy aquí. Todo bien. Te llamaré este fin de semana.

Lola next.

Todas las personas aquí son altas. Pero like... super tall. Como Shaq.

Shower.

Xiomara groaned and sat upright. Getting out of bed was the last thing she wanted to do, but she had been traveling for nearly forty-eight hours and desperately needed a shower. She unzipped her suitcase in search of her shampoo and bodywash. Pulling out her favorite fuzzy sweats and hoodie, a sharp corner caught the skin of her knuckle.

Xiomara unwrapped the item slowly, carefully. The glass was still in one piece, no cracks or scratches. She sighed in relief.

Her fingers dragged over the smooth gilded edge, taking in every millimeter of the photo. Javier's black ostrich skin boots shone in the sunlight. The boots had been a wedding present from a cousin years ago. Xiomara breathed deeply. The tears had long dried up, leaving her head empty and light. She held the frame against her heart briefly, saying a quick hello before propping it on the nightstand.

The desert hadn't felt the same since losing him. Her mother begged her to return permanently, but the pain was still too consuming. She felt like her heart was ripping to shreds each time she smelled the iron-rich sand. It wasn't job opportunities that kept her from staying home; it was grief.

The water was steaming hot, turning her skin red. Xiomara let herself relax under the water, rubbing the knots in her shoulders and back.

She wiped the steam from the mirror. Her golden skin was dark and ashen under her eyes. The plane lights had deprived her of sleep. Her limbs felt heavy, and it took great effort just to towel dry her hair.

Wrapping her towel across her chest, she sat on the bed and leaned against the bed frame. She would've killed to be completely alone in the silence of her room and a dozing Anubis.

It was probably a good thing her cabin wasn't ready. She might not have met anyone until Monday. This was good for her. She needed to stop being so alone. Rosebud would make a good friend. Maybe Bunchberry could turn her into a people person.

Xiomara woke up at 7:43 p.m. still wearing her fluffy yellow towel. Anubis was stretched near her feet, snoring in his slumber. She groaned as she sat up, fingering the rat's nest of damp, knotted hair behind her head. Combing the tangles out, she finished it in a slightly messy braid. Taking a deep breath to prepare for social interaction when she was blisteringly tired, she opened the door.

"There you are!" Rosebud exclaimed as Xiomara emerged from the hallway. Anubis ran out behind her, headed straight for the kitchen. Rosebud gestured to a brown-skinned woman beside her. "This is my wife, Kate."

"It's wonderful to meet you." Kate wiped her hands on her yellow apron, leaning to hug Xiomara. "Welcome to Bunchberry." Her buzzed head was bleached pale blonde, giving way for her skin to gleam like metal.

"Thank you for letting me stay." Anubis barreled into Kate's legs, rubbing against her like a cat. "Anubis thanks you as well." Xiomara laughed while Anubis squirmed under Kate's fingers. If having a dog was good for anything, it was certainly a reliable icebreaker.

"Well, you couldn't exactly stay with me." Xiomara turned to the tall man stepping into the kitchen. He looked oddly familiar with his dark brown eyes, amber skin, and a smile eerily similar to Kate's. Chief Thomas. "It's nice to meet you in person."

"Oh!" Xiomara smoothed her messy hair and wiped her suddenly sweaty palms on her pants. "I didn't know you'd be here, or I would—"

"Yes, sorry." Rosebud stepped closer to Xiomara and pinched her finger and thumb close together in front of her eyes. "Slight oversight on my part. Chief Thomas is Kate's brother." She grimaced. "And I forgot you didn't know that. Nonetheless, this is family time, no work talk until tomorrow!"

"It's nice to meet you, Chief Thomas." Xiomara shook the Chief's hand before sitting at the kitchen table.

"Call me Ken, please."

Uh, *no*.

Chief Thomas smiled with all his teeth as he sat across from her. "What do you think of Canada so far?"

"It's beautiful here." Xiomara told him. "A little cold, though."

Chief Thomas laughed at her slight grimace. "Yeah, it doesn't get very hot up here."

"July gets warm enough for shorts." Rosebud shouted from the living room where Redbone music hummed.

Kate and Rosebud placed bowls of meat and peppers in the center of the table. The chicken had gorgeous grill marks and was covered in red and orange spices.

There was a bowl of grilled corn, peppers, and onions beside a terracotta tortilla warmer.

"I know fajitas are kind of American." Kate said. "But I had to be realistic with the ingredients I could get all the way up here."

Xiomara smiled. "I love fajitas. This smells incredible, thank you." She met Kate's eyes, hoping her voice communicated how much she appreciated their consideration of her.

"I had Kate bring home some chiles for you, too." Rosebud pointed to a small bowl filled with the chopped roasted green peppers. Xiomara's mouth watered.

Grabbing a warm tortilla, Xiomara loaded it with meat and veggies before slathering an entire spoonful of chiles on top. She finished it with a squirt of lime and a dusting of chopped cilantro and white onion before digging in. Spicy, sweet, fresh, crispy, everything at once. Perfecto.

"This is amazing, Kate!" Xiomara kept her hand in front of her mouth and continued eating, bouncing lightly in her seat.

"Thank you." Kate grinned. "Cilantro is impossible to find up here, so I grow some in our greenhouse."

"Oh my gosh, the greenhouse is the best thing we ever did." Rosebud interjected. "It was Kate's idea." Rosebud winked at her wife, pressing a proud kiss to her cheek.

"Do you grow a lot of crops where you're from?" Chief Thomas asked.

"Not really." Xiomara wiped her fingers on her napkin. "Mostly just cactus, agave, peppers, of course. It's so hot and dry that most plants can't survive. We have plenty of cilantro, though."

"What is your home like?" Kate asked Xiomara.

"Pretty much the complete opposite of here. Really dry, really brown, really hot." She took a bite of her rolled up fajita.

"Did you live in a city?" Rosebud asked.

"No, there aren't many cities that far north... other than Juarez." Xiomara smiled. "I grew up in a super rural area. There were miles between us and the nearest neighbor."

"Oh my gosh, I couldn't imagine!" Rosebud exclaimed. "We all grew up walking between each other's houses."

"I don't know…" Kate tsked. "Might've been nice to avoid some of that small town drama."

Rosebud rolled her eyes while Chief Thomas nodded.

"Oh, we were not exempt from small town drama." Xiomara shook her head. "Our drama just had a lag time of three days."

The trio laughed while Xiomara settled into her chair and sipped from her glass of water. She felt welcome here, a feeling she often found difficult to come by. It wasn't often she found herself in a town so welcoming to Indigenous Mexicans. Usually, at least a few people weren't happy to have her around. But today, she could feel their happiness like a beam of sun shining on her skin.

Chief Thomas started telling a hunting story, giving Xiomara the freedom to study his face. His brown skin was warm, his nose flat and wide like hers, with eyes dark as midnight. She wondered if he was mixed, as he reminded her of the vast array of her own cousins.

Anubis whined at Xiomara's side, pawing her foot while maintaining eye contact. Perfect timing. She excused herself from the table to walk Anubis, hoping that by the time she returned, dinner would be over, and she could go to sleep.

The chill of the night air felt clean against the skin of her face, her ankles tasting the cold between her leggings and slippers. Anubis sniffed the ground, investigating every new blade of grass.

Stillness settled around her, the breeze allaying completely. Noises assaulted her ears. Creaking, buzzing, rustling, crashing—the night here was loud. A shiver tickled down her spine at the mismatch.

Calling Anubis inside, Xiomara turned tired eyes to Kate, who sent her to bed on account of her long day of travel. She bid goodnight to the siblings and excused herself. She slept soundly, her dreams empty.

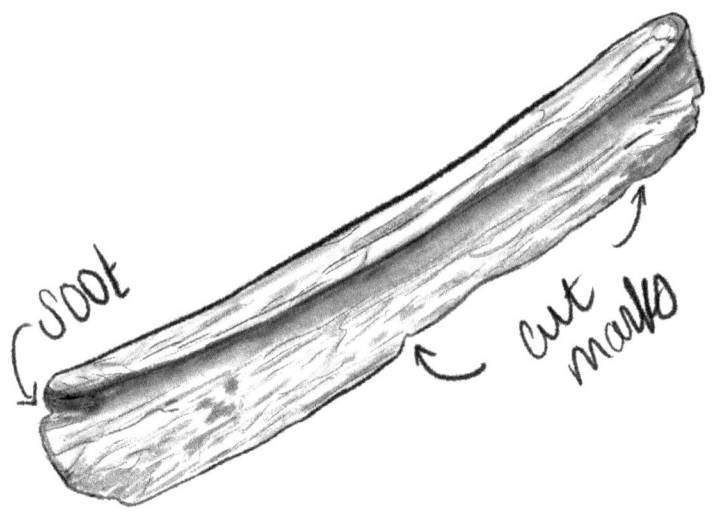

CHAPTER 2

The café smelled of coffee and bacon. At seven in the morning, the place was mostly empty. Though it had been empty when Xiomara had lunch here the day before as well. At home, she had lived too far from a town for a café. Was it always low on customers?

Xiomara took a seat at the bar, waving to the waitress when she held the coffeepot.

"Do you have any cinnamon?" Xiomara wrapped her hands around the filled mug, absorbing the heat into her hands.

The young waitress bent behind the counter, only the blonde buns on the top of her head visible. She handed Xiomara a shaker of cinnamon and walked away.

"What's the cinnamon for?"

Xiomara turned toward the voice, meeting warm brown eyes tucked behind the soft folds of crow's feet. With dark, weathered skin and a denim jacket almost as supple, she knew he was a farmer. He reminded her of her own father.

"I like it in my coffee."

"Just coffee and cinnamon?" The man asked.

"No." Ripping open the brown sugar packet, she watched the crystals sink. Stirring it with the thin wooden stick, she poured milk into the center of the whirlpool. "Cream." She set the stick down. "Cinnamon." Xiomara held the small saucer over her mug and tapped it three times with her fingernail, the cinnamon spreading evenly over the tan-colored drink. "Perfecto." She brought the mug to her lips, sipping the flavorful coffee.

He gestured to the young woman behind the bar top. "Let me get some cinnamon, too, please." The waitress nodded without looking up and topped his coffee when she brought the ingredients.

"What do you think?" Xiomara asked, hoping the old man liked her coffee.

"It's delicious." His lips turned up, and he took another sip. "Don't tell my son I put sugar in it, though." He winked as he brought his pointer finger to his mouth.

"I can keep a secret."

"You're not from here." The old man took his omelet from the waitress, sprinkling black pepper over the yellow eggs.

"No." She wiped her hands on the napkin across her lap. "I was hired to do the excavation and curation of the settlement artifacts."

"You're the famous archaeologist everyone has been going on about."

Xiomara blanched. "Everyone?" It came out in a whisper.

He graced her with the gift of ignorance to her hushed voice. "So, who do you belong to?"

"I'm Apache, from Chihuahua," Xiomara answered.

"I thought there weren't any Apaches left in Mexico." His brows pulled together.

"You thought wrong."

The old man smiled broadly. "I like being wrong."

"Hi, Uncle!" a ringing voice sounded from behind Xiomara's shoulder.

"Good morning, Rosebud." He kissed her cheek. "Busy day?"

"You know it." Rosebud exclaimed, pushing her glasses up her nose.

"Don't let them stretch you too thin." He stood slowly from his seat, white knuckles pushing against the counter for stability. He placed a comforting grasp on Rosebud's shoulder, then shook Xiomara's hand. "Nice to meet you, doctor."

"I'm not—" He was gone before she could explain she did not yet have her doctorate.

"That's Uncle Muskwa Yellowbird." Rosebud stole a slice of toast from Xiomara's plate. "Do you call elders Uncle in Chihuahua?"

"Sorta." Xiomara laughed. "All our elders are my uncles."

Rosebud threw her head back, laughing. "Honestly, that's how it is here, too."

Xiomara finished her simple breakfast while Rosebud ordered an iced coffee to go. Coffee to go only meant one thing; the meeting was happening soon. Her nerves were manifesting in sweaty hands and armpits. Xiomara made a mental note to keep her arms down.

The waitress set Rosebud's coffee on the table while Xiomara asked for the check. "Oh, Uncle already paid for you both."

Rosebud smiled as if she had expected it. Xiomara pulled a few Canadian coins out of her wallet and tucked it under her plate. "Thank you."

Rosebud bumped Xiomara with her shoulder as they crossed the street. "Are you ready to kill this meeting?"

"Claro que si." Xiomara smiled despite her nerves. She was a hardworking archaeologist, but this was an enormous job. Relocating an entire settlement, including remains and building a museum to house the uncovered artifacts, was... *intense*. Even without the cultural significance, it was a monumental job with tons of pressure. The settlement was quaint, and it had never been looted. Once it was excavated, it would be the most northern woodland site in Manitoba. Nothing in the world could compare to a site like this. She was determined to prevent any and all loss. If that was even possible.

It was an incredible thing to be part of. Incredible, but nerve-wracking. She had been communicating with the team for a year, preparing to excavate. Today would be her first time meeting them in person and presenting her excavation and preservation plan to the tribal council. She straightened her back, running her clammy palms across her jeans, hoping to rid them of the excess moisture.

Xiomara followed Rosebud into the conference room, taking a seat against the wall next to her. A familiar face peered at her from across the room. Uncle Muskwa was a council member.

Xiomara offered a hug to David, an Apache student attending college in Winnipeg. He had been a star student at the field school she led last summer, so she had recruited him for this job. "How was the drive into town this morning?"

David was staying in the next closest town, Junebug Crossing. A fan of Chinese food and overpriced coffee, David was a city boy at heart and had denied residing on a reservation.

"It was horrid." David grimaced. "I think I'll have to take them up on a room at the inn. I am not doing that long of a drive before sunrise."

"I think that would be a great idea." Xiomara squeezed his hand. "It will be nice to have someone I know nearby."

A booming voice filled the room. "Good morning, everyone." Chief Thomas entered, a coffee in hand. "I hope everyone has welcomed our new archaeologist, Xiomara Chavez, to town." He looked around, making eye contact with each council member. "As you know, Yellowbird Island is slowly eroding into the river. Xiomara is here to work with us to curate a museum with the recovered artifacts and relocate the remains to a new mound location chosen by the council. Xiomara, please show us your preservation plan."

"Thank you, Chief Thomas." Xiomara rose from her seat and stepped toward the laptop next to the projector. "It is an honor to be here with you. As many of you know, I've been working in archaeology for almost a decade. I grew up in the field, helping my father with our tribal museum as a child. It is one of my most treasured memories, and I am thrilled to work on creating this with all of you." She clasped her hands together in front of her sternum. "I'm honored to be here to help preserve your history. Our plan is to perform a complete excavation of the settlement with analysis and curation."

She moved to her first slide, an overview of the LIDAR analysis showcasing the hypothesized outline of the settlement. "Once excavation is complete, we will relocate the remains." She flipped to a photo of a large grass covered burial mound near the settlement. Tucked into the grass beside the trees, the mound was sizeable and thought to hold at least two individuals. "Ideally, I would ask for a spiritual or community leader of yours to guide us through this. I can help handle the logistics of safely moving ancient human remains, but I would prefer to have a community member lead as we are dealing with a burial. We will leave the remains as undisturbed as possible, transporting them with all the artifacts present." She turned to another slide, a mockup of the rebuilt mound showcasing the layers inside. "Lastly, we will replicate the mound to exact measurements."

"What plans do you have for building the museum?" asked an older woman with long white hair.

Chief Thomas interjected, "Calehan will be designing the museum connected to the casino. The two will share a gift shop."

The council members nodded at Chief Thomas's explanation. Rosebud gave Xiomara a thumbs up from the corner of the table.

"So..." Chief Thomas leaned forward, resting his elbows on the table. "Who has questions?"

Xiomara took a steadying breath as voices rose around the long table.

Calehan idled on the sidewalk as he waited for his father to exit City Hall. Technically, his father could drive, but he preferred he didn't with his bad hips. The roads out here could be hard to navigate, and Calehan wanted to minimize his father's stress as much as possible.

Finally, he saw his father's long braid, streaks of silver bolting through like lightning. Muskwa exited the building, hugging Rosebud and another much shorter woman. The woman's smile was wide, short square teeth shining. His father patted her twice on the shoulder, squeezing it once before retreating.

"Hey Dad, who is that?" Calehan pointed toward the woman with his chin.

His father gripped the handle of the door and climbed inside the truck. "Oh, that's the archeologist they brought in for the dig. She's Mexican Apache or something."

"What's her name?" Calehan squinted as he peered at the newcomer.

Muskwa clicked his tongue. "I can't remember. Something with a Z, I think."

"How long is she staying here?" He watched the woman smile at Rosebud. Calehan could see the laughter on her face, even though he couldn't hear it.

"Why are you asking so many damn questions? Got a crush on her or something?"

Calehan rolled his eyes, but kept his mouth shut. The archaeologist was beautiful. She had shoulder length, ink black hair with blunt bangs across her forehead. She wore the face of her ancestors in the desert brown shade of her skin, her black eyes, and the short, wide nose. She was alarmingly small. Rosebud loomed over her, the size difference between the two bringing a laugh to his mouth.

"I need you to run the horses this weekend, son." Muskwa said. "My hip just isn't doing well this week."

"Of course." Calehan took one last glance at the archaeologist before pulling away from the curb.

"Are you coming to the Spring Bash tomorrow?"

Calehan did not want to attend the town party. Every year in the first week of spring, Bunchberry hosted a seed exchange with neighboring tribes. The exchange helped everyone prepare for the growing season. He didn't much like crowds. Nor did he enjoy the small talk and tribal politics that were so common at gatherings.

"The archaeologist will probably be there." His dad wore an ornery smile.

Calehan turned up the radio in lieu of a response.

Muskwa had been wanting him to marry for nearly a decade now, ever since he came back from college. With his twin sister already married with kids and his younger siblings venturing off to college and careers, Calehan felt like a black sheep. It wasn't that he didn't want to get married; he just didn't want to marry anyone from Bunchberry. He was never going to escape the island and make something of himself if he did that.

Calehan couldn't simply get on a plane and see the world. He had responsibilities here. After his mother passed, he graduated from school early and went to work. With an ailing father, younger siblings, and a slew of horses and dogs to care for, he needed to be here for his family. Nataani was only fifteen, and the idea of leaving him behind ate at his stomach.

It had been his youngest brother who had encouraged him to apply for the job in Spain in the first place. Now, almost a year later, the offer letter hung on the fridge, unsigned. His father needed him, his siblings needed him, even the town needed him for this project. Leading a campus build in Spain was a dream come true for him, a real step in his career, but guilt plagued him at the thought of leaving. Who else would take care of his father and their ranch, along with his rambunctious siblings who were constantly moving around? Joy, the youngest sister, was the only sibling set on staying home forever. She had expressed multiple times that Calehan should go off to Spain and leave her to tend the ranch, but he couldn't bring himself to do it. Joy was too young to understand the burden of taking over the family ranch. There would be no more weekend relay races for her if he went to Spain. She had too much life left to live before she got locked down like him. Besides, relay winnings weren't even enough to keep the lights on.

A cloud of dust climbed up the sides of the truck as Calehan turned down their long driveway. He could see Joy tending to the cows. He slowed as they passed, Joy jumping into the bed to catch a ride to the house. She had graduated from high school the year before and insisted on postponing college so she could stay on Bunchberry with her horses. Calehan hoped she would eventually reconsider.

"These kids are so lazy these days, always wanting rides everywhere." Muskwa scoffed.

Calehan rose an eyebrow. "Dad, you know you used to try to do all your chores on horseback. It doesn't get lazier than that."

Muskwa let out a long, loud laugh, gripping his son's shoulder as they passed through the collapsing chicken wire they called a fence. Their land stretched out in boundless shades of green. The small herd of dairy cows stood grazing in the pen to the left, the horses standing along the tree line at the far right. Nearing the house, they passed their small flock of chicken and ducks, wandering their open pen beside Luna, one of their many livestock guardian dogs. With an all-black coat and black, piercing eyes, many people thought Luna was at least part wolf. Her clumsiness told Calehan she was all dog.

Slowing to a stop in front of their house, Joy jumped from the truck bed and opened her father's car door. "How was your meeting, pops?" She kissed his cheek and helped him from the truck.

"Oh, you know, same old, same old. The archaeologist is very sweet."

"Still glad you're not Chief?" Joy teased.

"Every day." Muskwa stepped inside, pausing to remove his shoes before heading toward the kitchen.

"He's doing a lot better, you know." Joy turned to Calehan as the door shut behind them. The siblings toed their shoes off in mirror image of each other.

"I have eyes."

Joy waved a hand dismissively. "You know what I mean."

"I do." Calehan gently pushed his sister toward the kitchen.

Nataani was seated on the small brown couch playing video games, nails painted a glittery black to match the controller. His voice rose as he ribbed his friends about a missed shot.

Joy headed for the shower while Calehan snatched the controller and put his brother in a headlock. "Is your homework finished?"

Nataani pulled at Calehan's arms, trying in vain to reach the game controller firmly in his older brother's stretched out hand. Calehan loosened his grip slightly, letting Nataani speak. "It's Friday, I don't have any homework!"

"I'm not sure that's how that works," their father said from the kitchen.

"Do your homework," Calehan said, releasing Nataani but keeping the game controller.

Nataani grumbled under his breath and pulled out his schoolwork. Calehan took to the basement stairs, his arms full of kitchen towels to add into the never-ending dirty pile.

Partially finished, the basement was insulated, but the drywall remained unpainted, and he was pretty sure the carpet covering the cold concrete floor had been there since the 70s. He pulled the wet clothes from the washer and stuffed them into the dryer. He refilled the washer with his siblings' clothing, rolling his stiff neck as he closed the lid.

Shuffling to the couch, Calehan stretched on the threadbare cushions, the springs pressing into the flesh of his hips. He let out a sigh, his mind cloudy with responsibilities. How was his dad going to get by if he moved away? With the ranch and the kids, he could never keep up. Calehan scrubbed his face up and down with his hands. He loved his home here on reserve, but he was so much happier elsewhere. The thought stung his tongue, bitterness filling his mouth. His time at school in Winnipeg was some of the best in his life. He loved the access to diverse restaurants, plenty of groceries, and the anonymity of a large town. No one was anonymous in a town of four hundred.

This museum would be the first building design he'd made since he moved home. There wasn't exactly a need for new anything on Bunchberry, a place that looked nearly identical to itself 200 years earlier. It wasn't even his idea. It was necessary in order to not lose another piece of their history. He pressed his forefinger and thumb into his temples, rubbing in small circles. There could be worse places to live than Bunchberry. He needed to remember that.

Taking a deep breath, he stood and headed up the stairs to help his father with dinner. Rounding the corner, a trilling laugh filled his ears. Juniper, his twin, stood across the island, watching their father hold her young son.

"Joining us for dinner?" he asked, throwing his arm around his best friend turned brother's neck. Clover gently elbowed Calehan in the stomach in greeting.

"I brought bannock." Juniper smiled sweetly.

"Did you make it, or did Clover make it?" Calehan implored, side eyeing his snickering brother.

Juniper ignored the quip and walked away to take a seat at the dinner table. Muskwa handed Calehan his baby nephew and began serving dinner. Frankie let out a happy squeal and reached for his uncle's face.

"She's not that bad of a cook, you know." Clover made a half-hearted attempt to defend his wife.

"Boiling pasta does not count, brother." Calehan took baby Frankie to the kitchen table. Settling his nephew on his knee, the family passed the food around, ensuring everyone had been served before digging in. Calehan, an ever-doting uncle, let Frankie have a piece of his bannock to chew on. The one-year-old was surprisingly picky with his food, but never passed up a piece of bannock.

"Clover is going to come over this weekend to help run the horses while I take Nataani into town." Juniper addressed Calehan and her father from across the table. Baby Frankie smiled at his mother's voice. "He needs to pick a suit for prom."

"Your first prom, little brother." Joy pinched his cheek. "Are you excited?"

Nataani swatted her hand away.

"What color are we thinking?" Clover asked his nephew.

"I think it should be crimson, but I'll know the one when I see it." Nataani squinted as if examining invisible clothing in front of them.

Joy nodded, dirt-stained fingernails clutching her fork between only two fingers. "Can I come with you guys? I would hate to miss the fashion show."

"Obviously." Nataani spoke through a mouthful.

"We just have to swing by Costco on our way home," Juniper added.

A string of no's rang from the two youngest Yellowbirds, who hated their eldest sister's 'short Costco runs' that seemingly never ended. Juniper tugged on Joy's long messy braid.

"So did you meet the new boss today?" Clover was the only other licensed large machine operator on the island and would assist Calehan with building the museum.

"No." Calehan skewered a piece of broccoli on his fork. "Dad met her, though." Nonchalance owned his face while anticipation thumped in his heart. Jealous didn't cover the way he felt about his father meeting the archaeologist. Something about her had settled into his mind, claimed ownership of a piece of him, and tied his thoughts to her.

"Oh yeah?" Juniper turned toward their quiet father. "So?"

"So what?" Muskwa sipped his water and smiled at his carbon copy of a daughter. She blinked back at him, used to his affinity for Dad jokes. "She's very sweet and very smart. What else do you want to know?"

"I don't know." Juniper let out a sigh. "Do you think she is going to do right by us?" Her eyes were wide.

"Undoubtedly."

Chapter 3

Xiomara tucked another unruly piece of hair into her braids. The humidity was killing her; she felt sticky no matter how often she showered.

Stepping into her sand-colored huaraches, she joined Rosebud and Kate in the living room. The two were on the floor with Anubis, playing tug of war with his favorite blue rope toy.

"Are you going to bring Anubis to the bash?" Rosebud looked up at Xiomara.

"No," Xiomara answered, perching on the arm of the couch. "He doesn't really care for crowds. Anubis is a bit of an antisocial dog."

Kate patted his back. "I understand the feeling." Scratching behind his ears, she stood and reached for Rosebud. "You two ready to head over there?"

Xiomara nodded while Rosebud stood and smoothed out her pink strawberry patterned dress. Kissing Anubis's furless snout, Xiomara turned on the radio for ambient noise while he was alone and slipped out the door. She climbed into the backseat of the sedan, watching the others hop in. Kate reached for Rosebud, settling their arms together on the armrest. Xiomara pulled her eyes away from the sight, a chill running through her veins at the memory of Javier tucking her hand into his while they drove the miles between their houses. A raven's caw drew Xiomara's eyes to the window. The river roared outside, filling her head with rushing water.

Kate parked in the dirt next to Chief Thomas's red Escalade. Xiomara could see his dark hair, a head above most of the crowd, as he mingled with everyone. Dressed in slacks and a button down, he looked out of place amongst a crowd of t-shirts and regalia.

Rosebud grunted. "He couldn't have worn jeans?"

Kate smiled at her wife, wrapping her arm around Rosebud's frilled pink shoulders. "Not everyone can have as great of style as you."

Rosebud scoffed "Obviously."

Kate met Xiomara's eyes as the two burst out laughing. The air tinged rose around them as their laughter mingled with that of the crowd. She could feel the good medicine all around them, lifting her spirit.

Chief Thomas waved and made a beeline for his sister. Kissing each of their cheeks, he greeted them quickly before asking if he could steal Xiomara from the other women.

"There's quite a few neighboring tribal members here who would love to meet an Indigenous archaeologist." His white teeth shone in the sun.

"Uh." Xiomara clammed up. "Yes, of course."

"Great." Chief Thomas stepped to the side, gesturing to Xiomara to join him. "I will see you two later."

Xiomara glanced over her shoulder at Rosebud, catching her squinting eyes before Kate pulled her into a kiss. They headed toward the food, and Xiomara crossed her fingers that they placed the horchata she made last night in the shade. She was hoping to make a quick escape from Chief Thomas and return to her friends soon.

"Xiomara…" Chief Thomas' voice brought her back to the present. "This is Chief Tanya Burns, of the Blue Sky Ojibwe." Xiomara shook Chief Burns' hand firmly.

"I'm very excited to see this museum you'll be building." Chief Burns' blonde hair hung down her back in a braided ponytail.

"Well, it should be complete by this time next year, so you'll have to stop by and check it out." Xiomara smiled while another weight settled onto her shoulders. An all Indigenous-led excavation and curation had never happened before, and Xiomara felt like the world was watching her.

"Certainly." Chief Burns said. "My late husband was our archaeologist. I met him while we were both at University in Winnipeg, so I brought him home and put him to work." Her blue eyes sparkled.

"Wow." Xiomara was a bit shocked at the woman's willingness to share. "I would love to read some of his findings, if there's any available."

"Oh, absolutely." Chief Burns patted Xiomara's upper arm. "I'll get your email from Chief Thomas on Monday."

Xiomara went to thank her, but a resounding shout of, "Mom!" filled the air between them.

"Ope, duty calls." Chief Burns waved to the two of them before searching for her daughter.

Chief Thomas was leading her to another person when his assistant interrupted, pulling him away. "I'm so sorry, Xiomara." He palmed her tricep. "I will come find you as soon as I'm done."

"Don't worry about it." She waved him off and beelined for the drink table. Xiomara crossed her fingers that the sweet rice drink still tasted fresh. Filling her paper cup, she closed her eyes as the sweet cinnamon transported her home.

"Hello. Nice to see you again."

Xiomara turned, finding Muskwa.

"Hi, Uncle." Xiomara leaned forward and kissed his cheek. "Would you like a drink?"

"Sure, I'll have what you're having."

"Oh, you'll love it!" Xiomara exclaimed, setting her drink on the table to serve him. "It's horchata. We make it from rice, cinnamon, and a Mexican sugar called piloncillo." She handed him the frosty white drink and a straw. "I brought some with me, just in case."

Calehan found his father in front of the beverage table, a paper cup in his hands.

"Only one, Dad." Calehan appeared from behind his father. "You have to be careful with sugar."

Calehan felt the stranger evaluate him. Heat seeped from her gaze, bringing a blush to his skin. Her sunglasses sat atop her head, allowing her to drink him in as openly as he was doing to her. The air rippled between them like the heat scorching along his skin.

"Hi." He reached forward, shaking her hand. "I'm Calehan. Nice to meet you."

"Xiomara." Her smooth accent stuck lightly to parts of her tongue. "I hear you're our large machine manager?"

He nodded. "I worked for a construction company in the city during college before opening my own here on the Rez." Calehan shifted closer to her. "It's mostly snow plowing and fixing drywall, but every once in a while there are projects like this."

"Chief Thomas mentioned you're designing the museum?" She tilted slightly, looking up at him, her eyes squinting against the sun.

"I am." Calehan grimaced slightly. "I have a bachelor's in architecture, but I don't use it much." He glanced away from her, scanning over the growing crowd.

"Well, this will be fun, then." Her eyes flashed wide, a grin taking up her face. "You can design something unique but with enough space for my catalog."

"I'll see what I can do." Calehan dragged a hand across his jaw in an attempt to hide the grin tugging at his lips.

"It's the first museum I'll ever work on from creation." Her words came out wistfully.

"Really? I heard you have a family museum in Mexico?" He took a moment to gaze at her up close for the first time. Xiomara was an oasis of bronze, her thick braid so inky black he couldn't see through it. Her bangs tickled her almond-shaped eyelids. The only way he could see her pupil was when the sunlight shone across her face, tiny golden red highlights then visible in her iris. She stole every drop of water from his body, his mouth dry and heavy with his tongue.

"My Dad built it before I was born. I never really got to contribute much." Xiomara pushed a line of dirt with the inside of her foot. "This is a dream come true for me." She took a sip of her horchata and smiled at Calehan, "So don't fuck it up." Popping her straw into her mouth, she turned, braid swinging across her back in retreat.

Muskwa rejoined Calehan and smiled at her retreating back. "I like her."

"Of course you do. You love when people boss you around." Calehan said.

"So do you." Muskwa snickered.

Joining the family for the round dance, he hoped his father would keep his suspicions in his chest. He wasn't in the mood for his dad's signature snickers and exaggerated winks. Juniper would be dancing with Frankie for the first time, wearing beads both Calehan and Clover had worn as children.

Calehan evaluated the crowd, looking for Xiomara. She was seated on a blanket with Kate and Rosebud, sharing watermelon slices and frybread while they waited for Grand Entry. Frankie ran over to his aunt, taking a bite of the watermelon Rosebud had been eating. Calehan could hear Xiomara's laugh in the shape of her mouth.

A man sat beside Xiomara. Calehan couldn't see his face, but he recognized the tribal seal pinned to his shirt. Chief Thomas always had a thing for Spanish-speaking Natives, like his mother had been. It was a common plight of the *My Mother Died When I Was A Kid Club* that Calehan had only grown out of after attending therapy during university. Kenneth had been much younger than Calehan when his mother joined the Spirit World. He hoped Nataani didn't continue the trend.

Calehan whooped when Juniper entered the circle. Frankie held tight to his mother's neck while she and Clover danced in with the others. Calehan admired the different regalia types, some dancers traveled hundreds of miles to compete for the coveted prizes. The winners of each category would go home with a cash prize and a seed bundle. Every visiting nation would contribute local seeds, wishing fruitful years on the dancers. He recognized Pueblo hoop dancers and Dine men and women dripping in turquoise. His eyes pulled constantly toward Xiomara, his curiosity piqued in a way it hadn't been for years.

He dug out his smartphone to take photos of Frankie dancing on his own, following Juniper and Clover around the dance circle. Calehan's smile spread over his entire face as he watched Juniper walk with Frankie, encouraging him to stomp his feet with as much fervor as his tiny body had. Muskwa received Frankie warmly when he ran out of the circle at the stop of the music. Calehan was so caught up in photographing his family, he didn't notice Rosebud and Kate approach them.

"Look at my nephew!" Rosebud's voice came out in a squeal, Frankie tucking into her ribbon skirt while she fluffed his hair.

Calehan covertly searched for Xiomara but couldn't find her. He rejoined his family in conversation, hoping she would reappear.

The air was full of delicious scents. Native chefs cooked up all kinds of Indigenous cuisine with some offering fusion options, like carnitas frybread and wild boar sushi rolls with blueberry wasabi hot sauce. It blew Xiomara's mind with all the options presented before her. A desire to try everything creeped into her belly, and she fought with herself to choose only one or two items.

Chief Thomas found her wrist-deep in boar sushi rolls while in line for a piece of frybread. "Need a napkin?"

She smiled with her lips together, taking the white paper from his hand. Freeing herself of the sticky wasabi, she thanked him. "I seriously can't resist; there is so much food here I've never seen before."

Chief Thomas' smile grew. "The Spring Berry Bash is our biggest event of the year. There's a group from Hawai'i that comes every other year. There's only like two seeds they can legally bring, but they cook such delicious food."

"Oh wow, I wish they were here this year. I don't think I've ever had Hawai'ian food." Xiomara popped the last mutton roll into her mouth.

"Well," Chief Thomas said, "you will just have to come back next year." Before Xiomara could reply, they were at the front of the line. Chief Thomas ordered them each a sweet frybread and stuffed a fifty into the tip jar before he drizzled honey over each piece. She squinted at his back as they walked toward the chairs, tossing her empty sushi tray in the garbage. He hadn't given her a chance to offer to pay for herself. The frybread wasn't expensive, but it still felt like a gesture she shouldn't accept from her boss. Was he always like this or was it some kind of show for everyone?

"Here." He pointed with his lips at a pair of empty chairs. She took her plate of honeyed frybread from him as she sat.

"Thank you for the frybread." Xiomara kept her voice even and gentle.

"Don't mention it." He shook his head and dropped a few napkins in her lap. "You can't tell anyone this, but I prefer frybread to bannock. I'm a traitor."

"No, you aren't." Xiomara scoffed. "I don't really like spicy food." She shrugged as he gaped at her. "It's fine, but I'm not going to go out of my way for something spicy, like regular is fine to me."

Chief Thomas shook his head. "I think yours might be more egregious than mine."

"Aye." Xiomara looked at him over the top of her sunglasses. "You better chill, or I'll snitch. I am currently living with your sister."

Chief Thomas's hands went up, palms out. "You're right. Kate would definitely blackmail me with that."

"Hey, you've got to stop stealing my roommate." Rosebud sat in the empty chair facing them, ripping a piece of frybread off Chief Thomas' plate. She licked the side of her hand where the honey dribbled past her grip.

"Here you go, babe." Kate's soft voice crept over Xiomara's shoulder as she joined them, Indian tacos piled high in her hands.

Rosebud squealed and offered a drink to her food-bearing wife. The two tore into their meals, ripping off pieces of frybread in each hand, one to eat and one to scoop toppings. The group settled into an easy moment of silence while they savored their NDN classic.

"When are you leaving for the city?" Kate's voice was soft, but the wind carried her voice to their ears.

"As soon as First Dancers are announced." Chief Thomas scrubbed the edge of his shaved jaw, glancing over the couple's heads at the crowd.

"Wow, brother, you aren't staying for cleanup? Typical man, eh?" Rosebud kicked his mahogany-colored moccasin with her pink leather clad foot, beads jingling against each other with the force.

He pinched below her knee with his thumb and forefinger. "I always clean up, jerk."

Rosebud stuck her tongue out at him, a piece of lettuce stuck to the corner. Kate and Xiomara shared a look that quickly devolved into laughter.

"I swear, the last thing she needed was another little brother." Kate squeezed Rosebud's thigh.

"I didn't know you were the oldest, Rosebud." Xiomara got strong only child vibes from her.

"Yep, I'm the bully firstborn." She dusted her hands off above her empty plate and settled in her chair, crossing her arms leisurely across her chest. "I'm only four years older than Clover."

"Six years older than me." Kate fanned herself as she peered at her vieja.

"Saucy." Xiomara wiggled her shoulders in their direction.

"Only way to describe us." Rosebud swatted Kate's beaded earring out of the way and pressed a kiss to her wife's cheek. "Oh! That reminds me! We need to buy you your first pair of earrings."

Xiomara trailed behind an eager Rosebud as she led the way to her preferred earring maker. Dozens of items glittered in the sun before the vendor. Their work was spectacular, beads glittering where they were sewn into a multitude of shapes and patterns. Fingertips burning, Xiomara crossed her arms at her back to prevent herself from touching every item in front of her.

Kate rounded the table and hugged the seller. She was seated in a camping chair behind her items, leather clutched in her palm, a needle between her fingers.

"It's her first pair, Auntie," Kate pretended to whisper into the woman's ear.

"Well, if it's your first pair, I think you should go big." Chief Thomas gestured toward a pair of large hoops beaded in gold and green.

"How big you got?" Rosebud popped onto her tiptoes to peer at the tables covered in jewelry and accessories.

"I've got just the thing." Auntie reached under the table and produced a cardboard box slightly larger than her hand, then offered it to Xiomara.

Xiomara opened the box. A pair of large, beaded hoops glittered against the white stuffing. Square shaped turquoise blue beads held tight to the hoops where orange triangles with tiny yellow flowers sprung from them like painted water lilies. Xiomara let Rosebud press the hoops to her ears.

"They're incredible." Admiration wrapped her words.

"Wow." Chief Thomas looked up from where he was examining beaded watch bands. He let out a low whistle. "Talk about a statement for a first pair. You look great."

"She knows." Rosebud answered.

Xiomara continued peering at the earrings, her fingers tracing over the orange peaks of the tiny pyramids.

"How much?" Chief Thomas opened his wallet, stepping beside Xiomara. His hand rested at the small of her back, the heat from his skin seeping through her shirt. She froze. This was starting to feel intimate.

"No need!" Xiomara waved him off with a hand. "I can pay."

"It's a gift." The old woman smiled warmly at her, pressing Xiomara's outstretched hands into her chest.

"No, I can't accept this. It's too much—"

Chief Thomas cut her off. "She loves it, Auntie, thank you." His hand wrapped around Xiomara's elbow, guiding her from the table while Rosebud and Kate debated their own purchases.

She thanked the beader once again, waving goodbye as she followed Chief Thomas toward the other vendors.

Once out of earshot, she stopped dead in her tracks, Chief Thomas bumping straight into her back. "Are people giving me free things because of you?" The new earrings swung gently from her quick movement.

"Um..." He hesitated. "I don't know."

Her eyes remained narrow as they bore into his face. "Are you sure?"

"Yes?" Chief Thomas blinked at her. "I mean, I don't know *for sure* it's because of me."

Xiomara shooed him away gently. "Go do your Chiefly mingling and let me pay for my things." She wiggled her fingers in the direction of the crowd and graced him with a small smile before disappearing among the other shoppers.

Xiomara took her time moving alone throughout the crowd. She purchased a juniper scented soap made by a local beekeeper, a piece of frybread made from taro flour, and a red jasper coyote fetish. He reminded her of home.

She wandered toward the dance circle where the celebration was winding down. Rosebud and Kate were nowhere to be found, so she joined the crowd standing on the far side of the circle. There were currently seven couples on the dance floor, dancing head-to-head or cheek-to-cheek in tight, stomping circles. Something was tucked between them, but she couldn't tell what the dark object was from this distance. She pushed her sunglasses up and squinted.

"It's a potato."

She looked up beside her and saw the tall man who had been with Uncle Muskwa before. Calehan. "What's a potato?"

"The thing they're holding with their faces. It's a potato. For the potato dance."

"Potato dance." Xiomara repeated, looking at the dancers. "I like it." She smiled at him warmly, their shoulders brushing.

"The winners are said to be together forever." Calehan watched the youngest couple drop their potato.

"Oh, yeah?" She peered at him from the corner of her eyes. "I hope they all chose their partners wisely."

"Teenagers aren't exactly known for their wisdom."

"You are right about that." She smoothed the end of her braid. "I've been that stupid teen."

"Who hasn't?" Calehan said.

The final couple standing was rewarded with resounding applause, the two of them joining in as they cheered for the two blushing teens. Calehan was about to speak again when a woman appeared beside him, a crying baby in her arms.

"Help," she pleaded to him.

Calehan gathered the crying boy in his hands and shot Xiomara an apologetic look.

"Good luck with your bebesito." Xiomara took a step back.

"I'll need it." Calehan walked away quickly, muttering comfort to the little man. Xiomara watched the three of them walk away together. Was that his son? Was the young woman his wife?

Xiomara brushed away the disappointment at Calehan being unavailable. She was also unavailable, so there was no reason for her to be upset. This project had been more than a year in the making and she would be damned if she let a hot dude interfere with her efficacy. Her work contract included housing and Chief Thomas had been explicit about the timeliness of this project. There was no space for flirting with guys she wanted to see between her legs. With a quick deep breath, she searched for her roommates.

Xiomara spotted Rosebud's blue hair bobbing toward the parking lot. The dirt sighed beneath her steps as she followed.

Kate was talking to the people parked next to them. "See you at eight!" They waved to her as they drove away.

"What's at eight?" Xiomara asked, watching as Rosebud kissed her wife's cheek before climbing into the car.

"Annual bonfire at our place. Everyone comes."

"Oh gosh." Xiomara leaned her head against the back of her seat. What exactly did "everyone" mean?

"Do you want to make the guacamole?" Rosebud turned nearly a full one-eighty to look at her.

"Claro que sí." Xiomara said. Kate pumped her fist in the air a few times, cranking the radio up to the classical stylings of *Hit Me Baby One More Time*.

"Hola, Anubito, ¿cómo estás, mi amor?" Xiomara squatted, taking Anubis's face between her hands and scratching behind his ears. "Ven." She wandered outside while he searched for the perfect pee spot.

The grass tickled the soles of her feet where she stood watching the sky change color. Flossy pink and orange clouds migrated across the sky while it turned from blue to purple. She watched Anubis run around the backyard, chewing blades of grass and attempting to catch lightning bugs in his mouth.

She brought him inside and served Anubis dinner, then joined Kate at the island where she found ten avocados waiting for her. "How many people are coming?"

"Oh, probably only forty or so."

Xiomara's gaze blurred as her eyes widened. Ten avocados it was then. She could feel the ache starting in her wrists just looking at them.

"Do you have a food processor?"

"Oh, I wish!" Rosebud's voice was clear, despite being in a completely different room.

"What about a potato masher?" Xiomara held her breath.

Kate smiled and reached into the drawer behind her, presenting the masher to Xiomara like a trophy.

Xiomara held the masher in front of her face. "It's you and me, baby." She pointed her finger between the masher and herself. "Let's do this."

Together, the three women prepared an array of snacks and side dishes, only dropping a few pieces to Anubis in the process. Xiomara had to be firm on the abundance of treats that Rosebud and Kate would've happily given Anubis for all of eternity.

Letting her hair down, Xiomara changed into leggings and a hoodie. The nights were windy and cold, so she wrapped her feet in wool socks and slid into an old pair of Javier's Birkenstocks. Worn from a decade of use, the shoes molded around her feet. She dressed Anubis in a sweater, his grey hairless skin cold to the touch. He bolted toward the backyard as soon as she opened the door. Alone in the kitchen, Xiomara set to tidying the counter space for drinks.

"Hello again."

Xiomara looked up from the mess on the counter, a bottle of rum in her left hand and tequila in her right. "Hi!" she stuttered out, meeting Calehan's light brown eyes. He was looking down at her full hands. "I was putting these out... not drinking them both."

Calehan took the liquor from her with his long fingers, holding both bottles in only one hand. "I don't judge." He turned and placed the bottles in the center of the island.

Xiomara perched at the edge of the counter, gliding her eyes across his lengthy frame. "Thank you."

Calehan stood well over a head taller than her, his shoulder still a few inches above her head. He peered down at her, close enough she could smell the sweetgrass on his skin. They really did grow them tall up north.

Rosebud called her name from outside, breaking the moment between them.

"Duty calls." Xiomara smiled, grabbing her lemonade on the way out the door.

Outside, Xiomara joined Kate and Rosebud where they were roasting marshmallows over the raging fire. Anubis jumped up and nestled into the blanket between them. Kate handed her a skewer stacked with three marshmallows.

"Do you like your marshmallows roasted or burnt?" Rosebud asked.

Kate scoffed. "Just because it catches on fire doesn't mean it's burnt."

Xiomara's marshmallow trio caught fire.

"Blow it out!" she squeaked, gently bumping Xiomara's shoulder.

Xiomara laughed and shook her head no. She let it flame for a few more seconds before pulling it from the fire and blowing it out. She squished it between two extra large pieces of graham cracker, a slice of chocolate on top. Rosebud grabbed Xiomara's stick and toasted her own marshmallow.

"I see you belong to the burnt category." Rosebud laughed as she pulled her barely toasted, still cold marshmallow from the fire. "Perfect."

Xiomara and Kate exchanged a look while Rosebud returned the poker. A tall man broke through the smoke of the fire, taking a seat beside Rosebud.

"Hey kids." His voice was monotone and deep like the night.

"Xiomara, this is my brother, Clover, and..." She looked around the party briefly, before nodding toward a woman talking to a group Kate had described as clan cousins. "That's his wife, Juniper."

"Calehan and Juniper are twins," Kate filled in.

Twins. There were plenty of twins in her community, but she had never guessed Calehan was half of a whole. "So, Calehan is a brother to all of you."

Kate, Rosebud, and Clover nodded. Xiomara was going to need a family tree. Clover waved them over, Juniper introducing herself before joining Clover in his recliner. Calehan took the seat beside Xiomara, offering her the slightest upturn of his lips.

"Hey, where's my baby?" Kate squinted in a playful glare, glancing between Clover and Juniper.

Juniper laughed. "He's having a sleepover at my dad's."

"Mom and Dad needed a night off." Clover rested his hand on Juniper's bum.

"Oh God, I am right here." Calehan grimaced, covering his eyes.

"It's been fifteen years; you should be used to it by now." Juniper teased her brother.

Clover smiled at his wife as if she held up the sky. Turning to Xiomara he explained, "We're high school sweethearts. She chased me as soon as she turned sixteen."

"*Me* chasing *you*?" Juniper exclaimed, laughter tumbling from her open mouth. "Absolutely not."

"I don't know," Calehan interjected. "I remember a lot of lingering looks when we were kids."

Juniper's loud *ha!* echoed around the fire before Calehan interrupted again. "On *both* sides."

Clover whispered a laugh of his own. She pinched his chest softly and snuggled into him. Juniper's husband was built like a brick house and took up the entire chair. He wore his hair shaved to the scalp on the bottom, and the long hair on top tied into a smooth braid. About the same size as Calehan, he towered over Xiomara. Juniper wore her black hair long and straight, her smile and eyes impossible to tell apart from her twin. She too, was at least a head taller than Xiomara.

Narrowing her eyes, Xiomara glanced around the fire. Everyone here was somewhere close to six feet or six hundred feet tall. Xiomara felt miniscule. She didn't think five-five was all that short until she arrived here.

Xiomara was pulled from her thoughts with a tug on her marshmallow poker. She looked up to find Calehan stringing two marshmallows onto the pointed tip. He met her eyes with a slight smile before gently placing them in the orange flames.

"So," Xiomara spoke softly, "do you have kids?"

Calehan nearly choked. "No." He hid his cough behind a laugh. "I don't."

"Damn near came close." Juniper snickered from above Clover's head.

Xiomara widened her eyes and shot Calehan a look.

"It wasn't... I didn't," Calehan attempted to defend himself. "My girlfriend from high school got pregnant almost immediately after we broke up."

"Dodged a bullet then?" Xiomara asked quietly. "Or missed a chance?"

"Dodged a bullet." Calehan took a sip of his beer. He held the bottle firmly, his pointer and middle fingers nearly obscuring the label.

She stared at him, the corner of her mouth lifting before she returned her gaze to the flames.

"What about you?" His voice was low, the crackling fire mixing with his tenor in her ears.

She shook her head. "I still feel like a kid myself sometimes."

"Me too." Calehan said. "Thirty-two years isn't enough to figure it all out."

Her laughter warmed the space between them. "Maybe the next thirty will seal the deal."

"I sure hope so." The two held each other's gaze in contented silence.

"Hey, whisperers," a voice person called across the fire. "We're playing *Never Have I Ever*, eh?"

"We're listening." Calehan and Xiomara held their hands up in mock surrender, sharing a look before focusing on the game.

"It's your turn, cousin," the person pressed, jutting their chin out at Calehan.

"Never have I ever kept bees," Calehan responded immediately.

Xiomara was certain her eyebrows were touching her scalp, but her bangs hid her surprise. She looked at his profile while he stared humorously at the game instigator who was now chugging their beer.

"You youngins better remember who's bigger than you." Clover propped his glass out in front of Xiomara, Calehan reaching over to tap his bottle to Clover's. His shoulder brushed hers, the smell of fresh sweetgrass invading her nostrils.

Calehan's eyes met hers as he settled into his seat. "Your turn."

She looked into the sparkling night sky while she thought. "Never have I ever...ridden a motorcycle."

"Damn, do dirt bikes count?" A lean blue-eyed woman stuck her tongue out when Juniper nodded, forcing her to sip her drink.

By the time it was Rosebud's turn, Xiomara was standing strong, having only taken two sips of her lemonade during the game.

"Never have I ever..." Rosebud dragged her eyes around the circle, narrowing on Xiomara. "Been to Mexico."

"I will remember this betrayal." Xiomara sipped her drink while she awaited the next turn.

"Never have I ever won a potato dance." Kate wiggled her eyebrows.

Xiomara clapped along with the group when Juniper stuck her straw in Clover's drink so they could take their punishment together. Calehan attempted to hide his sip, but Xiomara's eagle eyes caught him.

"You've won a potato dance?" She couldn't conceal the surprise in her voice.

"He and Clem won a few times, didn't they?"

Xiomara turned around, finding a redheaded woman smirking at Calehan.

"What are you doing here?" Juniper squealed, extracting herself from her husband and throwing her arms around the newcomer.

The twins surrounded the woman, obscuring her face from view. When they finally released her, Xiomara got a good look at the woman. The bridge of her nose and shape of her teeth matched those of Calehan and Juniper.

"Buffy, this is Xiomara, the archaeologist here to build the museum." Calehan introduced her.

"It's nice to meet you." Buffy took Calehan's chair and skewer, filling it with four marshmallows.

"My little sister here is a senior at the University of Winnipeg." Juniper ruffled Buffy's hair, then went inside.

"What do you study?"

"Social Work." Buffy leaned back in the chair while Calehan perched on the arm. "And business. I want to work with non-profits serving Indigenous people."

"That's incredible." Xiomara was too soft for social work. It killed her to not have full control over an outcome. "It is not an easy field to work in."

Buffy met her eyes, a knowing look shared between them.

"Maybe she will have something to add to your museum someday." Calehan said, still perched on his sister's chair, yet taking up every spot of air next to her.

"Ah, it's your guys' museum. I'm just organizing the inside of it, really." Xiomara brushed the compliment off. Museums belong to the community, not the curators. If only the Europeans could get on board.

"All right everyone, it's time." Juniper patted Clover's arm as the group rose from their chairs.

Xiomara hesitated briefly, unsure of what was happening and if she was involved.

"We're making our offerings." Calehan too her hand, pulling her from her chair.

Looking over her shoulder at him, he was barely visible in the diamond speckled sky. "You know..." Xiomara turned around to face him. "You could've told me you were a champion potato dancer."

"It didn't seem pertinent at the time." He stared at her.

"You mean the time when we were standing there watching the potato dance?" She raised a brow.

"Yes."

Xiomara sidled close to his chest. "You're funny." Poking him once in the chest with her finger, she took three steps backward before turning around and taking off in a jog.

"Are you coming?"

Calehan ran to catch up to her, bumping her shoulder with his as they joined the others. Setting his beer down on a tree stump nearby, Calehan took Xiomara's hand and placed it palm up on his own. A pinch of tobacco fell into the center of her palm, another pinch making a home in his.

Xiomara followed him to the water's edge. Peering down, she edged her way close to the cliff so she could see the water below. Calehan wrapped an arm around her and pulled them three steps back.

His voice was breathy like the wind and deep like the water before them. "The earth is much softer here than in a desert." She thanked him with a squeeze of his bicep, turning toward the water. Xiomara let her shoulder rest against his arm as they prepared to place their offerings.

Taking a deep breath, Xiomara let her eyes wander over the landscape while a prayer sang through her head. Dios, she was so lucky to be here, in a place like this one. The moon's gaze was so bright she could see the landscape carved into the painted night sky. The air tasted different up here, a cold taste that felt like ice filling her lungs. Her eyes ran across the tops of the trees where they met the ink violet sky. She admired the pale dimpled face of the moon before closing her eyes, thanking the ancestors of the land now welcoming her. She let the tobacco fall from her palm, the wind skirting it across the water before the current swallowed it whole.

Xiomara finally brought her eyes over to Calehan, finding him watching her, his gaze a tickle of sea spray on her skin.

"Thank you." She gestured to the water with a quirk of her head. She knew he didn't have to share his offering with her, and the intimacy of the action was not lost on her.

Xiomara opened her mouth to speak when Juniper threw her arm around Calehan's shoulders. "Drive us home, little brother."

He leaned away from his sister, scrunching his nose when her curls met his skin. "I'm older than you."

Juniper put her pointer finger up. "Time is a circle."

"Come on, you three!" Clover's voice bellowed through the night, beckoning them toward the fire. Goodbyes sounded throughout the backyard as people prepared to head home. Not a huge fan of hugs, Xiomara hung back slightly, dancing around everyone as she carefully evaded a multitude of embraces. Calehan kissed the cheeks of Rosebud and Kate, corralling both of his sisters and herding them toward the car.

Inside the house, Xiomara's fingers stung. Her eyes drooped too low for a shower, so she peeled her clothes off and dove beneath the covers, pulling the crocheted blanket on top for good measure. Anubis tucked into the blankets at her feet. She joined her dreams quickly, her desert at home painted with the violet night sky of Bunchberry.

Her eyes focused on the full moon, shining so brightly the mesas shone purple in the inky night. Javier's voice swam in her head, rushing through her ears and surrounding her like a waterfall. She could see him standing among the nopales, calling her name.

Mi vida. I've been waiting for you.

CHAPTER 4

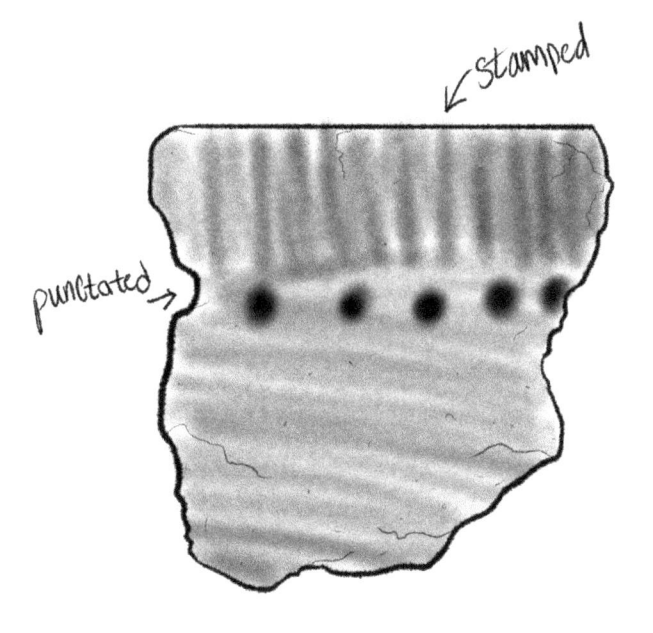

"Who wants the aux?" Rosebud brandished a mint green cord.

"I got this." David took the cord from her and plugged it into his phone.

"I hope you like Bad Bunny," Xiomara whispered to Rosebud, "because that is all he plays."

An hour later they were pulling off the ferry and onto Yellowbird Island. Xiomara's eyes were wide as she looked out the window, holding off a blink in the fear of missing anything. The trees were so dense on the island she couldn't see through to the other side, birds darting through sunbeams.

Xiomara saw the mound first, eyes drifting across the rounded edges as she said a silent hello to the ancestors resting inside. Climbing from the parked car, Xiomara laid her eyes on the site that had made a home in her thoughts the past year. To anyone else, it was an overgrown hill. Only she could see the secrets the earth concealed.

"Hello." The awe whispered between her lips and stirred the spirits around them, her happiness palpable in the air.

Chief Thomas led the group in prayer, Xiomara adding cornmeal to her pinch of tobacco and cedar. She watched the offerings mingle in the wind as they carried across the island and site, her whisper of honor trailing along with it. She couldn't contain the smile on her face as she turned toward the group, finding Calehan watching her. She blushed.

"Are you ready?" Chief Thomas bumped her shoulder with his elbow.

"Absolutely."

He clapped his hands together in front of his chest. "Take it away, doctor."

Xiomara stopped herself from correcting him in public. "David, can you grab our things from the trunk?"

The interns joined David at the car, whisking the catering into coolers.

"Today is day one of three survey days." Xiomara guided the group toward the table nearby. She placed an outdoor bed under the shade of the table for Anubis, where he promptly curled up for a nap. "We will be doing ground survey, topographical mapping, and artifact collection and cataloging." She quickly tasked the interns and equipped them with stakes and twine before sending them off.

Calehan spread the blueprints on the table in front of them, Clover placing rocks in the corners to hold it still in the breeze.

"I like to work east to west, so I will have you uncover this section here first." She used a red pencil to mark a portion of the blueprints. "And the second section once the rest of the interns arrive." Their first round of interns were high school and college aged Bunchberry residents. Therefore, they only had three interns. The following five would join them in the summer from surrounding Nations.

Calehan inspected the area she noted on the paper, small dots marking where Xiomara suspected to find artifacts or structures.

"We planned to bring the machines up here Friday." Clover leaned his hands against the table. "Ready to dig Monday. How's that sound?"

"Perfect." Xiomara said. "Now, let me show you what I need from this GPR." She spent a half hour orienting the brothers to using ground penetrating radar in an archaeological context before sending them off to complete the digital mapping of the site. The mound would have to be mapped by her hand later.

Chief Thomas moved to stand beside her. "Anything you need from me?"

"Will an elder be present to break ground on Monday?" Xiomara led him to the table of blueprints, thumbing open a green leather notebook. Tooled into the leather was a floral design, sweeping across the cover as if it were alive. Three flowers pointed in four directions, their leaves facing opposite their queen.

"Nice notebook." Chief Thomas tapped the bottom cover gently with the side of his knuckle. "My father and grandfather will be present to honor the site and prepare it for disruption."

"Three generations." Xiomara raised her eyebrows over the top of the gold aviators on her nose. "Lucky us."

"I think I'm the lucky one." Chief Thomas sat on the table, a lopsided grin hanging on his face, pointed straight at her.

Xiomara escaped with a quick murmur of needing to supervise the interns and escaped the charged silence. Maybe she was just imagining things. He was sweet and kind to everyone she had seen him interact with. Maybe this was just how he was naturally. Nothing to overthink about.

The youngest intern, Nataani, was off in the trees quite a few meters from the site. She stopped by David, asking him to check over the interns before following Nataani's red shirt into the forest. She could see him walking slowly, turning his head from side to side.

"Hi, Nataani," Xiomara called out as she got close, not wanting to startle the boy from his thoughts.

"Hi, Doc." He didn't turn to look at her, still focused on his surroundings. She watched as he opened and closed his eyes, sometimes closing them for short periods of time. "Sometimes I can hear them."

"Me too."

Nataani brought his brown eyes to hers, widened to show nearly the entirety of his caramel colored iris. His mouth dropped open in shock.

"There's this one site I worked on in the US." She joined him in the small tree break. "It was in southern New Mexico, a tiny temporary settlement. It was my first excavation in college, and I was doing my best to be perfect."

She looked at the sky, blue peeking through the break in the leaf coverage. "We hypothesized it was a single family, on a migration. They didn't stay long, likely a few months. But they loved that little rock outcropping they made their home." Xiomara sat on a downed log nearby. "We found petroglyphs, some humanoid figures, a dog, and two animorphs. And a few feet below that, there were more glyphs. They were obviously done by a child, and they were so faint." She let her voice soften as if it was the pressure of the child's carving hand. "I almost missed them. We think they drew their family, two adults, one with swirls and one with a braid, a child, and a baby. We had to do tons of scans just to see them. They were so light."

Xiomara closed her eyes and conjured the memory of first seeing those carvings by her knees. "I had been hearing laughter for days. I thought I was going insane or had food poisoning or something. But once I saw that, I knew. Their laughter was all around me." Opening her eyes, she found Nataani watching her from his own downed log, "Ever since then, I find if I take the time to listen, they will always be heard."

Nataani smiled, his crooked teeth making him appear even younger than fifteen. "I can't wait to learn their story."

"Me either, bud." She stood and dusted off her pants. "Don't wander too far, okay?"

"I won't." Nataani jumped from his log and began wandering again.

When Xiomara emerged from the trees, she saw Calehan looking over Rosebud's shoulder at the tape measure in his hands. "How's it going over here?"

"Great!" Rosebud swatted her brother away like a fly. "We're finishing the perimeter now."

Xiomara looked around her at Calehan. "You're up."

Calehan turned the machine on. It looked oddly like a white lawn mower with oversized wheels. He looked back at Xiomara, a briefcase-type laptop open in front of her.

"Are you some kind of James Bond or something?" Calehan nodded at the bulky black machine.

"I wish, but no. They just refuse to make things smaller." Xiomara stood beside him, the open spy laptop balanced in her arms. "I'm ready when you are."

Gluing her eyes to the screen, she settled at the edge of the proposed perimeter. Anubis circled three times before lying at her feet.

Xiomara took notes and screenshots over the hour Calehan pushed the radar across the site. Colored lines filled every frame of her vision. She had only stolen one glance at his broad shoulders when he passed her, reminding herself to focus on work and not her incredibly hot coworker. Rounding up the interns, she built a scene and told the story of these people through those colored lines.

Xiomara clapped her hands and sent everyone to lunch. She turned to Calehan, the sun was right above his head, painting him with a golden halo. "Hungry?"

"Starving." He gestured in front of him with his hand. "After you."

Clover handed each of them a plate as they joined the circle of camping chairs. Thin sliced buffalo was served in an open-face bannock, topped with green chiles and sliced cheese. Anubis munched on a few cheese slices and strips of grilled buffalo. Chief Thomas was standing with his sandwich off to the side, phone pressed to his ear. David sat beside Xiomara, cataloging the surface debris he had collected throughout the morning. He leaned over, holding an item out for Xiomara to peer at. Mouth full, an excited hum rumbled in the back of her throat.

"What is it?" Nataani asked, watching their interaction from across the way.

"A pottery sherd," David answered, passing it to Nataani.

He inspected it eagerly, turning it over in his hands and rubbing along the soft edges. Nataani paused when he noticed a raised area on the edge, angling it in the sunlight, straining to figure out what it was.

"It's a fingerprint." Xiomara said.

Nataani's mouth dropped open, along with the other interns. Calehan and Clover's eyebrows shot up, both straining to see the artifact. One of the older interns took her cellphone out of her pocket to take a few photos of the sherd, filming a video of placing her finger in the print of her ancestor who lived nearly hundreds of years before.

"It's not uncommon to find sherds with fingerprints in them. I've found dozens, but it never stops blowing my mind."

Smiles grew as the sherd made its way around the circle, each person spending time honoring this gift their ancestors had left them. She loved watching the attentiveness in their eyes, the way each one held their breath as they touched it. She could practically see the beats of their hearts as they aligned their fingers to the print.

David passed a few more artifacts around the group: a broken awl, a piece of what they thought to be a scraper, and a seashell with a hole in the center. It had likely been ornamental, a piece of jewelry or something worn on the clothes or hair. The interns were delighted by each find. She could see the excitement growing in every new item they touched. Her archaeology bug was caught when she first watched *The Mummy*, but these kids were catching the bug from their own family.

Chief Thomas eventually joined everyone for lunch, looking over Rosebud's shoulder at the awl she held between two fingers.

"These are some incredible finds, Xiomara," Chief Thomas complimented.

"Thank David." She poked him with her elbow. "He found all of these artifacts today."

"Cheers to David!" Chief Thomas raised his water in the air, laughter infecting everyone as they raised waters, teas, and diet Pepsi.

Wrapping up their lunch, Rosebud and Calehan packed their trash into the bed of his truck while Clover took soil samples. Islands were always a bit dicey, water consistently reaching across the land for its other half. Sometimes they would find underground streams or rivers wide enough to collapse. Thus, he needed to probe and sample the land around the site to ensure it would be safe to dig.

Xiomara loaded her things into the trunk, sweat dripping from her brow. Stifling humidity made the mild heat insufferable. Chief Thomas appeared in her peripheral vision, heading in her direction. She dragged the back of her hand across her lip, wiping the moisture from her upper lip.

"You did well today." Chief Thomas leaned against the closed trunk beside her. "Will you be in the office tomorrow?"

"Yes, David and I need to go over our findings from today." Xiomara looked around for David, hoping he could give her moral support.

"I'd like to see what you come up with." Chief Thomas squinted. "I'll meet you in the lab at lunch." He patted her arm as he walked away with no chance for Xiomara to answer him. She was normally pretty strict about lunch hours being work-free, but she hadn't had the chance to argue.

Xiomara loaded Anubis into the backseat where David sat with his head back, eyes closed under his hat. She looked for Rosebud, finding her half inside Clover's truck, long legs kicking in the air.

She slid from the truck and winked at Xiomara, then ran to the car.

"We're going to dinner tonight," Rosebud whispered once they were on the road.

David popped his head up in between the two of them. "Why are we whispering?"

"Oh, sorry." Rosebud shook her head as they drove onto the boat one by one. "We try to keep things on the low so Kenny—I mean, Chief Thomas—doesn't feel left out." The car shook as the boat lurched away from the dock. "He doesn't realize how weird it is to hang out with your boss, let alone your Chief."

The car rocked lightly as the boat churned through the water.

"He's our brother, so he thinks it's the same as when we were kids," Rosebud explained. "But things are different now."

"No one wants to drink with the boss," David added before leaning against the seat beside the napping Anubis.

"Should I stay home then?" Xiomara met David's eyes in the rearview mirror.

"Obviously you're an exception." His eyes rolled so far back in his head, she was certain they would come up from below.

"You're our coworker," Rosebud argued, laughter filling the car. "Kenny just doesn't know how to turn off the *Chief* part of himself yet, and no one likes a chaperone."

"You're a cool boss." David winked at Xiomara through the mirror, referencing their favorite movie to watch in the field. "Now, will there be any cute boys there?"

Xiomara groaned while Rosebud excitedly launched into detailing all the single men of Bunchberry.

↙ paint

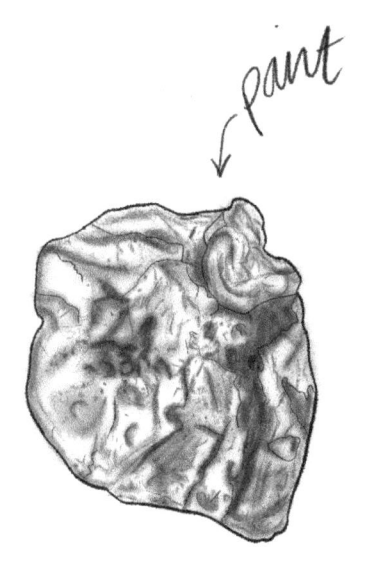

Chapter 5

    Xiomara entered City Hall with Rosebud, who was suffering from a severe case of the Mondays. Her influence on the mug selection in the employee kitchen was evident. There was a mug oddly shaped and painted as an orange cloud, one that was shaped like baby Yoda, and a vintage one with Winnie the Pooh. Xiomara took the oddly shaped orange cloud and breathed in the bitter steam.

Rosebud led her down a long white hallway. Photos of Bunchberry through the years lined the walls. She admired a black and white one with a man standing strong in the center with a war bonnet on his head. The man held a striking resemblance to Calehan. Written in Cree, she could only decipher the date 1883.

"Chief Running Bear." Rosebud smiled at the photo. "Best known for keeping the Dutch off Bunchberry for more than a decade."

Xiomara was impressed. That was no easy feat for any Native community, especially one as isolated and resource-rich as Bunchberry.

Rosebud led her downstairs to the basement where they would temporarily house the artifacts. Xiomara instantly felt the dampness and grimaced. She would have to talk to Chief Thomas about regulating the storage. Humidity accelerates deterioration, and being that the site was already humid, this room needed to be dry as a bone.

The basement was one large room, sinks and storage on one end, computers and books on the other. At the far end of the sinks, there was a pink door. Xiomara suspected Rosebud had something to do with the color choice.

"Chief only let me paint the door." Rosebud pouted. "Otherwise, I would've made your office incredible."

Xiomara patted her on the shoulder in shared misery for the certainly boring room she was about to enter.

Oh.

It wasn't bad at all. A sliding glass door to the right let in sunlight where she could access the porch and grounds of City Hall. It did have terrible gray tiles, but the walls were clean and white. Her pine desk faced the door. Rosebud decorated her desk, even placing a polaroid of Anubis in a small frame.

"Rosebud." Xiomara rounded the desk to hug her friend. "This is incredible. Truly. Where did you even get a photo of Anubis?"

Rosebud shrugged. "I have a polaroid camera. I took a few photos of him the other day."

"I love it, thank you." Xiomara squeezed her hand. Rosebud glowed like an award winner.

"You deserve it." Rosebud's eyes crinkled under her blue bangs. "You get settled. I am going to go fetch David." Rosebud's boots clicked on the tile as she walked away.

Xiomara placed her bag on the desk, letting a sigh fall from her mouth. She was overwhelmed. A new job, two new roommates, an office, a museum... When would she get a chance to just breathe?

Sliding the door open, she stepped outside. The air was cool on her skin, unsettling at this time of year. She was used to the air practically steaming by now. Bunchberry had a permanent breeze on top of its chilly temperature that demanded she bring a jacket everywhere with her. Xiomara missed the oppressive desert heat. It didn't feel like summer without it.

A low whistle sounded behind her. She turned to find David leaning in the open glass door.

"Does this count as a corner office, jefa?" David joined her outside, slipping easily into one of the rocking chairs on the porch.

"That wall goes to a utility closet so..." Xiomara shrugged, her smile stuck to her face.

"¿Estás nerviosa?"

"Claro que sí." Xiomara waved a hand in the air at him. "We're digging up a burial, a home." Her eyes roved over the green grass. "I can't make any mistakes."

David laughed at her. "No eres humano si you don't make mistakes." He nudged her in the shoulder. "You're not a robot."

"Can we get a robot?" Xiomara asked, only half serious.

David ignored her. "Aye, they got any artifacts down here already?"

Xiomara shook her head. "I haven't looked yet." She hurried inside behind David, the two tip-toeing as though their search would be forbidden. She followed him across the large room to the storage at the back, away from the sunlight. The shelves were empty.

"Maybe the drawers?" David asked.

Xiomara's heart dropped when she slid open the first drawer, and it was empty.

"Maybe they don't have anything." She opened a few more empty drawers before moving to the next section.

David searched through a few more drawers before calling out, "Jackpot!"

Xiomara ran to him, her heart beating rapidly. David was huddled over the storage, pulling all of the drawers open. Xiomara peered over his shoulder and shuddered. The artifacts were haphazardly piled into the top three drawers of the otherwise empty cabinet.

She nudged them around gently, grateful the drawers were lined with soft black fabric. Some of the items were recent, but the others were certainly prehistoric. Xiomara set a few red ochre painted pottery sherds together, thinking they may find their matches amongst each other.

A few hand axes were spread across the second drawer, no wrappings to speak of, though their remains were visible in the dent circumventing the stone. She palmed the smallest one; it was dull and weathered on the wide end where her fingernail caught in the knicks from years of use. Turning it in her hands, she ran her finger through the groove where it was once tied to a wooden handle—a handle someone would hold when they cut vegetables from their vines, chopped the heads from fish, and settled at night beside its owner. She rubbed the skin of her thumb under a small notch in the underside of the axe head. A diagonal line ran between three dots, two above, one below. She suspected the owner had carved it into the stone, identifying who it belonged to. Xiomara squeezed the stone gently in her palm, thanking its original owner.

"Look, there are shells in here." David brought Xiomara out of her thoughts as he presented her with a pendant that appeared to be a mother of pearl.

Xiomara took the pendant in her hand, picking the dirt out of the drilled hole that would've been home to a thin leather strap. She turned it over a few times, sliding her finger over the soft curved edges. Xiomara imagined the bead maker, slowly grinding the shell against a stone again and again until it no longer sliced the finger of its admirer. She wondered who the owner was. Did they trade for the pendant, or was it a gift? Was the wearer a man or woman? An adult or a child?

"We should see if the tribe has the budget for genetic testing. I wonder where the shell came from." She was always happiest with an artifact in her hands. Her eyes were almost glassy in the way they roved over the few items in the drawers.

"How much do you think we will pull from the site?" David asked.

Xiomara paused, picturing the site in her mind. "I think we are going to fill this room, maybe more. The museum curation will be difficult with the number of artifacts."

David's eyebrows met his hairline as he whistled. "I've never worked on an un-looted site."

Xiomara squeezed his shoulder. "It is a feeling unlike any other." They shared a giggle of excitement.

A voice sounded behind them, and both David and Xiomara let out a scream of surprise and turned toward the door.

"Oh my gosh, I didn't mean to scare you." Chief Thomas smothered a laugh.

Xiomara kept her hand to her chest as she joined him in the middle of the open room. "We can get a little focused."

"I'll knock next time."

David watched from where he stood beside his own desk. Narrowing his eyes, he looked between his boss and her boss.

Xiomara crossed her arms over her chest. "Actually, I'm glad you're here." She looked for David. "We'd like to consider some extra artifact testing. Is there any space in the budget?"

Chief Thomas chuckled. "We haven't even started, and you want more money?"

"Yes." Xiomara toyed with the end of her braid as she thought of what to say. "I anticipate we will find items without clear origins and with some extra tests, we can sometimes see where it came from."

"Sometimes?" Chief Thomas raised his brows at her.

"Organic matter doesn't always stand the test of time." Xiomara tapped her fingers on her crossed arms.

"I will see what can be done with the budget," Chief Thomas replied. "Now, tell me, is the office to your liking?"

"Rosebud did a fantastic job, as usual," Xiomara answered, stepping back to perch on a desk. "Anything you need, David?"

"I don't think we have enough empty metal cabinets." David sat at the desk Xiomara perched on.

Chief Thomas grinned. "You all are doing important work. It's my job to provide the tools you need."

"I will be sure to thank the tribal council for their support," Xiomara joked, recalling the multiple budget plans she produced for them. Their approval was required for all aspects of the project, but it was the budget that took the most work. Some members were more inclined to funding archaeology than others. Her idea to build a museum with the artifacts was the only way she got approval for excavation. She had originally been hired solely to rebury the mound dwellers, with the site lost to the water. Showing them a museum would bring further per diem convinced the council to allow her to excavate the untouched site.

She crossed her fingers in hopes Chief Thomas would find space in the budget for the extra testing. If the site had any signs of trade, she wouldn't be able to rest until she knew just how far they had traveled.

Rosebud's boots clicked on the stairs before she came into view. "I brought our lunches," she called out before she saw them, pausing on the stairs when she saw Chief Thomas. "Sorry Chief, didn't know you were here." She gestured to the three bags in her hands.

"I was just leaving," he replied. "I have a last-minute lunch meeting. Not to worry, I will crash your party another day."

The three were silent as Chief Thomas left. Rosebud tiptoed over, slightly hunched as she handed them each a bag.

"Let's eat outside." Xiomara nodded at the porch.

They sat at the long rectangle table on the edge of the concrete. The wood was slightly uneven, a large crack down the middle. Xiomara took advantage of the sunshine and sat on the end of the table directly in the sunbeam.

Rosebud and David dug into their turkey sandwiches while Xiomara reclined in her chair, tilting her chin up to welcome the light.

"You and Anubis are both like lizards," Rosebud teased as she watched Xiomara bask in her beloved sun.

"I'm committed to getting my vitamin D," Xiomara said, keeping her eyes closed.

"You might have to switch to supplements come fall." Rosebud kicked the side of Xiomara's foot. "Sometimes we go days without sunlight."

Xiomara felt her heart drop to her feet. It was impossible to imagine waking up to the dark. She could feel the seasonal depression looming. Hopefully the excavation would yield plenty of artifacts to keep her busy during the winter.

Xiomara moved into her office quickly, carting two boxes of books and a mound of field notes down the stairs. This morning was quiet in the lab. She was certain David was taking advantage of the shorter workweek and was still sleeping. A sigh of relief sagged her shoulders when she dropped the boxes on her desk.

The last year spent preparing for this excavation had allowed for her to amass a significant amount of Cree and Canadian archaeology books. She unloaded the books onto the shelves behind her. They took up almost the entirety of the available space.

She took lunch at her desk, deep in the scans of the site. Xiomara was up to her eyebrows in field preparation when a knock drew her from the laptop screen. Calehan stood in the doorway, filling every inch of open space. "So, this is your fancy office, huh?"

"I don't think I said the word 'fancy'." She glared at him over the top of her computer screen. Dressed in jeans and a flannel, his wide chest stretched the fabric thin. Saliva pooled in her mouth at the sight. Dios, he was captivating.

"It looks pretty fancy to me." Calehan said. Heat rose in her cheeks as he took the seat in front of her.

She chewed the pen cap in the corner of her mouth. "You going to build me a fancy office in that museum of yours?"

"I'll see what I can do."

Calehan glanced at the blueprints on her desk, small pink pencil scratches where she thought she wanted things to go. Xiomara quickly covered the sketches.

She sat back in her chair, her next words coming out in a whisper. "I don't know what I'm doing." She avoided his eyes, instead staying focused on the chicken scratch she had ruined his gorgeous blueprints with.

"You know more than me." Calehan leaned in his seat. "I think I've only been inside one museum in my lifetime."

Xiomara concealed her surprise at his admission. She couldn't imagine a life without a tangible way to remember the past. She felt almost ashamed to know she had likely seen and handled more Cree artifacts than he had. Her fingers itched with guilt.

"It's hard to imagine the layout without being in the space." Xiomara shrugged, nerves eating at the acid in her stomach.

"I'll take you there," Calehan said.

"Right now?" she asked.

He nodded and stood.

"I don't have a car yet," she said.

"I'm aware." The bemused look on his face made her laugh.

Xiomara stood, a flabbergasted smile overtaking her face. Calehan crooked his head back and clicked his tongue, beckoning her to follow him. Hastily grabbing her things, Xiomara joined him in the hallway, where he held her doodle-ruined blueprints tucked under his arm. He must've slid them off her desk as she packed her bag. Sneaky man. Xiomara plotted a way to steal them back and destroy them permanently.

Calehan held the door open to his truck, offering his hand to Xiomara as she climbed in and settled into the comfy bench seat. She took note of his belongings while he walked to his door. A leather bag hung from the rearview mirror, stretched full of stuffing she suspected was tobacco and cedar. His weathered denim jacket was on the seat between them, the cuffs stained permanently rust brown from the Bunchberry earth. A notepad was open on top of the jacket, a rough sketch of a hogan facing up. The car smelled like the woods... like *him*. She reached for her seatbelt as Calehan slid in beside her.

She saw why he kept a bench seat in his truck. Calehan stretched his legs out wide, allowing his knee to press against the gearshift, his thigh taking up half of the cushion between them. His knees fit evenly beneath the dash, despite the length of his femurs. Xiomara kicked her legs straight up, toes tapping the underside of the dash.

"It's just across the bridge." Calehan pulled onto Main Street.

The baritone in his deep voice vibrated through the truck cab as they drove the long road between the trees. He turned the radio on low, the music filling the quiet cab.

"So, are you the reason a bear got into my cabin?"

Calehan laughed. "No way. I locked those doors." He waved his hand dismissively. "Don't worry about it. With Anubis there, bears won't come around."

"I hope not." She grimaced.

"Where'd you learn English?"

"I went to graduate school in New Mexico," Xiomara explained. "Where'd you learn your Spanish?"

Calehan's eyes widened.

"I heard you talking to David the other day. You're not so bad."

"Thanks." Calehan focused on the road again before speaking. "My mother was from Arizona. Her dad's family spoke Spanish, so we learned a little from her as kids." He shrugged. "And I took it in school."

"No French?"

"No French," Calehan confirmed. "Seemed hard."

"My dad taught me English, too," she said. "He passed before I went to college, so I kind of had to learn English."

"How old were you?"

"Seventeen." Xiomara examined his stoic face. "How old were you?"

"Fifteen." Calehan kept his eyes on the road. "Nataani and Joy were babies. They don't really remember her. Are you an only child?"

"Yep." Xiomara sighed. "I have cousins, but no siblings. It's just me and Mom now."

"I'm one of seven."

Xiomara's mouth dropped open. Calehan laughed, his eyes crinkling in the corners.

"No wonder you're so quiet." Xiomara said.

"You think I'm quiet?"

"Don't you?"

Calehan shrugged.

"How often are you designing buildings for the tribe?"

"Pretty much never."

"Oh." Xiomara's brow furrowed. "What else have you designed?"

Calehan cleared his throat. "A few parking lots, a kitchen, your cabin."

"You designed my cabin?"

Calehan nodded.

"I feel special."

"Don't get used to it."

Xiomara swatted his arm with her fingers, laughing with him when he finally met her eye. "Speaking of my cabin, do I get to move in soon?"

"End of the week." Calehan said. "Promise."

The ride was over too soon, disappointment dropping like a cliff in her stomach. Xiomara admired the construction in front of her. The frame was built, but it was hollow inside. The windows weren't in yet, and the drywall wasn't up, but it was *real*. Her breath held in her chest, and she reminded herself to breathe every three seconds.

One.

Two.

Three.

Calehan opened her door, offering a hand as she climbed from the truck. Daylight surrounded him, shining down a bit too much like a god.

A beaming smile overtook her face. "I didn't realize construction was so far along."

Calehan kicked at the ground, the quirk of his lip barely visible before he turned his face from hers.

"I had a floor plan idea, too." Without stairs into the doorway, Calehan reached up and vaulted himself inside. "Can I show you?" He offered both of his hands to her.

Xiomara hesitated. The floor was as high as her chest. She wasn't the shortest person on the planet, but she certainly couldn't reach the step on her own.

Calehan dropped to one knee in front of her, offering his hand. "Come on." He reached forward farther, gripping her shaking hands, and she jumped. Stepping back quickly to bring her over solid ground, Calehan held her suspended in air.

With their eyes locked on each other; electricity coursed through them at every spot they touched. Finally, Xiomara looked away, wiggling her feet where they hovered above the floor. Calehan released her slowly, his hands inching down her back, letting her slip to the ground.

His heartbeat thumped against her chest. Xiomara stepped back first, her fingers brushing his soft shirt as she pulled from his embrace.

"So..." Her tongue felt heavy in her mouth. "Your floorplan?"

"Right." Calehan spoke raspy and low, like smoke carried by the breeze. He shoved his hands into the pockets of his jeans. "You know Winter Counts?"

Xiomara nodded.

"We would have the welcome desk and everything here, then the exhibit would start in this back corner." He led her to the back left corner of the huge room. "You could start with the oldest artifacts and circle around the entire room until we reach the newest at the center. We would keep this entire space wide open for you to display whatever you desire."

The deepness of his voice tickled down her spine. Whatever she *desired*.

"To keep the circle intact, we would build a staircase going down to the basement, where you could display your archives."

Her archives. Dios, she felt like he was talking dirty to her in the way he read her mind.

"And they would exit inside the casino gift shop." Calehan said dejectedly, but Xiomara understood. The casino was their biggest money maker. If the tribe wanted to keep the museum alive, they had to utilize the casino, too.

They stood in silence for a while as Xiomara walked around the space, visualizing the exhibit in her head. She could feel Calehan's eyes watching her every move.

Finally, she faced him. "It's perfect."

"Really?" His eyebrows shot up.

"It is far better than any ideas I had." She grimaced at the thought of her doodles and reminded herself to burn them. "Honestly, Calehan." She waited for his coffee brown eyes to meet hers. "I'm blown away."

Calehan felt heat creep up his neck and quickly averted his eyes from the cause. The way Xiomara was looking at him made his palms itch. Shoving his hands into his pockets, he continued telling her about his plans.

Xiomara giggled at his elaborative speech. "I think you've got it figured out, Cal." His nickname rolled off her tongue where it touched the top of her mouth, her accent dripping down that one word. "I don't think you need me."

Wrinkles formed between his eyes. "Of course I need you." An eyebrow rose behind the curtain of her bangs, and Calehan froze. Fighting to keep his expression neutral, he tried to distract her from his confession. "I need you to find some artifacts, for one." Calehan held his breath as he watched creases form at the edges of her eyes. A smile split across her face, laughter tumbling through. She punched him in the arm gently, turning away to look at the space once again.

"Where are you going to put my fancy office?" Xiomara looked up through her thick, pure black lashes.

Calehan gestured behind him. He outlined the walls with his arms. "Corner office, two windows, south facing." A knowing smirk took over his face. "It's going to be the warmest room in the building."

"I love it already." Xiomara stepped into the center of his invisible rectangle. He imagined her in the office. "Can I paint it pink?"

"We can paint it any color you want." Calehan answered without hesitation, his voice steady as it reverberated in the hollow building.

"In that case"—her lips quirked up at the corner—"I'm thinking… wallpaper."

"Okay, I didn't say I would submit to torture." Calehan backed away from her slowly, hands up.

"You already agreed!"

"I said we could *paint*." He laughed at her mock outrage, her arms crossed tightly, hip jutted out in defiance. A shiver rolled down his back. He loved her ferocity. Clearly, she was willing to fight for what she wanted. And so was he.

"It's going to be dark soon." Calehan offered his hand. "Come on."

"I'm going to break a bone because of you." Xiomara reluctantly sat in the doorway, dangling her legs over the edge.

"Come on, it's not so bad." Calehan gripped her waist, lifting her easily to the ground. Pulling away, his fingers brushed the skin of her hip exposed from their movement. He gulped.

The truck rumbled to life while Xiomara kept her eyes glued to the construction. He watched her fingers tap against her thigh, her excitement visible.

"Calehan?" Her voice was soft in the cab, sweet where it traveled through the air, tickling his nose like cotton candy. "I couldn't be happier. Seriously."

She was going to knock him unconscious baring her heart like that.

Calehan was thankful they were stopped when he glanced over at her. Round doe eyes peered back at him, her smile toothy as she gave him a taste of her happiness. He nodded, resting his hand on the bench seat between them. Fire licked up his arm when she took his hand in hers, squeezing firmly.

They rode in comfortable silence, Xiomara commanding the aux cord to play a few songs in Spanish. He hadn't heard them before.

Calehan turned up his family's driveway, watching Xiomara from the corner of his eye. She was focused on the window, taking in the land and horses. He hoped she wasn't disappointed by their simple ranch. Materials were hard to source up here. The more basic, the easier it was to fix. It did, however, leave many of the properties on Bunchberry looking a bit like sheds.

"This looks like a painting." Her voice came out in a whisper.

Calehan wasn't expecting her face to be as serious as it was, bringing a startled laugh from deep in his chest. "It's just home."

"How many horses do you have?"

"Ten," he answered. "Do you ride?"

She nodded. "We have four on the rancho."

"Do you miss them?" He turned left at the main house, heading toward the toolshed behind it. From this side of their land, he could just barely see the house where it sat on the next hill. She didn't need to see his humble home just yet, though.

Xiomara shrugged. "You get used to being away after a while."

Bringing the truck to a stop in front of the barn, one blue door swung half open in the breeze. They climbed out of the truck. He watched Xiomara from the corner of his eye as she wandered around. Turning the key in the ignition, Calehan brought the Jeep forward.

"We need to switch vehicles?" Xiomara questioned, squinting into the driver's window at him.

Calehan shook his head. Opening the door, he stepped to the side so she could see into the cab. "It's yours... while you're here on Bunchberry, at least."

"En serio?"

He nodded.

"Thank you." Her voice came out like a whisper, her arms settling around his neck.

Calehan held her to his chest, his fingers grazing the soft flesh of her waist. Kissing his cheek, she pulled away to look him in the eye.

"Would I be dreaming to ask if there is a backup camera in there?" Xiomara raised her eyebrows.

"You're lucky I got you a working radio." Calehan watched her laugh, his joining smile tame on closed lips. He could watch her laugh for hours.

"My deepest gratitude." Xiomara bowed mockingly in front of him.

"I hope you like tribal radio. It's the only station we got out here."

"I'm not sure why I expected anything else." Xiomara sighed. "Did you give me an aux cord at least?"

"Obviously." Calehan mocked his offense. "This is Bunchberry, not medieval times."

The quiet air around them rattled with the sound of an engine, Nataani appearing from behind Calehan's truck. He was shirtless atop a red ATV with a white dog in the basket behind him.

"Hey Doc!" Nataani waved to her.

"I'm not a doctor," Xiomara clarified.

"But that's what everyone calls you." A goofy smile hung on his lips as his eyes flicked between them.

Xiomara stepped closer to Nataani. "Who is everyone, and what are they saying?"

Nataani's eyes narrowed at Calehan while he leaned close to Xiomara's ear.

Panicked, Calehan interjected quickly. "It's a small town, and you're brand new. People are curious, that's all."

"Curious is one way to put it." Nataani snickered, earning a shove from Calehan that knocked him off the ATV. He bounced back quickly, popping up beside the dog still seated in the basket.

Nataani scratched the white pointed ears of the fluffy dog, beckoning Xiomara over.

"This is Ghost." Nataani pointed to the dog. "Cally had a Game of Thrones phase."

"That sounds about right for you." Xiomara smirked, looking over her shoulder at the stoic man.

He shrugged, putting his brother into a headlock and pulling him into the grass with him. Nataani was nearly as tall as his older brother, but he was built lean and long, while Calehan had settled into his stature, layers of muscle thickening his body. His arms were as large as his little brother's head. Blue veins bulged across Nataani's face as he tried to escape Calehan. Xiomara was laughing somewhere behind them. Releasing Nataani, he gave him one final shove before turning to her.

"Do you know the way home?" Calehan asked.

Nataani cut her off. "Yeah right. Dad already saw her."

Xiomara furrowed her eyebrows as she peered at Calehan in question. He sighed before answering. "He wants you to stay for dinner."

Her smile tugged higher. "What are we eating?"

↑ cut marks

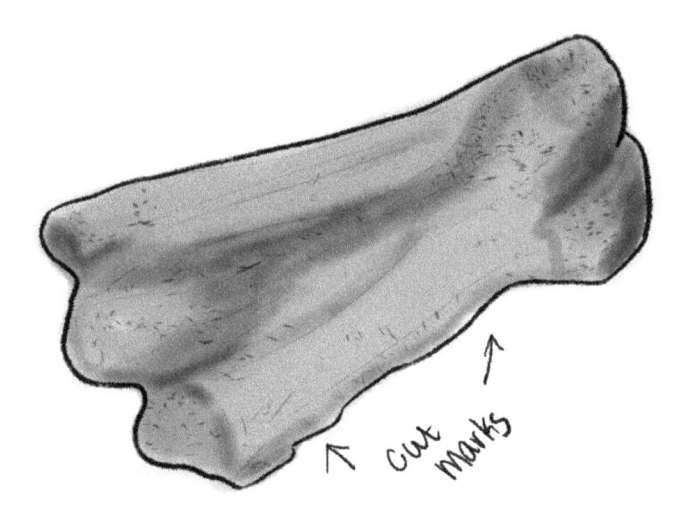

Chapter 6

Calehan climbed into the driver's seat of the white Jeep, beckoning Xiomara inside. She glared at him.

"You're going to drive my car?" Xiomara crossed her arms in the open passenger door.

"I don't recall giving you the keys just yet," Calehan retorted.

Laughter bubbled out of her chest as she climbed in beside him. Xiomara curled her toes inside her shoes, butterflies tickling her belly.

Calehan followed behind Nataani on the ATV, parking the Jeep in front of the main house. They both paused for a moment, looking at the front door left ajar after Nataani and Ghost ran through. Xiomara wondered if this was regular small-town hospitality or something more. She shoved away the thought. Her focus was supposed to be on work, not hot Native men.

Calehan brushed her arm, bringing her back to the present. The silence should have unnerved her, but she felt strangely relaxed in his unspoken communication. Calehan rested his hand at the small of her back as he welcomed her into their home. Guiding her to sit on the bench beside the door, he bent on one knee and began removing her shoes. Shocked into stillness, Xiomara could do nothing but watch as he carefully pulled her feet free. Calehan placed them neatly to the side, tucking the laces inside. She watched as he removed his own before guiding her with him to the eat-in kitchen.

Xiomara felt at ease in their simple home. It wasn't too unlike her own. The walls held dozens of photos, some behind glass, some stuck up with tacks, others tucked between the glass and wood of the frame. The gray couch was lived in, Ghost currently leaving a layer of white fur where he rubbed against the cushions. The kitchen was at the back of the house, avocado green cabinets lined three walls of the room, a white table in the middle.

Muskwa bent over a large pot, steam brushing his face while he stirred. The smell was decadent, hanging heavy in the air. She guessed it was game meat with the tickle of grass invading her nose.

"Hey, Dad." Calehan put his arm around his father's shoulders, looking into the pot with him. "It smells good."

"There's bannock in the oven." Muskwa smiled as he caught sight of Xiomara. She stood awkwardly inside the kitchen, leaning against the cabinets in an effort to be out of the way.

"We're eating fancy tonight." Nataani winked at Xiomara while he set the table. She joined him, unstacking the glasses he set out.

Calehan gestured to a seat for her, pulling it out as his father brought the pot of stew to the table. Joy barreled in the back door, dirt dried to her wrinkled kneecaps, grass sticking out of her braid.

"Is that bannock?" She beelined for the oven. Calehan moved quickly to bar her until she washed up. Joy caught sight of Xiomara and stopped short. "So that's why we're eating bannock tonight." A wicked smile curled over her lips, and Xiomara's ears turned hot.

Calehan gripped Joy's shoulders and turned her toward the sink.

Xiomara wound her fingers together, feeling out of place without a task. "Can I help with anything?"

"No." Father and son had indistinguishable baritones in their rejection.

Palms up in surrender, Xiomara took the seat Calehan pulled out for her. She leaned back in her chair and watched him wrap the bannock in a flour sack towel, placing it in a woven basket. She admired his back under the thin shirt he wore, the muscles rolling as he moved throughout the kitchen. He took the seat beside her, serving everyone a piece of bannock while Nataani filled their bowls with the steaming soup.

Calehan's father said a quick prayer before they dug in. Xiomara smiled at the taste of the soup, a gamey deer stew with wild rice. It was a homey flavor that instantly settled over her like a blanket. They made it with goat in Chihuahua, but she loved deer almost as much.

"How was school?" Muskwa had a voice that was deep and slow moving. The most mundane words sounded like stories from his mouth. He looked at Nataani expectantly.

"Fine." Nataani sighed as though the question was a nuisance. "The year is almost over."

Nataani shoveled the soup into his mouth, scooping seconds before anyone else had finished. Teenage boys were always like that. They could have a grocery store in their living room and would still eat as though it were closing. A small rock sat in her stomach at the thought of her cousins. They were nearly as tall as the corn when she left. How tall would they be when she returned?

"Just a few years left, little brother." Joy pinched the joint of his neck and shoulder, bringing a yelp of pain from him. She snickered and stole a piece of bannock from his plate.

"What did you think of the site?" Muskwa tipped his chin up at Xiomara.

"It looks great." She perked up, sitting forward in her seat. "We'll be ready to break ground next week."

"Feeling the pressure, Cal?" Joy teased her older brother, who offered her nothing more than a blank stare.

"I know what I'm doing." Calehan filled Muskwa's bowl with more soup.

Xiomara could see his nerves in the tick of his jaw, the pinch of his eyes, and the rigid stick-straightness of his back. It put her at ease to see him nervous about the project, just as she was.

"Will you be coming on excavation day?" Xiomara asked Muskwa.

"Dad will be doing the honoring with a few other Elders," Calehan answered, while his father chewed.

"Oh!" Xiomara's eyebrows rose. "That's wonderful."

Muskwa told her of the last groundbreaking when they built the casino. Joy and Nataani began bickering again, Joy ripping out a small chunk of Nataani's arm hair in retaliation. Nataani screeched in pain, bouncing a piece of bannock off Joy's head. Ghost swooped it off the floor before she could retrieve it. Muskwa looked hard at each of them, his firm stare settling them quietly into their chairs.

A new piece of bannock wedged its way onto Calehan's plate as Xiomara took a second piece for herself. He looked between her and the bread for a moment, as though he was surprised to see her place food on his plate. She buttered her bread and popped it into her mouth.

Dinner wrapped up when Nataani let out an infectious yawn that circled around the table.

Xiomara kissed Muskwa's cheek as he pressed the foil-wrapped leftovers into her hands. "Thank you for dinner, Uncle."

"You drive home safely." Muskwa squeezed her shoulder.

"I'm going to take her," Calehan told his father.

"Good." Muskwa patted her hand. "Drive carefully, the bears are awake."

Calehan nodded, kissing his father's cheek goodnight before guiding Xiomara out the front door.

Nataani followed them onto the porch. "Can I come?"

"No." Calehan didn't skip a beat.

"Come on." Nataani leaned on the hood of the Jeep. "I want ice cream."

"It's a school night." Calehan looked straight at Nataani. "Go inside."

Nataani threw his head back with a groan before heading inside. Xiomara giggled at his reaction. It was one she knew well as an only child, always left out of the adult activities.

Xiomara wrapped her arms around her middle. The air had cooled considerably while they ate dinner, a chill settling into her bones and bringing a rattle to her teeth. Calehan opened the door and ushered her into the vehicle.

"One thing to remember..." Calehan paused while she adjusted the mirror and seat to her liking. He reached between her legs. Xiomara froze in shock. Calehan ran his hand under the dash and dropped the steering wheel lower. "The brake can be sticky." Bringing his hand out from under the dash, he reached across her lap to grip the parking brake. "Just jiggle it a couple of times, and it should unstick."

Xiomara nodded as she watched the muscles in his arms ripple across his skin under the yellow car light. Why wasn't he shivering like her? Heat rolled off his arm where it brushed her sweater. Calehan worked the brake a few times until it settled, his wrist grazing Xiomara's jean-covered thigh when he pulled away.

"Ready?" A voice sounded behind them, Xiomara jumping at the intrusion. Joy climbed into the passenger seat beside her. "I'll ride with her, and you can follow us." Joy rolled her eyes as the two blinked at her. "I know the way to Rosebud's house; I wasn't born yesterday."

Calehan wrinkled his nose, closing the door on Xiomara before climbing into the truck to follow behind her.

"So..." Joy smiled deviously at Xiomara as they drove through the gate. "What do you think of my brother?"

Joy certainly didn't pull any punches. Xiomara coughed.

"He's very smart." Xiomara racked her brain for adjectives other than drop-dead-gorgeous. "And welcoming." She still hadn't sussed out his relationship status yet and blabbing to his littlest sister that she would bone him likely wasn't the way to find out. God forbid he was dating someone, and Joy was using this car ride to scare Xiomara off. Ay dios mio, this is exactly the thing that would happen to Xiomara. She attempted to breathe slower. And quieter.

"Ah." Joy waved her hand in the air dismissively. "Everyone has been waiting for you to arrive for weeks. Of course they're welcoming."

Xiomara laughed to fill the silence.

"Seriously, though?" Joy paused. "Everyone has been really happy you're Indigenous, too."

Xiomara breathed deeply; there was a nuance to Indigenous archaeology that was often lost on non-Natives. Xiomara found that people often forgot these sites, these artifacts, these remains, belonged to a people whose family still lives today. There was a level of respect and consideration she brought to all of her work that wasn't even a thought amongst her non-Native peers. Xiomara swallowed as she remembered the callousness with which some archaeologists treated sites, as if they were not also a home.

"I wouldn't be here otherwise." Xiomara nodded firmly, a shared understanding of the gravity of the project. "You should come up to the site one of these days."

Joy shrugged. "I'm thinking about it."

"Why don't you come when we break ground?" Xiomara thought it would be nice to have her there when both her father and brother would also be involved.

Joy shrugged. "Eh, maybe. Depends on how the horses are that morning." Joy glanced at her. "But I'll try."

"I think you'd enjoy it." Xiomara let the topic go as she asked Joy to tune to her favorite radio station for her. Joy reminded her there was only one. "I thought Calehan was just messing with me."

"Sorry." The delight on Joy's face showed she was not sorry in the least. "He wasn't lying."

Joy navigated Xiomara to Rosebud's house on the other side of Main Street. Calehan's headlights never left her rearview mirror. Xiomara parked the Jeep in the dirt to the side of Rosebud's sedan. She couldn't help but glance in the mirror again, hoping she could see far enough to view Calehan's eyes.

Xiomara and Joy climbed out of the Jeep, Xiomara waved goodbye to the teen. Her heart hammered as Calehan sauntered toward her.

Calehan led her to the porch, his warm hand settled into her back. He walked her up the steps, watching as she pulled out her key, turning it in the lock.

"Call me if the Jeep acts up or anything," Calehan told her, taking a step back.

"I will." Xiomara answered, frozen in front of the unlocked door. "Thank you for taking me home... and dinner, and the car, and everything."

"No need," Calehan answered. He stood before her a moment longer, blinking a few times before turning from her. "Goodnight, Xiomara."

Calehan continued walking backward, his eyes on the sealed door until he reached the truck. He climbed inside, staring straight ahead. Calehan could practically feel Joy vibrating next to him. "Don't start."

"Calehan and Xiomara," she started singing as he pulled out of the driveway, "Sitting in a tree."

Joy droned on and on about his unrequited love for their new town archaeologist. He didn't have the heart to tell her to stop, considering she was right. He thought of Xiomara incessantly. It was annoying, really, to have no control over his own thoughts.

"She likes you, too." Joy snickered at his deeply focused face. "Did you not know?"

"How do you know?"

"Um, I have eyes." Joy deadpanned. "You should've kissed her on the porch. Bet she would've kissed you back."

Calehan grumbled internally. "She's my boss."

"You're so dramatic." She waved her hand in the air as if Calehan was a fly buzzing by her ear. "You're *coworkers* with the same boss, Chief Thomas."

Right. Chief Thomas. His boss, who would absolutely not approve of a workplace relationship between Calehan and the archaeologist who was specifically *off-limits*. Chief Thomas had claimed he didn't want anyone making her uncomfortable when she would be living on rez, but Calehan suspected he didn't want competition for himself. This was the kind of sly game Kenny had always played. Being a modern chief suited him, that was for sure.

"Let's be honest, brother." Joy looked out the window as they drove along the pasture. "Kenny is a dork, okay? Sure, he's a chief. Sure, he's pretty hot—"

Calehan made a face of disgust.

"What? It's just a fact." Joy waved him off again as he parked in front of the main house. "All I am saying is you clearly have a chance with Xiomara." The siblings climbed out of the car. Calehan rested his palm on the hood as he watched his sister reach the front door.

"Take the shot, Cally." Joy flipped him off and locked the door behind her.

Calehan scoffed as he turned to walk home. Flipping the bird was one of her favorite adult achievements, alongside her stubborn choice not to attend university. Joy was a champion Indian Relay rider and was slowly making a name for herself. Out of all the Yellowbird siblings, she was the one who was most adamant about rejecting further education. Calehan was proud of her for sticking to her guns, but even if she was the best relay rider in history, she'd never make enough money to support herself. Relay race winnings rarely amounted to more than a thousand dollars. Even if she won a race every weekend, the winnings wouldn't even cover expenses. Calehan wanted more for her than a life of living paycheck-to-paycheck.

Joy had a choice. She chose not to go to university. She chose to stay home. She chose to buy a truck instead of driving the Jeep.

Calehan would never rob her of the gift of choice.

Instead, he would stay here. He would care for his father, his other siblings, the horses, the goats. He could be Calehan Yellowbird forever. But given a choice?

He wished to just be Calehan.

← ornamental

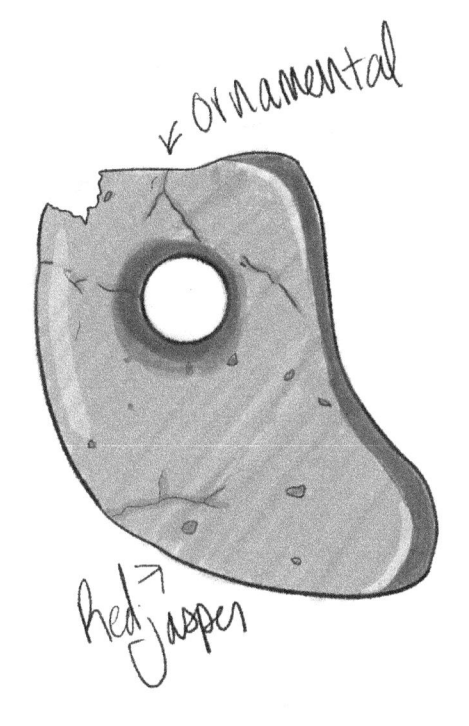

red jasper

Chapter 7

The sun still peeked through the trees and over the hills, kissing the water. Xiomara sat in the Jeep with David beside her. Rosebud, Kate, and an enormous amount of catering sat in the sedan. The ferry was packed to the brim.

The Elders were here to honor the land and prepare those who remained for the disruption of an archaeological excavation. Xiomara wasn't used to such a busy site. Numerous people milled about, each new face bringing a bead of sweat to her lip. Interns took notes and watched David's every move. The Elders stood to the side with members of the tribal council, focused looks on each of their faces. Other members of the community had come to the island to witness the groundbreaking, leaving them with a small crowd of camping chairs and picnic blankets full of people.

Xiomara stood off to the side beneath the shade of a tree. Glancing up, Xiomara caught Calehan looking at her. Xiomara squeezed her eyes tight for a brief moment.

Hi.

Calehan squeezed his eyes back at her, *Hi.*

She blushed at their secret communication, attempting to hide it by pulling her cap down lower. Xiomara stepped back and bumped into Chief Joseph.

"Oh! I'm so sorry, Chief." Xiomara straightened, hoping she hadn't caused him any harm.

Chief Joseph simply rubbed her arm, bidding her a good morning. Flames of shame licked up over Xiomara's body. She had let herself get distracted by a man, and here she was stepping on retired Chiefs! Xiomara took a moment to snap herself out of this rose-tinged haze Calehan had wrapped her in.

Focus, she told herself. Now was not the time for romance. It was time for making history. The tribe deserved her full attention and commitment to the excavation.

Xiomara joined David and watched Muskwa gather his offerings in his palm. Calehan took from the same leather satchel. Their identical brown eyes slid shut along with everyone else. Xiomara took a deep breath and closed her eyes. Their voices surrounded her, warming her like the sun. She tried to see blackness behind her eyes, but shining from the dark was Calehan, praying to her alone.

Afterward, she sprinkled a pinch of her own offering, watching the breeze carry her promise into the water. Birds sang while the trees danced with the wind. Water brushed the earth beneath her feet, gently coaxing the dirt from its home to join the turning river. The land was ready.

Laughter tickled the shell of her ear. The wind pulled and pushed the sound around her. It was them, and she hoped they were happy to have her. Thanking them one last time, she stepped from the cliffside. She gasped, immediately meeting familiar almond brown eyes.

"We're ready when you are, boss." Calehan's voice eased the crease from between her brows.

"I'm not your boss." She looked at him pointedly.

Calehan put his hands up, palms facing forward. "Whatever you say."

Xiomara quickly scanned the perimeter of their spray-painted grid, double checking her already triple-checked work. There would be no room for errors. She knew the site was low enough it would be unlikely to reach anything via machine. But that what-if feeling never really went away. She worried there would be something on top, that the quick removal could collapse any remaining structures, that everything could go completely, horribly wrong.

Xiomara looked up to Calehan where he sat in the machine. She paused, peering at him, arms crossed over her chest. He waved her closer. Gripping the bars on either side of his face, she climbed up two of the three steps.

"You'll need to be really careful." She chewed her bottom lip, a red welt forming on the dark skin. "If you go any deeper than sixteen inches, you could damage the artifacts beneath the soil."

"I remember." He offered her a wide smile; she could see almost to his molars. "Don't worry, I'm a pro." Calehan bumped her crossed arms with the back of his hand, letting it linger for a moment. He dragged the back of his knuckles along her forearm. "Sixteen inches."

Xiomara peered at his face, the furrow in her brow releasing at his touch. She stepped down, watching him intently from beneath her tree.

Calehan cleared their pre-measured grid quickly, Xiomara waving once she was satisfied with his work.

Calehan emerged from the machine to inspect the ground. He watched Xiomara examine the freshly disturbed earth, trying to decipher whether he had pleased her or not.

"How'd I do?"

"Sixteen inches on the dot." Xiomara kicked the toe of his boot. "I knew you could do it."

"No, you didn't!" Calehan threw his head back in a laugh. "You doubted me until thirty seconds ago."

"Only on the outside." Xiomara shadowed her eyes with a hand.

He opened his mouth to respond when Chief Thomas gained their attention from the edge of the freshly open site.

"Nice work, Calehan. Glad to see you putting that degree to use." Clapping a hand on his shoulder, Chief Thomas stepped in front of Calehan, wedging himself between them. "Miss Chavez, excellent work, as usual. What are our next steps?" He clasped his hands together in front of his chest as though he was somehow involved in the process.

"David and I have a few things to do before we can let anyone into the site." Xiomara attempted to stem the interest Chief Thomas was gathering. David set a clipboard of notes in her hands. Her thoughts raced for an excuse why Chief Thomas could not be in the pit with her. She needed to make him feel involved while keeping him far enough away he wouldn't interfere.

"Chief Thomas, would you be able to rally the interns into sorting and cataloging the surface findings?" Xiomara let herself fall forward with an exaggerated laugh. "I think you get the best out of them, if I'm honest."

Chief Thomas took the bait, heading for the interns.

Xiomara and David got to work measuring out the individual grids for the team. They worked quickly together, moving as one after all their years in the field. Xiomara was grateful Chief Thomas had given her the budget for a team leader; she couldn't imagine doing this without David. If Xiomara was the sun, then David was the moon. Her polar opposite and twin flame at the same time. David often knew her better than himself.

Sitting back on her heels, she searched for Calehan, finding him at the other end of the site. He caught her looking for him. Xiomara dropped her gaze in an effort to hide the blush claiming her neck.

"I was looking for you." Xiomara tilted her head as she looked up at him. She heard him suck in a breath as she stepped closer. "How do you feel about sifting?"

Putting Calehan to work sifting dirt for her and David, she stepped into her pre-measured square and began digging. Using hand shovels and trowels, they sat in their sections and systematically placed soil in a bucket, layer by layer.

Xiomara filled her bucket first, palming a few items before handing the bucket off to Calehan. David climbed out to show him how to sift while Xiomara sat down in the dirt, pulling out her green field journal. She grabbed the clipboard beside her and spread the items over the white paper.

Admiring the artifacts before her, she made a quick catalog in her mind. A grin settled onto her lips. Red tinged pottery sherds were copious, piled high on top of each other. Xiomara sorted through the stack, pulling out the blackened pieces. One was thickly blackened, almost as though it had sat in the fire until the last coal burned cold.

"Hey Xo!" Calehan called to her. "I think I found something."

Xiomara stood, veiling her surprise at the nickname by furiously brushing her hands on her jeans. Butterflies tickled her belly, the sound of a name no one had ever called her etching itself into her thumping heart. She leaned over the basket to check the wire mesh. Calehan held the item in his palm in front of her instead. Gripping his hand with both of hers, she pulled him closer to her face.

Xiomara brushed off the wet dirt with her fingers, inspecting it closely.

"You found a projectile point!" Xiomara bounced lightly on her toes, her hand grabbing at Calehan in excitement. He let her catch his arm, leaning into her weight with a hand on her elbow.

David's face lit up. "A projectile point on the first day!"

"What does that mean?" Calehan asked, everyone crowding to look at the point.

"It's just good luck." Xiomara let out a sigh of relief. "A sign we're doing the right thing; that they want us here."

David took the point from Xiomara. She let her hand fall, Calehan catching it in his. She squeezed his fingers fiercely, holding it tight to her midsection before turning away to track the moving artifact.

A few of the Elders held the point close to them, sharing breath with their ancestors, giving them life once again. Juniper leaned down and showed Frankie, telling him the significance and importance of their cultural materials.

Xiomara could feel her face light up like a star as she watched the point bring smiles to the crowd. Answering questions as she went, the smile on her face never faltered. Once the crowd dispersed, Xiomara skipped to where she left Calehan in front of the sifting tray. She squeezed him into a hug, arms flat across his back. Pulling him closer to her, she stood on her tiptoes but still had to turn her head into his chest. Calehan squeezed her tightly to him.

"Xiomara, I knew I made the right choice in hiring you." Chief Thomas stepped forward. Calehan dropped his arm in an instant.

"I'm happy the council chose me." Xiomara said. Lettig him hug her before briefly before pulling away. Hugging Calehan had been a mistake. Now, Chief Thomas was entitled to equal treatment or she would have to admit her crush on her co-worker. Chief Thomas kept an arm around her shoulder, his palm damp against the bare skin of her arm. "Gotta draw it up." She wiggled the artifact in the air and tore from his grasp.

Xiomara rolled her shoulders back, knees creaking as she folded herself onto her foam pad. She was not a huge fan of hugging, and certainly not hugging her boss. Eyes on the dirt, she thought it over in her head. Almost everyone on staff was somehow a family member. Maybe this was just how he was with his employees.

She chewed on the end of her pencil, peeking over the dirt wall to watch Calehan. He had discarded his flannel button up when the sun reached the center of the sky, opting for his white undershirt instead. Shrouded in dappled sunlight, he made quick work of each bucket of dirt.

Xiomara jumped when he caught her watching him. Calehan smirked and looked away, returning to his sifting. Xiomara felt her chest start to warm, her cheeks quickly following suit. She buried her face in the notebook, hoping no one noticed.

Calehan *was* flirting with her, right? He was so kind and friendly; it was difficult to tell if it was flirting or personality. Was he like this with everyone?

Xiomara waved at David across the site, where he was identifying the small fragments on the interns' mesh. She touched the fingers of her right hand to her lips a few times, David nodding. He grabbed the bell off the table and rang it.

"Let's eat lunch, people!" he shouted, ringing the bell again for good measure. Xiomara grabbed sandwiches and hastily bodied him into the woods.

"Ay que haces?" David snatched his sandwich from her hands as they retreated from the crowd.

"Necesitamos hablar," Xiomara said. "Solos."

"Is this about your *lover boy*?" David fanned himself with a piece of lettuce.

"Shh!" Xiomara told him. "We're like three feet away."

"I think it's fine, jefa." David sat on a downed log facing the site. "So..." David stared at her in silence for a few moments. "Calehan?"

"How did you know?"

"You're like a little teenager around him." Xiomara choked on her sandwich. "I've never seen you blush this much in the entire time I've known you, and you've only been here a month."

Xiomara frowned. She didn't think it was that noticeable. *¡Qué vergüenza!*

"He watches you like a hawk," David continued on. "It's a little creepy, but I'm also kind of into it? He's hot, Xio, what can I say?"

Xiomara covered her face. "He's really hot," she groaned, throwing her head back toward the sun. Xiomara sagged against his shoulder.

"There's only one answer." He shrugged, jostling her head. "You've got to fuck him."

"Ay no mames," Xiomara laughed as she bumped him with her shoulder.

"I bet he's got a hu—" David was cut short by Xiomara's hand clamping over his mouth.

She glared at him pointedly before removing her hand. They ate in silence for a while, watching people mingle around the site. Xiomara eyed Muskwa where he stood away from the crowd.

His gray streaked hair was unbraided, swaying in the breeze before the burial mound. Muskwa reminded her of her father. Her dad would visit the family burial site often, spending time with them, talking with them, letting them see the world through his eyes. The gentle breeze broke when Frankie grabbed his grandfather's pant leg, asking to be picked up. Gripping his sandwich in his tiny hand, Frankie let his grandfather hoist him onto his hip.

"What are you doing all the way over here?" A sing-song voice cut through their shared silence as Rosebud walked up.

"Talking about boys," David answered. Xiomara glared, pinching his thigh above the knee until he squealed.

"Soplón," she hissed from her barely open mouth.

"Which boys?" Rosebud smiled wickedly. "I brought you lemonade." She handed them each a small cup.

David thankfully remained silent while Rosebud looked between them expectantly.

Rosebud held out another ten seconds before sighing in impatience. "Okay, I hope it's Calehan, but I guess it's fine if it's Kenny, but I don't really see you two together."

"Kenny?" David muttered under his breath.

"Chief Thomas, his first name is Kenneth." Rosebud shrugged. "His family is fairly religious."

David shook his head at Xiomara.

Xiomara gave in. "Yes, we were talking about Calehan."

"Thank God." Rosebud sat next to Xiomara on the log. "You guys would make such a cute couple. I've been saying it since day one."

"Ay dios mío," Xiomara whispered, eating more of her sandwich to avoid the conversation.

David and Rosebud fist bumped in front of her. She groaned.

"Relax." Rosebud patted Xiomara's knee. "You both are hiding it expertly. David and I are just paying extra attention in the hopes you get together."

"We're coworkers," Xiomara argued.

"Who cares?" Rosebud said, scrunching her face and throwing a hand into the air, swatting the wind away.

"I care," Xiomara said. "I don't want to lose my job."

"I don't think that would happen." Rosebud shrugged as though it was simple.

"Not sure I'm willing to risk it." Xiomara finished her lemonade and stood. "Come on, we got dirt to move."

David rounded up the interns while Rosebud and Kate prepared the Elders for the ferry back to Bunchberry. Xiomara took a seat at the table under the awning, multiple artifacts spread out before her. Each was accompanied by a brown paper bag. She picked up the black permanent marker and her field notes and settled to work.

Xiomara had tagged and bagged all the stone tools before she finally tore her eyes from the table. David was in her grid, slowly digging out what looked to be a ceramic pot. Chief Thomas was speaking animatedly to a few Elders who stayed behind.

"Hi," a faint voice sounded behind her.

"You made it." Xiomara smiled as Joy looked around, taking everything in.

"I rode in with the ferry to pick up the oldies." Joy shrugged, attempting to appear nonchalant. Xiomara could tell she was curious.

"Well, I'm glad you're here." Xiomara said even though Joy avoided her eyes. "So, do you want to torture your brother first or look at some artifacts first?"

"You can show me this stuff, I guess." Joy peered at the brown bags, straining to see who slumbered within.

"Calehan actually found the first one of the day." Xiomara looked for the bag holding his red artifact. "It's a chert bifurcated projectile point."

Xiomara turned Joy's hand face up and gently laid the point in her palm.

"This piece broke off." Xiomara pointed to the wide end, where one edge was missing. "But this end is still intact. That's how we know it is bifurcated."

"How old is it?"

"That can be hard to know for sure." Xiomara explained the intricacies of archaeological dating methods and the importance of strata in an excavation. "I would guess this is anywhere from nine hundred to fifteen hundred years old."

"Holy shit." Joy's deep brown eyes widened.

Xiomara crinkled her nose. "I know. It's almost impossible to imagine, right?"

"It's so small." Joy pressed her finger against the dull edge. Softened by a thousand years of rain and dirt, the edge was not as sharp as it would've been when used. Still, it was remarkably thin and felt sharp enough to cut. "How did they do this back then?"

"Pretty simple, really." Xiomara leaned against the table. "They would use a larger stone to hit against the chosen stone repeatedly until small pieces flaked off into the shape they wanted."

"But the notches?"

"We can only theorize." Xiomara's smile was gentle. "But perhaps an awl and many, *many* years of practice."

Joy shook her head in disbelief. Xiomara understood the mental mind-fuck she was currently experiencing. For so long, the world told her that they were inferior, unintelligent, and not capable of intricate invention like this. Decolonizing the mind was a lot different when they could hold the real thing in her hands. Her ancestors' capabilities and achievements could be tangible, untainted by the glamorized colonial history. Untainted by the desecration of looting. The projectile point she held in her hands had power both of them could feel.

Calehan came over, carrying a tray full of artifacts.

"Perfect!" Xiomara clapped her hands and took the tray from Calehan. She turned to Joy and explained the process of labeling an item, cataloging it, and preparing it for transportation to the lab.

Joy narrowed her eyes at the swiftness with which Xiomara put her to work. Calehan looked pointedly at his younger sister until she acquiesced and took the seat in front of the table. Xiomara smiled softly at Calehan's brooding gaze, bumping him with her shoulder in thanks.

"Come on." She walked backward as he followed her. "I can't do all this sifting myself."

"I don't know, you're pretty strong." Calehan squeezed her bicep in jest.

"Bullying my archaeologist, Calehan?" Chief Thomas materialized behind them, earning a start of fright from Xiomara.

Calehan turned around to face him, lips closed, jaw set, eyes dark. The two seemed equally in distaste of the other.

"Chief Thomas." Xiomara's voice pitched just a bit higher. "Would you like to participate?" She looked briefly around the site. "I could use another sifter."

Calehan glanced at the Chief's shiny black dress shoes before walking away.

"Maybe next time." Xiomara saved face for Chief Thomas. "Sites can get pretty dirty."

Chief Thomas watched Calehan shake the mesh contraption, dirt falling onto his feet. He turned to Xiomara and smiled. "Well, you will certainly be welcome to my help in the lab. I'm available anytime, right upstairs."

"Of course." Xiomara nodded and retreated to her grid. She should've asked Calehan to build the lab in the basement of the museum.

David popped his head over her shoulder, perched behind her on the balls of his feet. "Nataani is missing."

Xiomara stiffened, glancing around to see if anyone else had noticed the teen's absence. Focusing on Calehan, she hoped he would help.

"So listen…" She leaned against the sifting tripod, whispering to him. "Nataani wandered off. Any idea where he might be?"

Calehan paused his sifting, the answer already in his eyes. Quirking his head to the side, she followed him into the tree lines, gesturing wildly at David to take over sifting for Calehan.

"Don't worry," Calehan told her. "Nataani loves to wander, but he isn't stupid. He grew up here. He's safe. We'll find him quickly."

Calehan was right. Nataani hadn't wandered too far, but he had wandered up.

They found him lounging in a tree, drawing on a sketchpad. Xiomara already had a soft spot for this kid. His jovial personality and intensely focused curiosity had grabbed her heart immediately. All the interns had, but Nataani was making it really hard to be irritated at him.

"Hey, Nataani!" Xiomara called up to him.

"Hi Doc!" He waved down at them from his position high in the tree. "Is lunch over?"

Xiomara laughed. "Yeah bud. It's been over for a few hours now. You want to come join us?"

"Oops." His face was apologetic as he climbed down the tree. "Sorry. I lost track of time."

"No worries." Xiomara handed him a fresh Gatorade. "How about we stay in earshot for lunch from now on?"

"You got it, Doc." Nataani fist bumped her and took off running to join the other interns.

"He reminds me of you." Xiomara bumped Calehan's shoulder. "Just silently appearing and disappearing everywhere."

Calehan laughed. "I think he takes after Juniper more than me. The disappearing in the forest is definitely from me, though."

Xiomara giggled as he smiled down at her, all teeth, complete attention on her. She feared she was going to get used to this.

A blush rose over her cheeks and neck, his mere presence setting her aflame.

Lola.

She needed to talk to Lola. Her ravenous friend was committed to the single life until age thirty-five and would certainly be able to talk her out of this crush.

Back at Rosebud's cabin, she took Anubis out for a walk. She dialed Lola's number and waited for her to answer.

"Buena, Xiomara, he estado esperando tu llamada." Lola's voice was foggy across the line, wind blowing around her.

"Lo siento, the reception is ass out here." Xiomara chewed her lip as she wrapped an arm around her middle, fighting the cull from the sunset breeze.

"Why do you sound like that? Que pasa?" Lola sounded exasperated. "Out with it already your heavy breathing is tortuous."

"There's a guy."

"Obviously." A slap sounded over the line and Xiomara could picture Lola slapping against the steering wheel beside her.

"Ya, tu sabes, ya ya. Anyway," Xiomara shushed her ranting friend and continued, "The situation is we're coworkers."

"Who cares? You're only there for a year or two anyway." Lola's voice was still full of excitement and Xiomara felt as though she could hear her eyes rolling back in her head. "How hot is he?"

"Extremely." Xiomara squeezed her eyes shut against the memories of his muscled biceps flexing under the sun.

"Ay dios mio, Xiomara, why not? He's hot, you like him, what is the issue?"

"Te dije, tonta. We work together."

Lola sighed. "Do it anyway. Sneak around, be a little bad for once."

Xiomara let the silence stretch through the phone. Picking at the cuticle of her left thumb, she sighed heavily and leaned back to gaze at the darkening sky.

"Haven't you punished yourself enough, mi vida?" Lola's voice went soft and gentle, "Javi would want you to live your life."

"Yo sé," the words came out as a whisper, Xiomara blinking furiously to avoid tears. "When will it stop hurting?"

Lola sighed heavily on the phone, "Nunca. Pero it will hurt a lot less with someone beside you."

"I have you."

"Cabróna, I'm trying to get laid and shit not pull a Thelma and Louise." Lola scoffed, muttering about her desire to have a life partner with a penis.

"Fine." Xiomara let her head hang back on the seat, "Lolita...he has me down bad."

"What is he like?"

"He's gentle and friendly." Xiomara couldn't help the smile that overtook her face as she described Calehan to her best friend. Lola demanded a photo of him and then immediately declared they were perfectly fated. Xiomara disagreed on the basis her eyes were level with his nipples, but Lola argued that was also a pro.

"Xiomara, prometeme," Lola paused dramatically, "at least give him a chance."

"Lo prometo." Xiomara took a deep breath and went inside.

Organic material

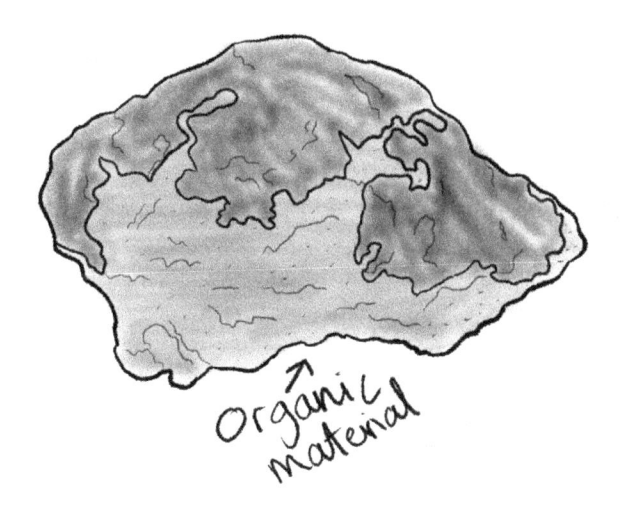

Chapter 8

The weekend welcomed her happily, sunlight teasing the black from her vision. Xiomara blinked against the bright light. She struggled to remember her dream, the memory quickly slipping away.

While she struggled to recall the evaporating memory, a rope wound around her gut and pulled taut.

Xiomara needed to go to the site.

They had left a partially uncovered ceramic the other day and Xiomara couldn't tear it from her head. If her theory was correct, that pot would have a marking similar to the hand axe and other ceramics they had found. She didn't understand the carving yet but she couldn't bring herself to stop wondering if this pot also bore the symbol.

Problem was she had no boat and no idea who could take her there other than Chief Thomas. She didn't want to give him the wrong idea by asking for a private adventure to their worksite on the weekend, so she thought of the only other person who seemed to know this land better than the chief. His sexual appeal and ability to get her immediately throbbing in her pants had nothing to do with her choice.

At all.

Calehan answered before the second ring.

"Good morning." His voice was silky and she guessed he had been awake for hours already.

"Hi." Xiomara hoped he couldn't hear the smile in her voice. "Am I interrupting anything?"

"Not at all." A horse brayed in the background and Calehan laughed. "Are you calling to make sure Nataani didn't wander away again?"

She laughed. "Actually I wanted to ask you a favor."

"I'm listening."

"I…" Xiomara trailed off, debating how to phrase her request without sounding like a late night psychic. "I was hoping to make it up to the site today to finish up a few things. I didn't know who else to ask."

She held her breath as the seconds ticked by in silence.

"I can pick you up in an hour."

"Yes! That's perfect! Thank you!" Xiomara stumbled over her words, surprised at his easy yes.

"See you soon."

Anubis tucked himself into the bench seat between Calehan and Xiomara. Sitting upright, he was tall enough to see over the dash. Calehan brought them to the ferry dock on the edge of Bunchberry Island. The ferry was waiting and they pulled straight on.

"What's in the cooler?" Xiomara nodded to the red ice chest on the floor between them.

"I brought lunch." Calehan said.

"Oh! I didn't even think about that." Xiomara said. "Thank you, again, for bringing me and lunch."

"Don't mention it." Calehan dismissed her admiration easily and pulled off the ferry at Yellowbird Island. "I was going to swing by anyway, your cabin is ready."

Xiomara squealed with delight. "I can't wait to see it."

The air was still around them, the trees breaking the breeze before it could reach the site. Calehan pulled the tarp off the east corner of the grid, exposing the two leftmost sections. Jumping in, Xiomara took her trowel and started to dig.

Calehan watched her from the edge of the site, Anubis dozing beside him.

"Hopefully I didn't ruin your Saturday plans." Xiomara murmured.

Calehan shrugged. "My only plan was your cabin anyway."

"Then...you're welcome?"

Calehan laughed then, his teeth shining in the sunlight. He stood and took her full bucket. Sifting the dirt in silence, he collected the few leftover items and brought them to her. He dropped the items into her waiting palm.

"How are you doing?" His question was quiet in the way a cat investigates in silence.

Xiomara looked at him, attempting to decipher what he was asking. His eyes were genuine as he peered at her.

"I'm good," she answered him. "I move around a lot, like the old ones." She joked, winking at him. "You get used to it."

"To being alone?" He looked at her with open curiosity, but she could see the whisper of sadness in his eyes. She shrugged and turned her attention back to the artifacts in hand.

"I'm never alone." Xiomara fingered a small bone shard. Blackened on one end, she suspected it had been dinner many years ago. "Just because we can no longer see them doesn't mean they aren't still here, all around us."

Calehan nodded, watching intently as she bagged the items. "Who were they?"

Xiomara looked up at his question, glancing around the site before answering. "We don't know enough yet, so I can't say."

"Come on," Calehan tapped her ankle with the toe of his boot. "I know you've got a theory already."

Xiomara rolled her eyes. "Fine." Settling back down onto her kneepad, she continued methodically removing layers of dirt.

"I was wrong before." Her eyes remained glued to the ground. "I thought this was a point-in-time but I actually think this was a continuous occupation. Well, partially." She glanced at him before continuing. "I think this might have been hunting grounds for a specific clan or family. Look, this sherd I found on the first day had these markings on it. Usually it's just damage from erosion, use, even just for fun. But yesterday I found three more items with the same symbol, including a hand axe."

"What do you think it means?"

"We might never be able to say," Xiomara sighed. She passed him another bucket full of russet colored dirt. "But I think it might be an identifier, possibly of the clan or the family."

Calehan nodded, emptying the bucket over the screen. "I'll ask my dad if he knows anything. What did the symbol look like?"

"It was a line with three dots. Two above, one below and the line is always at an angle." She held her hand out straight, turning it sideways and tilting it to demonstrate.

Calehan chewed his lip in thought, "Constellation maybe?"

"Pretty small for a constellation but it's possible." Xiomara sighed, recovering the grid and dusting her hands off. "That's the thing. We might never know."

"Does that bother you?" Calehan gripped the sift pole as she sorted through the items on the screen. "Having so many unanswered questions?"

Xiomara shook her head without looking at him. This was a constant question for her, especially as an Indigenous archaeologist. The western quest for knowledge had started the field of archaeology, but she exclusively operated under an Indigenous mindset. Knowledge was not her goal. She worked for preservation only.

"They tell me everything they want me to know." Xiomara bagged three red chert flakes. "Knowledge can be a burden as much as a gift. Like any parent they keep secrets from their kids." Rubbing at a piece of fossilized charcoal, she faced him. "Some things do not need to be remembered."

Calehan laid a blanket out between two tall trees, facing the calm water lapping at the shore. He offered Xiomara a bagged sandwich and pack of fruit snacks.

"I got hungry and ate the chips earlier." Calehan grimaced. "Sorry."

"Guess you owe me chips then."

"I guess so." His wide smile brought a blush to her cheeks. Calehan so rarely offered more than a smirk, much less an open-lipped smile and here she was; receiving multiple wide-open Calehan smiles. Xiomara felt special.

Javier had been like this too, shy with his smile. His right eye tooth turned out and lent him a slightly crooked grin. Javier had hated it, often showing those teeth to only her. It had been one of her favorite secrets, his smile.

Xiomara bit her lip as her appetite turned sour and acid rolled in her belly. Did she have space for two secret smiles in her heart? She struggled to picture Javier in her mind, the picture fuzzy – unfocused.

Clearing her throat, Xiomara stood and called for Anubis.

"Ready?"

Calehan looked down at the half eaten sandwich in her hand. His eyes lingered on her face until she broke the gaze to scratch Anubis.

"I'll ask Rosebud to drop your bags off."

Xiomara nodded and followed him to the truck, grateful for the thumping radio.

Halfway between Calehan and Rosebud's house, her cabin was nestled amongst a plethora of trees. Calehan had let her rest the majority of the ride, only speaking when she asked him if they could please listen to another song.

"Sure." Calehan turned the radio off. "I hope you have a good voice."

Silence stretched between them while Xiomara stared at him.

"I'm waiting."

"I'm not singing for you." Xiomara laughed in disbelief.

"Why not?" Calehan screwed his face up exaggeratedly. "You don't want to hear my voice I promise you."

"Yes I do." Xiomara giggled. "Sing me a song, architect Calehan."

"Are there any songs about architects?" Calehan stalled, "We should write one."

"Estoy esperando." Xiomara crossed her arms.

"Happy birthday –" Calehan cut off when Xiomara burst out into laughter, reaching over to gently push at his shoulder.

"I meant a real song!"

"That is a real song." Calehan argued.

By the time he was turning the truck towards the trees, she had forgotten the pit of guilt burning an ulcer into her stomach. Tucked between evergreens, her cabin was a simple rancher with a tin roof. The exterior was painted the color of sandstone after a rainstorm. The door and shutters gleamed a pale turquoise. a wreath of flowers hung on the door. A smile slowly climbed her face as she looked over at Calehan.

"I hope you like it."

"It's beautiful." Her wide smile infected Calehan, who offered her one in return.

The dirt settled around their feet as they walked to the porch. Calehan placed the silver key in her hand, gesturing to the door with a timid smile. Xiomara turned the key in the deadbolt, then the beautiful bronze handle, squeezing her eyes shut in anticipation when she heard the near silent *click*.

She pushed the door...and pushed again. It was stuck.

"Shit," she heard Calehan's voice behind her as his left hand lay against the door, above her head. The warmth of his close body teasing her back, he pushed the door open, the both of them stumbling forward through the opening. Xiomara's toes caught the doorjamb and she steadied herself with a grip on Calehan's forward reaching arm. He held her close in return, wrapping his arm around her waist to steady her.

"Gracias," Xiomara breathed, leaning her head back to look up at him, looming tall, his chin parallel over hers. Anubis whimpered below them, drawing their gazes from each other. She let him off the leash, watching as he ran through the house sniffing everything he could reach.

"Anytime," he smiled, releasing her and stepping to the side. "Allow me to give you the full tour."

He showed her around the quaint cabin, renovated with his thoughtful architect mind. A jack and jill bathroom joined the primary bedroom and hallway, making use of the sole bathroom in the one bedroom home. He installed a ceiling fan in the bedroom to make up for the lack of air conditioning though Xiomara was freezing even now, doubtful she would be using it.

Her bed was covered in a rust orange bedspread, the bed-frame and furniture a simple light oak. With angled wooden legs and flat geometric faces, the furniture was modern with a nod to the retro. She suspected Rosebud had some kind of influence in the decoration. She ran her hands over the sage green silk pillowcases, stroking the feathers of the dreamcatcher hung above her side of the bed.

"Rosebud is Ojibwe too," Calehan leaned against the doorframe, his brown eyes watching her carefully. "She made that for you last week with some turquoise from Kate's cousins in New Mexico."

"You all are incredibly thoughtful." Xiomara smiled at him over her shoulder.

Calehan shrugged, "We're happy you're here."

Her face burned as Calehan's eyes whispered desire where they slid over her face.

"I am too."

Their brown eyes met across the room, heat seeping through the space between them.

Xiomara looked away first, twisting the quilt between her fingers. Her chest felt warm, heat spreading through her body where he had looked at her.

"Come on," Calehan tilted his head back, "I'll show you where the firewood is."

Xiomara followed him through the living room where Anubis had made himself at home on the couch. He led her to the back, opening the double doors to a small pine colored porch. It was partially covered to the left, where a stack of firewood sat protected from the rain.

"That should be more than enough for summer." Calehan picked up one of the logs in just one hand, long fingers stretching wide, nearly touching where his pinky and thumb wrapped around. "I'll bring some more in a few months, before winter."

"I can chop my own firewood, you know." Xiomara crossed her arms over her chest. Truthfully, she was no wood chopping expert, and cutting a few pieces a couple times a year didn't really count in this circumstance. But she didn't need to rely on him.

Calehan looked her head to toe wordlessly, opening a small door under the porch stairs and pulling out an axe. Holding it straight out to her, blade facing him, he waited for her to take the axe. Xiomara crossed her arms and leaned around the blade to glare at him. The pink of his lips split by white teeth when his face broke into a smile as he swung the axe around to rest upon his shoulder. His raised arm lifted his shirt slightly, a peek of fair brown skin flashing before her eyes. "I'll show you how before winter."

"Fine." She relented.

"Speaking of," He sighed as his eyes looked out over the trees, "Can you shoot a rifle?"

"Of course I can." Xiomara huffed. She wasn't a city girl. "Pretty sure we have more predators than you do."

"I was just checking." Calehan held one hand up in front of his chest, palm facing her. "I put motion-activated alarms out there but just keep an eye out for bears."

"Aye, aye, Captain." She mock saluted.

"There's a rifle by the front door and one here, above the back door." He ushered her back inside the house. "Ammo is in the hall closet."

"Did you leave a map or should I be taking notes?" Xiomara pressed her back into the peninsula in the kitchen. Her arms were crossed over her chest, one foot resting on her knee like a flamingo.

"I'm happy to draw you a map," Calehan stalked towards her, eyes trained on hers. "I figured a museum curator would have a good memory."

"I have a fantastic memory." Xiomara scoffed, dropping her foot to the floor. "It's full of museum related knowledge." She tapped her forehead with her pointer finger. "No space for trinket knowledge."

"I hardly think of ammunition as trinkets." He wiggled his fingers in the air as he said trinkets. Xiomara found his use of air quotes unnecessary. The toes of their boots were touching, Calehan boxing Xiomara to the counter while his hands gripped the stone behind her.

Her mind was begging her to pull away but she was rooted to the spot. The race of her heart slammed in her chest and stole her breath. Chief Thomas had been explicit about the focus needed on the project and how distractions would be swiftly dealt with. She was ready to burn that memory from her mind.

Since Javier had started visiting her dreams, she felt like she was betraying him with her interest in Calehan. But she couldn't find a way to stop.

"My sister will be walking over here soon," Calehan told her, checking his watch.

Xiomara nodded, following him out to the front porch.

"This house, Calehan," she paused until he met her stare. "It's incredible. You're a wonderful architect."

He ducked his head, hiding a smile.

"I just built some walls." He laughed. "It's nothing."

"Well, if not for you I would still be rooming with Rosebud," she smiled and looked at her long, wooded driveway. "Instead of in my own house."

"I aim to please." He winked at her, starting down her porch steps. "I'm sure you are eager to unpack and settle in."

Xiomara watched him retreat from her, hoping against hope he ached to touch her the same as she.

"Cal," his name flew from her mouth before her brain had fully formed the word. He stopped where he was on the stairs, turning back to face her. Surprise was written all over his face.

Xiomara took a few steps forward, "Thank you, for all of this." She gestured around herself, laughing as he watched her. "I appreciate you."

Calehan nodded. Xiomara fussed with her bangs, hiding from his open gaze. Calehan grabbed her hand, pulling her back into him for a hug.

With Calehan a step below her, her eyes were almost level with his chin. She leaned into his hug, wrapping her arms around his neck and letting her cheek press to his. Xiomara felt his grip loosen and wrapped her arms tighter around his neck. Breathing in his warm tobacco scent, she felt Calehan hold her closer, lifting her feet from the ground.

His arms were everywhere. Worked from years of manual labor, they spread across every inch of her back, wrapping completely over her so that he could grip her hip and shoulder, holding her to him.

Xiomara held him so tightly to him her knuckles whitened. Gravel crunched in front of them, Joy appearing around the bend.

"Your sister is here," Xiomara whispered against his ear. His answering groan rumbled through her body as she laughed.

Calehan set her back down and leaned back to look at her, thumbing her chin. She felt stripped bare under his gaze as it toured her face, tasting her features. He kissed her cheek, pressing his forehead to the side of her head for a brief moment. Xiomara turned her face into his and caught his lips with hers. It was over as soon as it happened, Calehan barely able to kiss back before she was pulling away.

His hand chased her, tracing along her arm as she slid through his grip, her fingers squeezing before she was out of his grasp.

"Hasta luego," she said, retreating until she was pressed against her front door.

Calehan staggered down the stairs, his eyes still on hers. His smile was wide, soft white teeth on show. "See you later." She watched from the porch as they pulled away, his hand waving goodbye out of the window.

Xiomara thunked her head back against the closed door. Did women get blue balls?

She opened her eyes and found Anubis watching her from the couch.

"Don't judge me." Xiomara sat beside him and scratched his chin. "You kiss him every time you see him." Anubis showed his belly in response. What a whore.

grooved

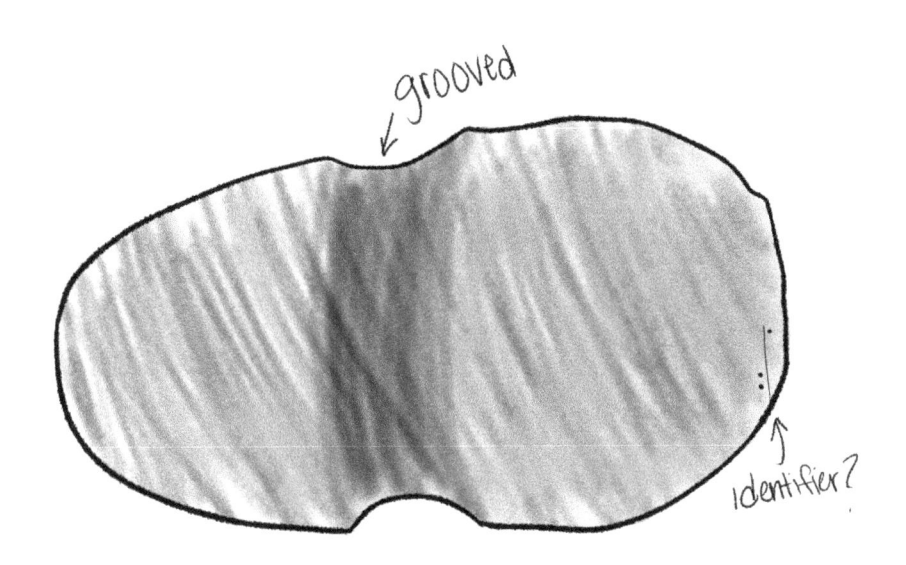

identifier?

Chapter 9

Stirring cinnamon into her coffee, Xiomara struggled to focus on the emails in front of her. Last night, her dreams were bright, vibrant, alive, and full of Javier. She woke up feeling like she hadn't gotten any sleep. The sun shone behind her closed eyelids the entire night, talking with Javier until her alarm rang. It was strange how easily he appeared in her dreams since the berry festival. For years she had been without him, searching for a sign that his spirit remained with her. She couldn't figure out what exactly had changed and brought him back to her.

"Good morning, Ms. Chavez." Chief Thomas accompanied his greeting with a firm knock on her open office door. "Could I steal a few minutes of your time?"

"Of course." She invited him to sit, pushing her laptop to the side to give him her full attention. Xiomara was digitally cataloging the artifacts and transcribing her field notes and really needed the break.

"The Elders informed me this morning of another site." Chief Thomas smiled when she did. "Would you like to see it?"

"Yes!" Xiomara was flustered, her hands wandering her desk in search of something to do. "I- yes, what--"

Chief Thomas interrupted her, grasping her hand. "Great. I've been really impressed by your dedication to the project. Small town drama can be an easy distraction sometimes."

Xiomara blinked at him. What an odd statement. Did he know about her and Calehan? Had he caught them flirting? She thought they had been nonchalant enough but maybe she was wrong. The Chief's statement felt like a not-so-subtle reminder about the significance of their project. Shame fled her bloodstream.

"We leave tomorrow morning." Chief Thomas stood and clapped his hands together. "See you at the casino at six am."

Chief Thomas tapped a couple times on her door as he left, his jovial whistle reaching her ears until the elevator doors closed.

Xiomara chewed her lip and stood, pacing around her office. She had a million questions she knew no one had an answer to. Not even her. A ground survey would not yield an answer to even half of her questions, but *a new site*? Another untouched site was something she could *not* pass up.

Rosebud found her outside half an hour later, pacing on the porch and scribbling in her green notebook. Setting their sandwiches on the table, she waited for Xiomara to notice her.

"What are you pacing about?"

"This new site." Xiomara shook her head as if the answer should've been obvious. "Do you know anything about it?"

"Not really," Rosebud unwrapped her sandwich, heart-shaped sunglasses covering her eyes. "It's far as fuck away, though. My brother is forcing me to come. Do you know how much I *hate* camping?"

"We will be camping?"

"Oh yeah. Did Chief Thomas not tell you anything?"

"He said to meet him at the casino tomorrow at six am. That's all I got."

"Babes…" Rosebud patted her hand. "We're going on an overnight trail ride. You need to pack dry." Xiomara zoned out as Rosebud continued talking.

She hadn't been on an overnight ride since she was a kid. Clover only had a few horses so it must be a small group going with them. "Who all is going?"

Rosebud chugged some sparkling water and answered. "Clover, Calehan, me, Kenny, his dad, Calehan's dad. I think that's everyone."

"Can David come?" Xiomara couldn't do a whole-site ground survey on her own. It would take days.

"Probably." Rosebud shrugged. "Ask Kenny. He'll say yes to whatever you want." Rosebud bumped Xiomara suggestively.

Xiomara grimaced. "Don't say that."

The Chief had been more hands-on in the last few weeks, visiting the site and meeting for debriefs with her weekly. She wasn't sure if he was interested in her or thought she couldn't do her job. He thanked her for her attention and focus, reiterating how important it was to ignore distractions. She suspected it had something to do with the easy way she and Calehan communicated, in polar opposite to the formal way she addressed the Chief. She and Calehan needed to be on their best behavior tomorrow.

"Shit, girl, you got the pick of the litter right now." Rosebud crunched her potato chip between her teeth. "I do favor Calehan, but I support you either way."

Xiomara grunted disapproval at her friend. "I do not want Chief Thomas."

"Good, 'cause Calehan is obsessed with you." Rosebud laughed at Xiomara's blush. "I mean it! The way you two look at each other could melt glass."

Xiomara bit into her sandwich, hoping that their attraction wasn't actually that noticeable. Calehan did frequently look at her as though he wished to devour her whole—mind, body, and spirit. Maybe she looked at him the same.

Finished with lunch, she climbed the stairs sluggishly, putting off speaking to Chief Thomas until the end of the workday. His secretary had already gone home, so she knocked on his open door and stepped through.

"Xiomara," he said when she entered the room, the smell of lavender tickling her nose. "To what do I owe this pleasure?"

"Nothing, really." She leaned one arm against the back of the chair in front of his desk, unwilling to sit and prolong her visit. "I was hoping I could bring David along to the new site tomorrow? I could really use his hel—"

"Of course," Chief Thomas answered before she had finished speaking. "Anything you need."

She took a step back. "Awesome, thank you."

He stood from his desk. "I'm about ready to head out as well. I'll walk you."

Damn.

They stepped into the elevator together, Chief Thomas pressing the button for the ground floor.

"How is your cabin treating you?" He leaned against the wall of the elevator, his long legs crossed in front of her.

"It's wonderful," she answered immediately.

"You're not too far from my property." Chief Thomas held her eye. "You should come over for dinner sometime."

She broke his gaze.

"Thank you for the offer." Xiomara slid by him and out the door he held open. It was a feat that she squeezed by without touching him. "Maybe once I'm settled in."

"Please don't hesitate to call me if you need anything." He followed her to her car. "I'm just up the road. Could probably walk between our houses."

Xiomara was glad to be facing the car, her eyes bulging. "Good to know. Thank you, Chief."

"You can call me Kenny." His hand curled around the edge of her open door, preventing her from closing it.

"I probably won't." She flashed a toothy smile, hoping against hope he would laugh and let her be.

"All right." Chief Thomas stepped away and put his hands up, palms facing her. "The offer stands. Drive safe." Stepping around the open door, he threw an arm around her neck and pulled Xiomara into a hug. He secured his other around the middle of her back, holding her securely against him.

Standing on her toes, she pressed her hand into the center of his back. She patted it gently, hoping he would release her. Finally, he pulled back and headed to his own vehicle. Closing the door behind her, the Jeep roared to life. Xiomara peeled out of the lot before he could catch up.

Calehan stood at the café entrance, the burning steam of fresh roasted chiles creeping up his jacket sleeve. He watched Xiomara smile, her hand pressing between Chief Thomas' shoulders and brushing along his back while they stood in an embrace. After a lifetime, they broke apart, and Calehan watched while they waved goodbye.

He should've known.

Of *course* Xiomara was enchanted by Chief Thomas. Who wouldn't be? He was tall and the women said he was handsome, but he was significantly leaner. Calehan was rounded from a life of commodity food and an adult love of carbs.

Chief Thomas wore the face of his mother, the dark brown skin to match. He looked more modern, with curls cropped close to his head. He was every woman's fantasy...unlike Calehan. A farm boy still working for his father in his thirties. What had he done that was even worthy of Xiomara's attention? He was stupid to think she'd want him when there was a chief chasing after her. Here he was, imagining a future and falling far too quickly for someone he had only kissed *once*.

Xiomara was an accomplished archaeologist, with multiple published papers and now two museums to her name. Calehan had a useless degree and dug holes for a living.

Muskwa interrupted his thoughts as he exited the café, fresh tea in hand. "What are you looking at?"

Calehan shook the thoughts from his head. "Thought I saw a hawk." He ignored the look of suspicion on his father's face and climbed in the truck.

At home, Nataani set the table while Calehan plated the food. Joy was at the casino for a girls night, leaving the Yellowbird men alone for a night.

"Decided if you're going to take that contract in Spain yet, big brother?" Nataani asked.

"You're so invested in this job I *might* take." Calehan toyed the idea over in his mind. He had put off signing the contract, and for what? Sibling guilt and a woman he had known for thirty days. Maybe he was being foolish.

Nataani scoffed. "You have to take the job."

He turned to Nataani. "Are you sure *you* don't want to move to Spain?" Calehan crossed his arms and glared at his baby brother.

"If you're asking me to visit you, I thought that was a given." Nataani walked away, tapping his purple-painted nails along his frosted glass of tea.

Calehan leaned back in his chair, rolling his shoulders in thought. What was keeping him here on Bunchberry, anyway?

With Joy staying home for at least the next few years, his dad would have plenty of help around the ranch. If he took the smallest lodging offered, he would be able to send a few hundred dollars home each month. Maybe this was in everyone's best interest. He hated to admit that Xiomara's interest in him had nearly kept him tethered to Bunchberry eternally. Regardless of her interest in him—or Chief Thomas—he needed to focus on himself and his family.

With a project as large as an entire college campus, moving to Spain would be worth it just for the future opportunities. A dream built itself in his head: the idea that no one in his family would ever have to live paycheck-to-paycheck again. Spain was more than just a job; it was a new life. Besides, who hadn't dreamed of living in sunny Europe temporarily? Sure it was the land of the colonizers, but lodging was included and the pay was handsome. It would be stupid to turn it down.

Taking a deep breath, Calehan nodded. Yes. This was the right thing to do. Three years of work away from his family could change all of their lives for the better. He had to do this for them as much as himself.

After dinner, he signed the job offer that had been stuck to the fridge with a beaded blueberry magnet and dropped the letter in the mailbox. This was going to be good for him and an incredible step in his career. He deserved a win.

Finally.

Walking from the mailbox, Calehan stopped to scratch his childhood horse. He stood almost as tall as the horse's midnight-toned eyes, reflecting a single white moon.

"Ready for tomorrow, Angel?" Calehan rubbed his wide nose, brushing some of the dirt off the horse's black hair.

Calehan leaned forward, resting their foreheads together. He had raised Angel from birth. Now almost fourteen years old, Calean had spent half of his life with Angel. He briefly wondered how hard it would be to bring a horse from Manitoba to Valencia. Would he have to ride a boat?

A trill rang through the damp air, startling the two apart. Angel chuffed and turned away, as if personally offended by the ringing.

"Hello?"

"Hi." Her voice stopped his heart in his chest. "Is it okay to give you a call? I can call Rosebud instead, if you're busy." Xiomara's words were ice white, rushing like rapids through his mind. "I didn't mean to interrupt—"

"You can always call me." Calehan pressed his fingers to his forehead, a grimace stretched across his face. Why had he said that? His heart was going to pound out of his chest. Hands gripping the fence, he worked the metal like a stress ball.

The silence hung between them on the line, neither sure what to say next. What had sparked her to call him? *Shit.* Was this a work call? Dirt flew out from his kicking boot; he had probably fucked something up.

"How is the construction coming along?" Her voice was featherlight, tickling his ear.

"It's going really well." His voice softened to match hers. "You should swing by sometime. Tell me what paint colors you want."

Her voice became louder with her laugh. "I am always available to boss you around."

Calehan had to take a deep breath to calm the rush of blood to his pants.

Xiomara didn't wait for his response. "I hear you are taking us on a hike tomorrow." After he confirmed her suspicions, she got to the reason for her call. "Rosebud told me I need to pack *dry*." She emphasized the word for him. "I don't know what that means."

Calehan laughed, suddenly glad she called him. She would've been miserable without proper clothing on a hike this damp. His voice was louder now. "Joy has some extra clothes. I'll pack you a bag."

"Really?" Xiomara's voice pitched higher, tugging his lips up with it. "That would be awesome, Cal. Thank you, seriously."

"I'll pick you up at 5:30." He could see her smile in his mind.

"You're the best." Her voice was sunny. "Buenas noches, Calito." Fire flashed across his entire body. That nickname set him aflame *everywhere*. He had to stop walking to catch his breath through the searing heat taking him over.

"See you tomorrow." He kept the phone against his ear until the screen went black. Calehan couldn't stop the hammering of his heart in anticipation of seeing Xiomara. Looking around, he set out to check on the cows before heading inside. Fire still danced across his skin, and he was sure he resembled a tomato. He needed the chilly night air to calm his heart. She had called him for help, not Chief Thomas. Maybe he had a chance, after all.

side notched →

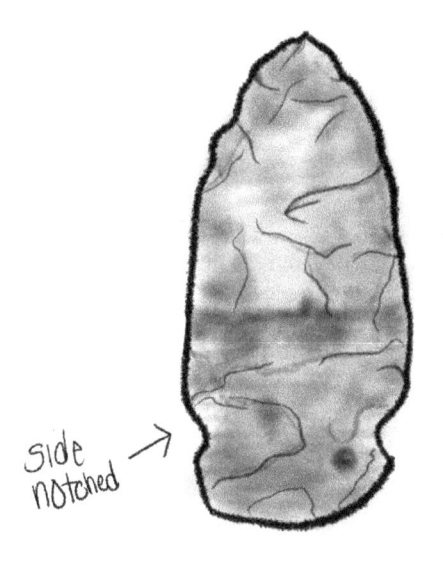

Chapter 10

Sun teased the edge of the land, desperate not to chase her beloved moon from the sky. Dirt swirled around the tires as Calehan parked beside Xiomara's Jeep. He grabbed the duffel bag beside him and slid out of his truck, ascending her stairs two at a time.

Xiomara opened the door before he could knock, her sweet cinnamon and vanilla scent overwhelming him and luring him inside.

"Good morning." Calehan hoped she couldn't hear his racing heart when he kissed her cheek.

He presented a jacket from the duffel bag and set a pair of cowboy boots down beside her door.

"I'll have you ride in cowboy boots." He watched her socked feet putter around the kitchen and couldn't help but imagine her doing that in his own house.

"You're telling me what to wear now?" She tilted her head to the side just a hair. Great.

Now his heart was in his ears. There was no way she couldn't hear it.

Calehan sat at the counter and accepted the cup of coffee she offered. "Where's Anubis?"

"I dropped him off with Kate this morning." Xiomara set her mug on the counter beside him. She dragged her gaze over his face and body and he could feel her eyes on him heavy as a hand. "I've never seen your hair down." Her fingers ghosted over the damp hair stuck to his cheek.

"It's still drying." Calehan explained. His mouth went dry at her touch, vision tunneling into her.

"I like it." Xiomara leaned in.

Calehan let her steal every thought from his mind. Her lips tasted like cinnamon, and he wondered if he would ever get used to the taste. It was strong, vibrant, and lingered on the tongue in the same way she did. Did he want to get used to it?

He worried he already was addicted.

Widening his legs, he tucked her in between them so she could be flush against his chest. His hands ached to hold her closer, to squish her into him until she couldn't breathe. Her giggle stole his breath away, and he kissed her until he was seeing white.

Finally pulling away, he rested their foreheads together.

"How long do we have?" Xiomara asked, her lips reddened.

Calehan checked his watch. "Ten minutes."

Xiomara grunted. "Not enough time." Kissing him chastely, she rinsed her empty mug out and set it in the sink. "What do you know about this site?"

Calehan leaned forward on the kitchen counter. "Not much. My Dad said it's a gathering place the old ones spoke of." He sipped his coffee as he watched Xiomara calculate every word out of his mouth. "It's in a swamp, sort of."

Her eyes bulged. "How cold is the water?"

"I'm not sure, but too cold to stand in when flooded." He waited for her response. "Is that a good thing?"

"If the site is submerged in a cold enough bog, there could be preserved organic matter. We could learn exactly what they were eating, growing, and burning. The possibilities are... vast... numerous... infinite." Xiomara gripped his shoulders, her face close to his. "It could be a great thing."

He couldn't stop himself from kissing her smile. Her excitement was infectious, and he found himself imagining the possibilities buried beneath the earth.

Calehan pulled away when he began kissing down her neck. A moan vibrated in her chest the same time it reached his ears and if he had been fifteen still, he would've came right then.

"We should get going." Glass cut his tongue while he shattered their moment. "Don't want the Chief thinking I've kidnapped you." Her bottom lip poked out in disappointment.

Xiomara clicked her tongue in disapproval. Calehan rinsed his mug in the sink, bumping Xiomara away when she tried to take over. Washing both of their coffee mugs, he placed them on the drying rack and wiped his hands.

He could feel her eyes stroke over his skin. Calehan regarded her similarly, itching to touch her with more than his gaze. A blush graced her cheeks when she met his eyes.

Calehan handed the neoprene dry jacket to her and shouldered both of their bags, loading them into the back of the truck. Opening the door for her, she gripped his outstretched hand and climbed into the cab. Her thumb stoked over the pulse point of his wrist as she pulled away, a shiver reaching all the way to his toes from her touch. Calehan walked to the driver's side with his head held high.

Calehan handed her the aux cord, effectively distracting Xiomara for the lengthy ride. She took it upon herself to introduce him to what she called *Norteño essentials*, giving him a quick class on *Xo's Favorites 101*.

Calehan took mental notes.

The casino parking lot was largely empty, only a few vehicles waiting for them. Mornings here were foggy, the dew settling into the air like bees onto a petal. She could see Rosebud in Clover's truck, a hat pulled low over her face. Xiomara guessed she was asleep. David was stretched across the backseat, mouth dropped open. Would she get to sleep, too? Measuring the bench seat with her eyes, she was pretty sure she could fit with her knees bent.

"Which horses did you bring?" Xiomara let her head fall against the seat, loosely lolling from side to side. Her eyes ran along Calehan's profile, cherishing his tall, broad nose. It stood proudly on his face, commanding even. She dreamed of running her fingers along the bridge, following it with her tongue. Did he taste the same as he smelled?

"Only the most well-behaved ones." His voice snapped her out of the scandalous thoughts, earning a fake punch to his arm as she pushed herself upright. "Stay here. I'll bring breakfast." Tying off his damp braid, he slipped from the car.

Calehan joined his father and brother, his back to her. Xiomara watched as the three men conversed, a long braid hanging down each of their backs. A glaze overtook her eyes. It must have been amazing to grow up in such a large community. She had always wondered what it would've been like to share a culture, a family with so many others.

The trio joined the other men, Chief Thomas crossing his arms as he spoke with Calehan.

Xiomara grimaced and sunk farther in the seat, peeking over the edge of the dash in hopes she couldn't be seen. She worried this would happen if she showed up in the same car as Calehan, but she hadn't been able to resist the flutter in her heart and the heat in her belly when he declared he would pick her up. How could she say no?

Crossing her fingers, she hoped Calehan would play it cool and the Chief wouldn't suspect that she had considered taking him to bed this morning. She sunk further into the seat.

Calehan regarded Chief Thomas. The Chief stared at him with his lips curved in a permanent look of disgust. A flower of pride bloomed in Calehan's chest, puffing it out, he stood tall.

"Joy loaned her some clothes, so I offered to bring them and give her a ride." Calehan's voice was even as he answered him. The bitter taste of a dare spread along his tongue.

"Why did you volunteer a car for her if you were going to be her personal chauffeur?" His glare was severe, but having grown up together, Calehan wasn't fazed. Kenny had always been like this. Calehan assumed it was because he found Calehan's quiet and laid-back demeanor threatening, especially when he accounted for their family history.

"Chief." Calehan stepped closer. "Bunchberry isn't on a GPS. How did you expect her to get here alone?"

Chief Thomas rolled his lips under his teeth. "Next time, check with me first. I'm responsible for her."

Muskwa interrupted, his laughter loud as he clapped Calehan on the back and pulled him into the other's conversation. Clover outlined their route on a topographical map at the direction of Muskwa and Chief Thomas' father, Chief Joseph. Calehan and his father had gone when he was young, and now the trail was impossible to see. Muskwa would have to lead the group with Calehan at the rear. This way, they had two people verifying the route.

Chief Thomas reiterated the plan, claiming the ownership of it to remind them who was in charge. He was putting on a show for the wrong group. Everyone here knew him from birth. No amount of bravado would intimidate them.

Calehan returned with a banana and breakfast sandwich for her, laughing when he opened the door to her scrunched up form. "Are you hiding?"

"Maybe?" Xiomara remained curled up as he pulled the truck onto the road, Chief Thomas leading them. Xiomara eyed Calehan while he drove.

"He thought I kidnapped you," Calehan said. Xiomara grunted.

"I told you he would think that." She plopped her food unopened on the dash.

Calehan hadn't expected that reaction. "What? Not a fan of the Chief?"

She shrugged. "He's my boss."

"That's it?"

"Yeah." She looked at him across the cab. "That's it."

Calehan nodded, furiously fighting a smile. "Good to know."

The remainder of the drive had Xiomara squirming in her seat. By the time they arrived at the farthest point for the cars, she was coiled tighter than ever and desperate to let loose on a horse.

Xiomara pulled on Calehan's jacket, his scent stuck to the fabric. He rounded the truck with her backpack, gesturing with his head for her to follow. Clover and his dad had tied up the horses outside the trailer, the majority saddled already by the time they joined them. Calehan led her to a pair of horses, one large and all black, the other a slightly taller white and brown paint.

Calehan packed the black horse's saddlebags with food and water, and Xiomara's backpack. The paint horse carried more weight, taking more water and her duffel bag.

"Where's your bag?"

Calehan looked her dead in the eye. "Our stuff is in the same bag."

"Oh." Xiomara ignored the butterflies that took over her entire body. They weren't exactly her clothes, which dulled the butterflies, but the intimacy of sharing a travel bag had a grip on her heart.

"This is Angel. He's your horse for the trip." Calehan patted the butt of the large black horse, scratching along his inky black spine.

Xiomara tipped her head to the paint behind Angel. "Is she yours?"

"Well, she's Angel's, really." Calehan double checked the straps across Angel's chest. "But yes, I'm riding Dreamer. She's a bit picky."

Xiomara understood her preference for Calehan over other riders. She felt the same. "They're bonded to each other?"

Calehan nodded, scrutinizing Xiomara's expression.

"So, you and I will be riding next to each other for this whole trip?" She stepped closer to him. "Did you do that on purpose?"

Calehan held still long enough that Xiomara worried she had gone too far and ruined it. He nodded slowly, barely dipping his chin.

His hand rested on the saddle beside her head. Her chest brushed against his stomach, breath sticking in her lungs.

Calehan looked down at her. "I didn't want you riding beside anyone but me." He sidestepped her frozen form, rounding Angel and untying his lead. Dropping the reins over the saddle horn, he waved Xiomara to him.

"You don't have a block?" She looked around, peering at the trailer in search of a step. Xiomara wasn't sure how she would get up there without one. She could barely reach the stirrup from the ground.

"What do you need a block for?" They exchanged confused looks before Calehan continued. "You have me."

He gripped her leg behind the knee, holding tight to her thigh. She pressed her weight into his hand, her leg rubbing against his broad chest. Pushing her up with his hand, she threw her leg over Angel and settled onto his back. Xiomara adjusted in the saddle, rolling her hips to find a comfortable position. Calehan palmed her calf comfortingly, guiding her foot into the stirrup.

He rounded Angel, ducking under his long neck to check her other stirrup. Guiding her foot, he slid his hand up her leather cowboy boot and onto the back of her thigh. Fingertips pressed into the meat of her soft legs; fire licked up her body from where he touched her. Calehan adjusted her saddlebags, rummaging around before stepping back to look them over from a new perspective. He nodded in satisfaction, patting Angel on the bottom.

"Walk him around a bit. I'll come find you soon."

She tapped Angel with her heel, letting the reins rest against his neck. Xiomara tipped her head to the golden sun, warming her face in the light. Angel walked languidly beneath her, lapping the open area between the trees. Rosebud rode up beside her, pulling her from her thoughts.

"I can feel my ass going numb already," she muttered to Xiomara, huffing where she sat on a stunning all white mare.

"You don't like to ride?"

"I'm an indoor cat, Xio." She pushed her sunglasses up her nose while Xiomara laughed.

She picked up the reins and guided them farther from the others. "Did Clover say anything about what Chief Thomas said this morning?"

"About Calehan having you in his car before the sun had risen?" Rosebud snickered, likely assuming more than the truth.

"He only picked me up." Xiomara sighed. "Nothing more."

"Lame." Rosebud clicked her tongue against her teeth. "Anyway, don't worry about Kenny. Cal will set him straight."

"What does that mean?"

Rosebud shrugged. "Calehan doesn't really care that Kenny is the Chief. He never yields to him, no matter how hard Kenny tries."

Xiomara narrowed her eyes. She hoped she was not a pawn in their intimidation game.

Angel turned and began bringing them toward the others. Calehan made eye contact with her, watching from where he tightened the cinch of a thickly muscled thoroughbred. She wasn't surprised to find Chief Thomas astride the huge animal. Calehan patted the horse and stepped away, heading straight for Xiomara.

He drew close, his hand reaching out to catch Angel's nose in his palm. "How's he ride?"

"Perfectly," she said, scratching the coarse mane where it disappeared beneath her saddle.

"Good morning, ladies," Chief Thomas called out as he rode closer, his father and Clover following behind. Rosebud groaned and clutched the thermos in her hands.

Calehan fell silent, his hand wrapped around Xiomara's leather covered ankle.

"Or not…" Chief Thomas laughed at Rosebud's facial expression.

A riderless Dreamer sidled beside Xiomara, Muskwa having untied her to join the group. The saddle atop her back was stunning—a mahogany red leather beaded with the colors of the eastern sunrise. Violet, coral, and pink, the flowers swirled into a rising sun across the saddle. It was beautiful, calling her eyes even as she tried to focus elsewhere.

"Have you decided if you will be staying through the winter?" Chief Thomas had given Xiomara the option to curate remotely over winter, knowing she may want to return to Mexico for the holidays.

"Yes," Xiomara answered. "Once we close digging, there will be hours of cataloging to do. There are far more artifacts than I imagined." She kept her eyes straight ahead, though she watched for Calehan's reaction. The uptick to his lips was nearly imperceptible. But she saw it.

"Have you seen snow?" Chief Thomas leaned closer, his button down open on his chest.

"Yes." She smiled. "A few times."

"Have you driven in it?" Chief Thomas nudged his horse closer to her. "It can be dangerous driving if you've never done it before."

Before Xiomara could answer, Calehan was passing her breakfast sandwich into her hand, his shoulder against the front of her saddle. He blocked Chief Thomas from getting any closer. Dreamer sidled up in search of both the boys, poising herself between Xiomara and Chief Thomas.

"Don't worry, Chief. She's got my Jeep." Calehan looked at the Chief directly, unwavering in his gaze.

"Well…" Chief Thomas turned his eyes to Xiomara "I'm next door and I'm happy to carpool once it snows." He offered a lopsided smile. "We can't have the lead of our project getting frostbite."

Xiomara laughed his comment off, refusing to show her discomfort on her face. Angel followed Calehan without prompting, taking her away from the Chief. Prodding at his back with his nose, Angel goosed Calehan as he swung onto Dreamer's back. He looked majestic atop the horse, his braid swinging lightly over the beading of his saddle. Xiomara curled her toes in her boots, forcing her breath out slowly through her nose in an effort to dampen the heat rushing up her spine.

Calehan brought them closer to the group, the horses falling in line beside each other. The toe of her boot brushed Calehan's jeans with their proximity. He was so close to her she could smell him. The scent of tobacco was strongest today. She guessed he had smoked in preparation of their journey. Black jeans did nothing to obscure the girth of his muscular legs, the stretch taking her breath with it. His hand was perched on his thigh, fingers spread wide where they dimpled into his thick flesh. Tearing her eyes from him, she shifted in her saddle, hoping no one was watching the flames take her cheeks.

"Muskwa and I will lead," Chief Thomas boomed from atop his paint horse. "We have about a six-hour ride to the campsite. Buddy system at all times, comprenden?" His eyes flicked to Xiomara. "Would you like to ride up front to see more clearly?"

"Um…" She fought for an excuse. "I'll be taking notes. I don't want to slow everyone down; I can stay in the back." She forced a bright smile on her face, hoping to sway any negative reaction to her rejection.

Chief Thomas nodded. "Skoden."

The group filed in easily, Muskwa and David chatting animatedly with Chief Joseph.

Xiomara let the reins rest on Angel's neck, trusting he would follow his lover. He did, the horses stepping in time with each other, walking so close their ears brushed every so often. Rosebud and Clover were chattering in Ojibwe before them, David grabbing leaves from each tree they passed. Xiomara closed her eyes, the tenor of their voices warming her spirit. The sun kissed her face when she leaned her head back, bangs falling to the side so the sun could shine through.

"You put a lot of trust in Angel," Calehan said, nodding at her hands palm up in her lap, her head tilted to the sky.

"Not really." Her eyes remained closed. "I trust you."

Xiomara smiled to herself, as though she could hear the blood rushing through his veins. She opened her eyes, watching his hips sway with Dreamer's steps. His light brown skin shone in the morning light. A dreamy haze settled over her eyes. This couldn't be real life.

Rays of light shone around Calehan, the sun caressing him with her touch. She highlighted him in a pink toned glow, stealing Xiomara's thoughts with the glowing caress. Xiomara shut her eyes again. The sun didn't choose lightly, and Xiomara trusted her instincts. If the sun liked Calehan enough to bathe him in pink, a color of love and life, maybe this would be worth it.

"What are you smiling about?" Calehan asked.

Xiomara shook her head. "Everything."

He squeezed her knee, eliciting a squeal of surprise.

"Shh," Calehan told her, his finger over his mouth. "You'll call the bears."

Xiomara narrowed her eyes. "You didn't mention bears."

"That's what I packed the rifles for."

Xiomara glanced at his saddlebags, only now noting the gun strapped to Dreamer. How had she missed that?

Teeth cut into her bottom lip. She hadn't considered there would be bears on this trip. That had been quite an oversight on her part. She hadn't worried much on Bunchberry Island; bears couldn't tear through walls. A tent, however?

"It's okay." Calehan laughed gently. "They won't come near us with all the noise you and Rosebud make together."

"Ay cabrón." Xiomara poked him in the thigh. "Are you sure?"

"Yes." He caught her hand, glancing forward to ensure Chief Thomas wasn't looking, and brought her hand to his mouth. He kissed her pulse point, then the crook of her elbow, and her palm, when she pulled away.

"You're going to get us caught," she whispered to him.

He shrugged. "We're adults."

"On a work trip." She eyed him narrowly.

Calehan nodded. "I will *try* to keep my hands to myself if you do."

Xiomara dragged her eyes over his long neck. The pink glow bathed him in light like her own personal sun. "No promises." She tipped her head to the side, watching as he shifted in his saddle. She loved making him squirm.

Halfway through the ride, Chief Thomas stopped the group for a break.

Xiomara lay in the grass beside Muskwa; the two stretched out like starfish in an effort to release their joints. Muskwa had lit a sprig of sage between them. The familiar scent felt like levitating. The leaves dappled the sunlight on her face, their whispered breeze lulling her nearly to sleep.

"So..." Xiomara turned to look at Muskwa. His face was resting in a gentle smile, and she hoped he wasn't asleep. "Did I hear Chief Joseph call you 'almost Chief' back there?"

Muskwa was quiet for so long Xiomara figured he was asleep. When he spoke, she nearly jumped out of her skin. "Chief Joseph is a funny man."

They let the silence stretch, and Xiomara figured he wasn't going to elaborate.

"Our family are the hereditary Chiefs of our nation." Muskwa's voice was so gentle it mixed with the voices of the birds sitting in the trees above them, reaching her ears as a song. "My grandfather was Chief when we switched to voting, and my father chose not to run. I chose the same…and so have my children, so far." His eyes were closed with memories. "Chief is not the same position it used to be. We are a modern people, no matter what we tell ourselves. A chief is a politician now, and I like to think us Yellowbirds are far too honest to be politicians."

"I think so, too." Her voice was gentle, sweetened by her smile.

"You guys want to eat or take a nap?" Rosebud threw her hands on her hips, tapping her foot as she looked down at them.

"Definitely lunch." Xiomara took Rosebud's outstretched hand, watching as Calehan helped his father.

They tore through their turkey and huckleberry sandwiches in record time, climbing into their saddles before the hard print of the seat had left their muscles. Chief Thomas waited off to the side as everyone got on the trail, claiming he had to bring up the rear for accountability.

Unease spread down her spine like cold fingers as Chief Thomas sandwiched Xiomara between him and Calehan.

Angel drew close to Dreamer. She glanced at Calehan, his gaze settling over her like a blanket, and she felt her heart rate slow.

"Seems like old Angel can't walk straight," Chief Thomas said, gesturing with his chin at her horse.

Calehan's gaze could cut steel. He didn't need to utter a word, though, as Xiomara immediately took offense to the statement.

"You want to trade him in for a new model, Chief?" Xiomara squinted. "Pretty sure this guy is an Elder." She scratched at the hair between the horse's ears, giving him an appreciative pat on the neck.

"You're right." Chief Thomas flashed an award-winning smile. "Is that why you chose to ride him?"

"Of course." Xiomara spoke without looking at Calehan.

Be nonchalant, she told herself.

"Speaking of old things…" Now was her chance to question him about the site. "Any ideas how old this site is? Is it possible it was previously under a glacier?"

"Yes." Chief Thomas tapped her ankle with his boot, white teeth shining in the afternoon light. "About three years ago my father and I noticed a few axe heads and projectile points wash up on the shoreline. It was the first time the ice had ever melted, and by the next year this place was almost impossible to get to."

Xiomara chanced a glance at Calehan, but he was staring straight ahead, his jaw pulled tight. She waited for him to meet her eye, but he didn't budge.

"This year has been remarkably dry," Chief Thomas continued. "I figured it was now or never."

"It sounds like it will be back under water soon." She offered him a shy smile. "This may be your last chance."

"Good thing I had you nearby." Chief Thomas winked. "It's not so easy to find a Native archaeologist for something like this."

"Don't I know it." Xiomara shook her head. Some sites were so deep in the desert, the topography hadn't been charted in decades. The risk was high, and the reward was abysmal. Desert landscapes either never changed or changed within hours. There was nothing in between. As a child, her father had taken them to the same petroglyph site every four years, leaving offerings at the natural spring below. By the time she moved home from college, it was gone. It got harder each year to keep track of what was natural destruction and what was developers.

Calehan watched her converse easily with the Chief while they shared the difficulty of getting employees to relocate temporarily. Xiomara sat stone straight, glancing back at him every few minutes. If she wasn't so clearly disturbed by the Chief's looming presence, Calehan would've laughed at her evasive answers.

"Would've taken valedictorian from him, too, if he'd been in the right grade." Chief Thomas shrugged, lips pulling down at the edges.

The sly dig brought Calehan to the present, a strange look on Xiomara's face. He raised an eyebrow at her.

"You were valedictorian?" Her voice was quiet.

"Not really." Calehan shrugged it off, as though his answer should suffice. He should've known it wouldn't be enough for her. She always wanted to know more. More about him. No one had wanted to know more about him before.

"I mean..." Calehan shifted uncomfortably under her expectant stare. Chief Thomas lingered over her shoulder, smirking at him. "I guess I was, if you want to call it that."

"What else would you call it?"

"Nothing better to do," Chief Thomas interjected. "Calehan didn't do any extracurriculars."

"Why were you in a different grade?"

"They moved me up one grade." Calehan watched her from the corner of his eye, unwilling to give Chief Thomas any reaction. It really hadn't been a huge deal. He had started tribal college a year early, finished his degree in Winnipeg within a year and a half, and took to working full time by twenty. His income was the only reason his siblings grew up with a present father, rather than one working eighty hours a week two towns away.

"I knew you were smart." Xiomara wiggled her foot free of the stirrup and tucked the toe of her boot into his calf. She pulled away when Chief Thomas spoke.

"It's not like a rez school is that hard." The Chief scoffed.

"Did you move up a grade, too?" Her voice dripped like mezcal joven.

"No." Chief Thomas bristled, straightening his back. "But I was lacrosse captain, basketball co-captain, and student council president."

Xiomara made a face of awe that didn't reach her eyes.

"What about you?" Chief Thomas said. "What did you do in high school?"

"Nothing." Xiomara said.

Calehan hid the smirk on his lips. People often thought she measured intelligence in the western way, with degrees and prestige, but Calehan knew that wasn't who she was.

"We were homeschooled together." She gestured, forming a circle in front of her chest, tapping her heart with her fingertips. "My cousins and I were homeschooled by our community and some of us went to college, and some of us didn't." She shrugged, looking forward. "There are many ways to learn."

"I admire that about you." Chief Thomas said the words emptily. "You really value traditional knowledge. Continuation of traditional knowledge is one of the most important things we can do, in my opinion. Of course, college degrees are important, too."

Xiomara laughed quietly, curling her fingers into Angel's mane. Reading her like a book, Calehan could tell she wasn't comfortable with the Chief's statements.

Luckily, Chief Joseph came to their rescue, calling for his son to come forward.

"I'm interested in reading your notes later." Chief Thomas nodded at Xiomara and rode ahead.

Calehan watched the Chief ride away, his eyes narrow in focus. It was plain to anyone that the Chief had some kind of crush on Xiomara, but today only reaffirmed that she didn't reciprocate the feelings. He didn't fight the pride straightening his shoulders.

Xiomara examined Calehan's profile. His face was blank, no semblance of emotion visible.

"You two don't get along, I gather?" Xiomara waited for Calehan to answer her question.

Calehan shrugged. "The Chief gets along with everybody."

"I'm asking about you."

"We're too different and too similar." Calehan didn't elaborate.

Shouting ahead called their attention, the group entered a clearing at the top edge of a mountain, clear high views all the way around. Calehan took Angel's reins and tied the horses at the far edge of the clearing, where they had fresh food and water.

Xiomara joined Rosebud and David, unloading food and water while the others set up their tents. Chief Joseph started a fire, rimming the burning logs in large rocks with a grate on top. They set out pots to heat dinner. By the time everything was ready, the sun had set and so had exhaustion.

Falling into the camping chair beside Rosebud, Xiomara sipped her mug full of stew. Chief Thomas offered her a piece of bread and took the chair on her other side. The deer stew was earthy and packed with root vegetables and wild rice. It set up home in the center of her belly and started slowly ticking her inner clock closer and closer to sleep.

Letting her eyes close for just a moment, she jerked her head upright when she felt coolness against her cheek.

"Sorry." Sitting upright, she apologized to Chief Thomas for the inappropriate head nod.

"Nothing to be sorry for." Chief Thomas smiled. "You're welcome to use me as a pillow."

Xiomara glanced across the fire at Calehan. He was looking right at her, his lips turned up just slightly when they made eye contact.

Rosebud noted the tension around the group and loudly announced it was time for bed. Grabbing her hand, she pulled Xiomara from the fire.

Xiomara crawled onto her sleeping bag on her knees, pulling at the backpack Calehan left inside for her. Grabbing her green notebook, she opened it to the front cover, where she kept a polaroid photo of Anubis and Javier. She hoped Anubis visited Javier in his dreams like she did.

"Is this island part of Bunchberry reserve?" Xiomara still wasn't clear where they were.

"It used to be." Rosebud wrapped a silk scarf around her head. "It's privately owned now."

"Did Chief Thomas buy it or something?" Xiomara was puzzled when Rosebud laughed in response.

"Well, this island belongs to the hereditary chiefdom." Rosebud said.

Xiomara furrowed her brow. "You mean Calehan's dad?"

"Yep. It's sacred land. They decide who comes and goes here, *not* Chief Thomas or Chief Joseph. In the old days, it would've been different. But now it's legally owned by Uncle Muskwa."

Calehan had his own island. It boggled her mind, the thought of having remains so close to home. Many of her ancestors' things were in museums in Spain. Even some of their most sacred items, like human remains.

She wrote her notes quickly, in a messy shorthand she would struggle to read tomorrow. By the time she was finished, Rosebud was fast asleep, light snores coming from her tucked in face.

It was then she heard it. Footsteps.

Tap. Tap. Tap.

Xiomara leaned forward and unzipped the flap just enough to peek out. It was Calehan. A small lamp illuminated one side of his face, the stars lighting the other.

Tilting his head at her, he grabbed her jacket from the tent floor. He slipped it over her shoulders and zipped it up to her throat. Calehan dropped to his knees in the grass before her. Taking her hand, he wrapped her fingers around the lantern handle and positioned it beside his head. Ungloved, his palm was warm where it wrapped around her calf, pulling her foot onto the edge of his knee.

Her knuckles went white. Xiomara closed her mouth, dry tongue sticking to the roof of her even drier mouth. Gently, he wiggled her feet into the boots, tying them easily, not too tight, and knotting it twice to ensure they'd stay out of her way.

Xiomara tried to thank him, but she couldn't open her sand-full mouth. Calehan brushed grass from his knees and stood.

"Can I have the lantern?"

Xiomara looked down at her hand, where she had the lantern in a death grip. Calehan had wrapped his own hand around them both. His thumb stroked over her tense knuckles, soothing the taut skin.

Nodding furiously, Xiomara dropped the lantern. "Sorry. Thank you for the shoes—tying my shoes."

Laughing quietly, Calehan took her by the hand and led her toward the horses. Angel was already saddled and waiting. Calehan hoisted Xiomara into the air so she could throw her leg over the tall horse. With a hand on either side of her, Calehan swung his long leg over Angel's back and tucked her into his chest. With a click of Calehan's tongue, the horse began to walk up the hill.

The smell of sweetgrass and tobacco surrounded her when she nuzzled into Calehan's embrace.

"Did you make a speech at graduation?"

Her question took him by surprise. "For valedictorian?"

She nodded.

"No." He spoke barely above a whisper. "My class was like eight people. No need for a speech."

"You could've told me how smart you are." She threw a glare at him over her shoulder.

"I'm not. Really. Kids skip grades all the time."

"You don't have to minimize things around me." Xiomara spoke softly. "I think you're smart either way."

The bushes rustled beside them, Angel side-stepping the trail until Calehan settled him.

"Is it a bear?" Xiomara whispered, wide eyes turned to him.

"No." Calehan rubbed soothing circles up and down her arms. "Bears don't typically make it to this side of the island."

A huff left her mouth. Calehan smiled and kissed her cheek, squeezing her waist tighter.

He tucked his cold nose into her hair. "I promise you are safe as long as I'm here."

Turning in his arms, Xiomara brought him in for a bruising kiss. He held her to him tightly, squeezing all the air from her lungs.

"Why do you taste like bear root?"

He offered her the widest smile she had seen on his face, all his teeth shining white. "I'm keeping you safe." He rubbed his nose against hers, dragging her in for a firm kiss. "I promised."

Xiomara elbowed him gently and turned her head to the side, presenting her smooth cheek to him.

"We're here," Calehan whispered in her ear, gently guiding her eyes toward the sky. He could hear her sharp intake of breath, the way her hands clenched his, her eyes glued open and trained on the green trail of light.

"Incredible."

"I know." Calehan said, breath ghosting over her ear.

"This doesn't look real." Xiomara's mouth hung open in awe. The lights danced across the sky, twisting and turning to show off their other shades of purple and pink. Calehan held her in his arms as she watched the sky, his gaze trained on her. She could see him from the corner of her vision, his smile ebbing in time with hers.

When she finally withdrew her eyes from the lights, Calehan laid the thick padded blanket on the grass, tossing another fluffier one on top. He unfurled compressed pillows and they watched them puff up on the makeshift bed.

"I saved you some chocolate," Calehan whispered, emptying seven mini chocolate bars from his pocket. She crawled onto the makeshift bed, tearing into the chocolate candy.

Xiomara smiled as Calehan sat beside her, letting her settle between his legs. She tipped her head against his chest, blinking slowly at him until his mouth met hers. Calehan's hand dragged over her arm, his palm warm where it curled around her shoulder. Wide hands allowed his thumb to sit gently into the dip of her collarbone. He drew a line up the center of her throat, hand caressing her neck, warming her like a honey tea. He still tasted of bear root, and she admitted he did make her feel safe.

Her body hummed in his possessive hold. Warmth radiated from him, and her neck began to sweat beneath his hands. Xiomara whimpered into his mouth, and he took the cue to flip her beneath him.

Xiomara wrapped her legs around him, bringing his hips flush against her. Her fingers tucked into the neck of his shirt, nails scraping over the meat of his shoulders. He wasn't close enough. She wanted to feel his skin on hers, no barriers between them. His heartbeat thumped heavily against her chest. She nipped at his lip with her teeth, sucking him into her mouth. Calehan pulled back with a throaty groan, licking down her neck sloppily, the chilly night air freezing the skin he left behind.

Every inch of her skin was on fire. Feverishly she tugged at his shirt, hands moving beneath the fabric to expose the flesh she craved. Calehan followed her lead and pulled his shirt over his head. Pinching his pec between her teeth, she bit down hard and released him only when he hissed and tugged her hair.

With her head held back, he dipped his fingers into the valley of her breasts, bunching the fabric of her pajama shirt in his hands and pulling it up enough to expose her breasts to the moonlight.

A groan fell from his mouth and shot straight between her legs. Simmering anticipation stretched between them, her heart beating in her ears.

Calehan gripped her hips and wrenched her into him, trailing his hand up her body to pull her face to his. Foreheads together, he smoothed over her mussed hair and cradled her face to his. The press of his lips this time was different.

Gentle, searching lips moved against hers. Her body sang where it met his fire-hot skin. She could feel his breath where his nose was against her cheek, his tongue gentle where it teased hers. There was no oxygen left in her chest, her heart hammering, sweat brimming on her skin. She feared she could not force herself from his embrace, even if the forest was burning down around them. In his arms, she was powerless to stray.

Xiomara tugged at his belt, opening the buckle to his jeans. Her pants vanished with his. His mouth wrapped around her cold-hardened nipple, the moan from his throat vibrating against her breast. Flames licked across her body, thighs itching to close and stem the throbbing between her legs. Xiomara jutted her hips up into his, her heel pressing into his back in a feeble attempt to bring him closer. He pried himself from her grasp.

Calehan pushed her legs apart. His eyes met hers, and he sat on his knees in front of her. Muscles rippled as he freed his long hair from his tight bun and gathered it into a ponytail. Eyes never wavering, Calehan rubbed himself against her.

Xiomara was seconds away from begging him to fuck her when he took one of her hands and wrapped it around his gathered hair. Her muscles clenched around air. He took her other hand in his, threading their fingers together on top of her breast.

"Cal…" Her voice was throaty, the sound she'd hear in the back of a smokers only bar. Disappearing between her legs, Calehan kissed her gently, gripping her breast when her body jumped in response. He ran his lips across her slit, teasing ever so softly, she wasn't sure if the touch was just a dream.

Her fingers tensed in his hair. "Por favor."

Calehan found her clit instantly, the swell of her skin presenting it to him like a pearl. Calehan rolled the bud into his mouth and sucked. Xiomara was acutely aware that she was a purveyor of continuous noise, but he was relentless in a way that she could not silence herself. He devoured her, his hand curling around her body to lock her hips to his face.

Xiomara released his hand, in favor of threading all her fingers into his hair, holding his face to her center. Calehan was red tipped and harder than a rock. Xiomara could just barely see him stroking himself below her, sending her over the edge. Her legs locked behind his head as she cried his name, her body moving to the same song.

A giggle tumbled from her mouth when she released him, a hand covering her face while he dragged wet kisses up her body. Calehan rubbed his nose over hers, back and forth. A kiss.

Tousling the bangs on her forehead, he kissed her like he was running a marathon. His lips moved over hers as though this one kiss could last for hours, could freeze time, and keep them here in this moment forever. She slid against him like honey, so slowly she would stick to him for days, impossible to wash off the rolling pressure of her touch. She smiled into his mouth as she grabbed his ass, palming his cheeks and giving them a ferocious squeeze.

"Your ass"—she squeezed him again and brought her hands together in an echoing smack—"está increíble." His answering laughter thundered through the trees.

Calehan dove into her mouth, his wide arms eclipsing her back. She felt nothing but him. Groaning into her lips, Calehan ground against her wetness. Xiomara tilted her hips, catching his tip in her entrance. She didn't hesitate and slid him inside her without preamble. They shared an open-mouthed sigh, settling completely into each other. Xiomara refused to open her eyes, wetness stinging her lids. He felt like coming *home*.

Xiomara held his face to hers, kissing him harshly, claiming him in every way. No matter how tight she held him, he held her tighter, pulled her closer, kissed her harder. He found a rhythm that matched her racing heart, his thumb ghosting where they were joined. She mewled when he sent her to the clouds. Calehan followed her quickly, licking into her mouth. Her name trailed from his lips, her eyes watching his smile—the one he reserved only for her.

Her tongue tickled his chin before she bit it gently, smiling at the sting of his hand against her ass. He tried to lift his weight from her, but she tugged him down. Xiomara wrapped her arms and legs around him, holding him tightly to her.

"Can we stay for a while?" Xiomara stuck her tongue out to lick his nose.

"Whatever you want." Calehan kissed her until the sun chased the moon from the sky.

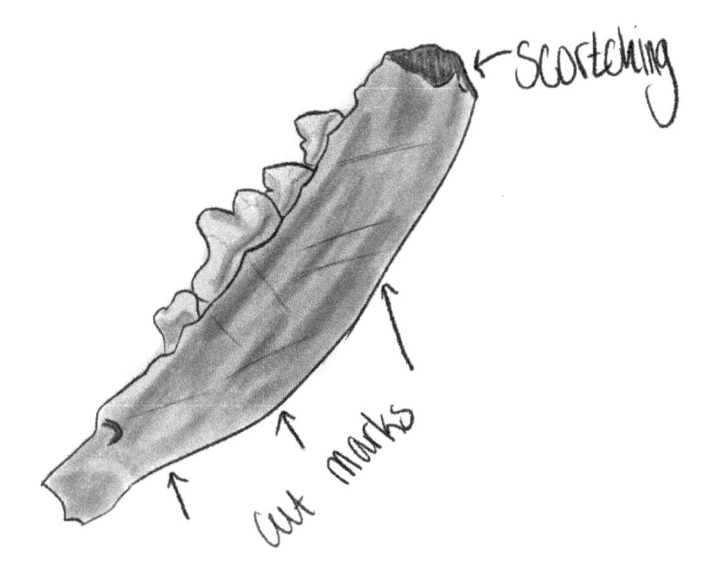

CHAPTER 11

Ice hung in the air. Her breath was white, opaque as paint. Xiomara needed to ask David what the elevation was and just how it was possible for it to be *this* cold. Leaving her pajamas on underneath, she pulled pants and a hoodie over her head. Tucking into her boots, she wrapped up in the neoprene coat Calehan brought her and pulled a beanie on her head. The Bunchberry tribal seal was beaded into the fold of the knit, the red berries firm under her fingertip. Two berries were finished, the third an unfinished outline. The beads were sewn with a white thread—sinew, she suspected. One of Joy's many projects, probably.

She slid from the tent and joined Rosebud by the crackling fire. Her hair smelled of smoke. It reminded her of home.

"Thank you." Xiomara sighed heavily, taking the mug of oatmeal with bare hands.

Opening her eyes, mushroom brown ones stared back at her. Calehan winked as she met his gaze, the corner of his lips pulling up. He was brushing Dreamer, feeding her extra snacks and electrolytes. He fed and groomed every horse they had while everyone else enjoyed breakfast.

Muskwa handed her a mug of coffee. "I couldn't sneak cinnamon, but I stole these from the café." He opened his hand to reveal a handful of mini creamer cups in an assortment of flavors. She thanked him and chose a French vanilla one, pleased she wouldn't be forced to drink it black.

"How did you sleep?" Muskwa sat in the camping chair beside her, draping a woven wool blanket over their knees.

"Pretty good." Was there punishment for lying to your elders?

"Sometimes people have trouble sleeping with how quiet it is here."

Xiomara laughed. "It is not quiet here. The bugs are so loud! Even the trees make noise."

Muskwa smiled. "Spoken like a true desert kid."

She returned his grin, wistful for her warm sky and dry packed dirt. "The desert is not silent, but she comes close."

"That it does." Chief Thomas poured himself a cup of coffee, finally returning from a phone call. "My mother used to say that the desert was so quiet it could carry you across time."

"It definitely feels like that sometimes." Xiomara watched a bird dive into the water in front of them, rising with a shiny fish trapped in its golden beak. She welcomed the distraction, the bird gathering the attention of the group. The black hole of her own thoughts opened wide and sucked her in.

Javier visited her in the dream world again.

It was starting to freak her out. Was there some kind of connection between Javier and Calehan? Javier only began visiting her after she met Calehan at the berry fest. Closing her eyes, she thought of them beside each other. She couldn't pin-point any resemblance. Javier's mother never changed her landline. Did she still have that old family tree? An investigation may need to be launched.

Xiomara brought herself back to reality with the bitter burn of campfire coffee.

It really wasn't that weird to see him in her dreams. She had waited for this. Years had passed without so much as a word from him, and now she had the audacity to complain about it.

Rolling her shoulders, Xiomara settled into her chair and stirred the mug of oatmeal, disappearing into her thoughts.

Javier had known. Even in her dreams, her inner thoughts and emotions hung above her like a neon sign that only he could see. No matter how hard she tried, she could never keep secrets from him. He braided her hair beneath the red mesa, the shade cooling their skin in the desert heat. Warmth seeped through her legs, residual heat leaking from the earth and into her spirit.

Javier tucked her head into his shoulder. Her eyes watched the empty blue sky. No way to mark time without a cloud in sight. There was no time in dreams.

Xiomara told Javier about Calehan. She told him of the way Calehan teased her, cared about her interests, the way he loved his family. Javier laughed when she recounted the way Calehan had told her of his museum plans. The shyness he presented to hide his vast knowledge. Pride bloomed in her chest when she told Javier how smart he was, that he skipped a grade and graduated early and started a career on rez before he was twenty-one. He congratulated everything. Calehan deserved even more, he said.

I like him, he told her, fingers woven into her hair.

How can you say that to your wife?

I have been waiting to see you smile like this, mi querida.

Xiomara hadn't felt as alone as she did opening her eyes that morning. Tears had dried on her face while she dreamed, sweat tightening her brow. Her molars ached from clenching her jaw in her sleep. Xiomara loved to see him in her dreams, but each time she woke without him hurt the same as the day he left her.

A gentle hand on her shoulder pulled her from the dream world. Calehan gazed down at her. His finger reached under her hair, grazing fleetingly across her neck. Xiomara took a moment to realize what he was doing, still halfway in her dreams. Calehan finished touching her as soon as he started, moving quickly to keep their involvement private as she had asked. She relaxed when he sat beside her, his presence warming her from the inside. He made her feel lighter. Just being near him perked Xiomara up, brought her back to the present. Her ears tuned in to listen for his voice.

"Do you camp often where you are from?" Chief Joseph broke the quiet of the morning, looking between David and Xiomara.

"Not much," David responded. "I'm from the city, and Tucson is way too hot."

"And you?"

Xiomara shook her head. "There isn't much to see but flat dirt for miles around."

Chief Joseph nodded, a smile playing across his face. He sipped his coffee slowly before asking her, "Are you a fan of rattlesnake?"

Xiomara covered her mouth as she finished her bite of elk sausage. "They're all right. Not my favorite."

"I don't have much taste for them, either." Chief Joseph relaxed into the camping chair, and Xiomara knew he was settling in to tell them another story.

A while later, their breakfasts settled deep in their bellies, they were prepared to hike into the site. Across the river and over a hill too small to call a mountain, the site was nestled into a frostbitten valley. Frozen under a considerable piece of ice for most of the year, they had a small window of time to see what slumbered beneath the water.

Xiomara walked Angel beside her, encouraging him to relax his puffed-out chest so she could tighten the cinch strap once more. Rosebud was still standing beside her horse, waiting until the absolute last second before she had to mount the mare again. Rosebud looked like she was walking around in someone else's body. Xiomara was used to her quirky skirts and funky dresses that showed off the artwork covering her legs. Instead, she was dressed in jeans and a Blink 182 hoodie.

"If your hair wasn't blue," Xiomara called to her as she and Angel walked over, "you'd look like a square."

"That is the meanest thing you've ever said to me." Rosebud wiped a fake tear from her eye and leaned her face dramatically into the horse's neck.

"The truth hurts." Xiomara squealed when she dodged Rosebud's punch. "I have a secret."

Rosebud tore the sunglasses from her face. "Did you get laid?"

"Que cochina, with everyone around?" Xiomara pressed her finger to her lips to shush her friend. "We took Angel up the hill to this meadow and spent the night there."

Rosebud's mouth dropped open, and her eyes bulged wide.

"Are you two ready?" Chief Thomas materialized behind them, both women jumping out of their skin.

"Can you walk louder?" Rosebud screeched at him, stomping her foot before throwing herself atop her horse. "Jesus Christ," she muttered, tapping her heel until the horse walked away.

"Sorry." He patted Angel on the rump and stepped closer to Xiomara. "I seem to keep startling you."

"I'm easily startled." She turned toward Angel, pulling the reins over his head. She paused briefly and stretched on her toes as she waited for Angel to drop his neck so she could push the reins up his head.

"Here, let me help you." Chief Thomas stepped forward, hands outstretched toward her.

"No need." She leaned heavily into Angel's side. The horse took her guidance and stepped sideways a few feet, giving Xiomara space to climb up. She gripped the stirrup and slid her left foot in, bouncing once before swinging onto his back. Giving Chief Thomas a tight smile, she clicked Angel forward to join the others.

David sidled up next to her.

"Él te quiere," he whispered.

"Well, he needs to stop," she muttered under her breath.

"Stop what?" Calehan and Dreamer joined them.

"Dios mío, do you all have super hearing?" Xiomara huffed, zipping her jacket up to her throat.

Calehan and David exchanged a look. They shuffled along one by one, Calehan and Xiomara side by side at the back—alone this time.

They rode in silence for a long while, each lost in their own thoughts. She finally looked over at him when she smelled the salmon jerky coming from his pack.

Reaching out, he offered her a bite-size piece of jerky. Xiomara leaned down and took the jerky from his fingers with her teeth. Her tongue peeked out and licked along the edge of his thumb as she tucked the piece into her mouth.

This ride was much shorter, though Angel fought her in entering the water. She was nervous about it herself, which didn't help the situation. Calehan brought Dreamer close to Angel, letting her bump into him, boots and saddles clanging. Encouraged by his girlfriend, Angel followed Dreamer easily across the small river.

They climbed the tall hill easily, Angel's footing careful and sure. Cresting the tallest point, she finally saw the swampy area waiting for them below.

Her heart sank to her feet. Or to the bottom of this river. Ocean? Lake? She didn't know anymore.

"I knew this year would be warm," Chief Joseph's voice was broken, carried to them only along gusts of the wind. "I hadn't guessed it would be this bad."

Water flowed in front of them, the valley completely flooded. The hill they stood on now had eroded partway, slipping into a steep cliffside. Early snow melts had flooded the canyon and brought the water levels almost to the surface where they stood.

Her heart sunk. Whatever remnants were left of the site were surely gone. The early melts had turned what was once a riverbank into a riverbed. Flood waters were incredibly destructive and could scatter artifacts hundreds of miles. This flood had likely raged beneath a thick layer of ice, trapping the pressure of the water and raking things across the rocky canyon.

Chief Thomas gathered the group with a promise of lunch.

Calehan made eye contact with her as they began to file away from the. She hesitated. Calehan was still on Dreamer's back, far from everyone else. He nodded at her once, the dip of his chin almost imperceptible. Clicking her tongue against the back of her cheek, Angel followed the others. Chancing a glance back, she saw Muskwa and Calehan dismount their horses and move towards the water. The breeze moved in and carried their prayer on its back.

An hour later, Xiomara found Calehan beneath the shade of a wide tree. Its trunk was wider than Calehan's shoulders, nearly obscuring him from view. She sat on the grass beside him, stretching her legs in front of her.

"How did I miss the fact that you're Chief Yellowbird's great-grandson?" Xiomara relaxed into the trunk of the tree, shoulder squishing against his.

"Mmm..." Calehan scrunched his eyebrows, looking up at the sky, "Probably because I didn't tell you."

"And you decided to withhold information for shits and giggles?"

"No." Calehan laughed. "This rez has four hundred people and the closest town only has a few thousand. It was nice to meet someone who didn't know I was a Yellowbird."

The fireside was not as jovial as the night before. Chief Joseph told them stories from their childhood. Lessons in consequences and duties.

Rosebud turned into bed early, and Xiomara jumped at the chance to go with her. Guilt sat like a stone in her gut at the thought of the lost site, and she wanted to enter the dream world. She wanted to see Javier, to let him remove that guilt stoning her to death.

Xiomara didn't dream.

incised →   ↙ soot

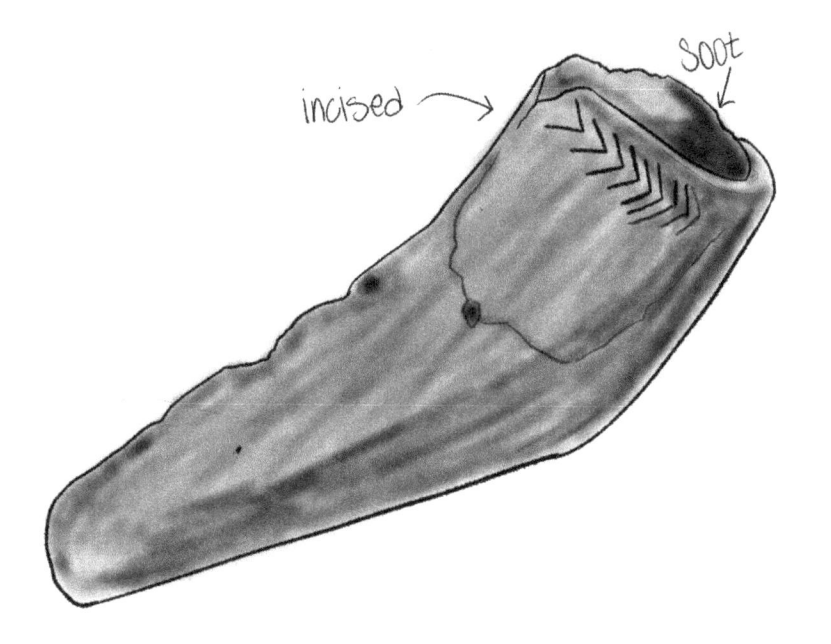

CHAPTER 12

The rain smelled different here, damper. Heavier. Xiomara sighed as her feet touched the ground. Pressing her hands into her back, she stretched the tense muscles in her body. Calehan took the horses and sent her to the truck, assuring her he didn't need any help. Lying face down on the bench seat, she yearned to curl up on a real mattress. Her face was tucked into the dark crevice of the bench, eyes closed. She felt the truck dip and shift as Calehan and his father packed their things.

Something tickled the inside of her ankle. Xiomara jolted in surprise. She relaxed when her eyes found Rosebud and not a giant spider crawling over her legs.

"Kate said she just dropped Anubis off." Rosebud winked at her over the top of her sunglasses. "Your cabin has great soundproofing, by the way."

Xiomara kicked at her friend, covering her reddened cheeks with her hands.

"I need you Friday night." Rosebud picked at her untied shoelaces. "There's this community dinner, and we're going dancing afterward."

"I'll be there."

"I know." Rosebud smacked her hand against Xiomara's calf. "Dress hot, yeah? Make Cally work for it a little."

Xiomara ignored her friend and flopped down onto the seat. Hopefully, their mutual torture was not noticeable to everyone else. She still wasn't sure that a relationship between her and Calehan was something they could be public about. If Chief Thomas' reaction was a sign, then she needed to be better at keeping this secret.

"Miss Chavez." She sat up at Chief Thomas' voice. "I'll see you in my office next Monday at eight. We need to discuss your budget."

"I'm supposed to be at the construction site Monday morning," Xiomara said.

"I'm sure Mr. Yellowbird understands you have other priorities."

"Our project is my priority, Chief." Xiomara held his eye. "But I am happy to make time for this as well. I will see you then."

Chief Thomas patted her ankle and walked away. His condescension smelled like burning sugar.

Xiomara pulled her feet into the cab, tucking them onto the bench. Resting her chin on her knees, she wrapped her arms around her legs. Chief Thomas unnerved her. She hoped that he hadn't noticed something between her and Calehan. She was grateful when his truck left first, two cars between them so that the Chief couldn't see her and Calehan.

"Penny for your thoughts?" Calehan's voice was barely above a whisper as he slid into the truck beside her, bumping her toes with his thigh.

"They're worth a quarter, at least."

"How about dinner?" Calehan pulled onto the road behind his dad.

"That was smooth." She laughed giddily, moving across the bench on her knees to look at him.

Calehan looked at her, dropping his arm to the back of the seat so that she had more space. Her knees wedged into his thighs as Xiomara wrapped her arms around his neck, dragging across the muscles of his shoulder and back. His cheek was warm where she pressed her lips into him, nosing his hairline when she tucked into his neck. He wrapped his arm around her back, holding her to him.

"Is that a yes?" he whispered, pulling at her belt loop.

"Sí." She leaned forward and kissed him. Calehan's eyes fluttered shut for a moment before they sprang open, mud pulling at the truck tires. With a laugh, Xiomara plunged her tongue into his mouth before she pulled back, biting into the skin of his shoulder. Crescent moons hung in his tan skin where her teeth had been. She kissed the mark and tucked her face into the crook of his neck.

Wrapping his arm around her, Calehan found the skin of her hip, thumb ghosting over her warm flesh. The dirt road stretched before them; the two fit together like two pieces to a puzzle.

But they had a long drive, and she needed a shower. She slid over and put her seatbelt on, but picked up his hand and placed it on her thigh, her hands toying with his fingers absentmindedly. Now that they had acknowledged their feelings to each other, the pull to touch him was painful to resist. She fought the urge to rest her head on his shoulder now that they were on the highway, worried Chief Thomas might see and demand even more meetings.

"Chief wants to meet with me next week." Xiomara told him.

His gaze stripped her naked as he processed her words. Calehan focused on the road, his hand pressing into her thigh in calming circles. She figured they calmed him more than her.

"I can handle him." Xiomara ran the tips of her fingers back and forth across his forearm. "I can see all the emotions on his face... unlike you." She eyed him closely, searching for an indication of what he was thinking.

He smiled without turning his head toward her, lifting his hand to trace the side of her face. Bringing her to his shoulder, he kissed the top of her head, holding her there.

Calehan drove slowly up her dirt driveway, doing his best to make minimal noise as items jostled in the truck bed. Xiomara kept her head against his shoulder, letting it roll back and forth over the unpaved driveway. He parked in front of her small house, resting his head on hers for a moment. Calehan turned into her, burying his nose in her hair and breathing deeply.

He jumped when he met her open eyes, probably expecting her to be asleep.

"You're cute," Xiomara whispered.

"Glad you think so." He kissed her nose and slid from the truck, pulling her out of the driver's door behind him. Grabbing their things from the truck bed, he followed her inside.

Anubis tore through the house, running in circles and using the furniture like trampolines. He was barking up a storm, yowling in between. Calehan encouraged him, running at him, smacking quickly across his bottom, and shouting along with his barking.

This was new.

"He loves you." Xiomara said.

"What can I say?" Calehan crouched down to get closer to the dog. "I'm pretty lovable."

"I guess so." Xiomara peered at him, fighting the blush on her cheeks. "Stay tonight?"

"If you'll have me." Calehan followed her into the bedroom, towing their camping bag behind him. "I should've installed air conditioning in here." Calehan sighed, wiping the fresh sweat from his neck.

"Yup." Xiomara groaned, pushing her sweaty bangs from her forehead. She stripped out of her clothes quickly, turning the shower to lukewarm.

"This is the hottest day on record." She heard the swallow in Calehan's throat. Reaching over, Xiomara wrapped her pinky around his. She understood. The desert suffered the same way.

"My father used to say, 'Indian land goes first because she is the most giving land on Earth.'" Xiomara could hear his voice in her mind. At the time, it was the hottest day ever recorded in their hometown and she was eleven years old, sweltering during a heatwave and temporary water ration. Her father saved them by telling the stories of their ancestors, bringing the kids into their true culture for the first time. Xiomara's lips curved in a small smile, sweat glistening the top of her lip the same as it had that summer day.

Xiomara peeled back the shower curtain and climbed inside. "Are you coming?"

Calehan didn't hesitate to follow her. The cool water shocked them both, each of them hesitant to immerse themselves in the stream.

Calehan submerged himself under the cool water first, undoing his braid and wrapping it up into a bun. Xiomara didn't hide her wandering eyes as she admired every curve of his soft body, following her gaze with chaste kisses across his skin.

His broad, rounded shoulders led into oversized biceps, wide and muscled from a lifetime of farmwork. His belly was soft as it relaxed under the water, her eyes traveling down to his strong, muscled legs with thighs larger than Xiomara's head. Her eyes dipped down to his suntanned feet before roaming leisurely up his water slick body, finding his eyes watching her in hunger. She squeezed her thighs together.

Their similarly dark brown eyes met, each unflinching. The shower seemed to suddenly become the same temperature as the rest of the house. So much for refuge.

Xiomara watched Calehan breathe deeply, his chest moving under the water. He silently crept towards her, cornering her against the cold tile wall. Hands on either side of her head, he molded himself to her, a gasp escaping her reddened lips when the cold tile touched her skin.

"Your skin is on fire." He whispered.

"So much for cooling off." Xiomara smirked, running her fingers slowly up his chest, smoothing the wet hair behind his ear with her finger. A growl-like groan rumbled in Calehan's chest when he kissed her. He ran his hands over her waist and hips, holding her still as he reached between her legs. A tortured, painful groan erupted from the bottom of his chest.

"Is all of that for me?" His voice stole her breath. It was deeper and hungrier than she had ever heard it. He kept his eyes closed, forehead against hers.

She nodded against his face, dragging her lips over his.

Using his height to his advantage, he pressed his thigh between her legs, lifting her feet slightly off the floor, leaving her perched on his slick, sparsely haired thigh.

He continued kissing her, lips opening and tongues meeting, he gripped her legs behind the knee and leaned her body further against his leg. Grinding her body against his thigh, Calehan's mouth found Xiomara's perked brown nipple, enclosing it in his oven hot mouth.

Twisting closer, Xiomara pulled him tighter to her body, her satisfied sighs tugging at his dick. He slid his right hand up her wet thigh, trailing his fingertips over her hip bone and reaching down between her and the tile wall. His spit lubricated fingers found Xiomara's tightest hole. Teasing it slightly, he felt Xiomara stutter against his thigh, a gasp tumbling from her open mouth into his. Pushing his finger slowly inside, she locked her feet behind his back, giving him purchase to grip her hip and aid her in her ministrations on his wide thigh.

Calehan was two knuckles inside her, reclaiming her mouth while he quirked his finger upward. Within seconds she was exploding everywhere. His entire body felt her orgasm, his skin tingling in response to her pleasure. Xiomara's head fell to the crook of Calehan's neck as she recovered from her climax.

She laughed lightly, a smile gracing Calehan's face as he asked her what was causing this delight.

"I just can't believe I came that hard just from...*that*." Her cheeks reddened slightly as his finger slowly eased from her bottom. He pulled her from the wall, turning her around to lean against his chest while he pressed his back where hers had been. He snuggled her into his embrace, his long arms covering nearly her entire upper body.

"I am happy to do it again if you like." He whispered in her ear, biting at her lobe gently.

She laughed out a scoff, he was cocky absolutely, but he had good reason.

"No." She said, stepping from his arms and pushing him back against the wall. Holding his gaze, she sank to her knees before him.

"Shit," fell from Calehan's lips.

Xiomara gripped his balls when he finished in her mouth, the two of them finally satisfied despite the stifling heat. Wiping the edge of Xiomara's lips with his thumb, he pulled her chin to his and kissed her deeply. He pressed their bodies together as if he was trying to bring every piece of their spirits into contact with one another.

"I need to kiss you like this everyday." Calehan declared confidently, looking deeply into her sleepy eyes. Her long, thick lashes held water droplets on the end, her eyes heavy as she tried to blink them away.

"I'll think about it." Xiomara winked.

Calehan reached the top of Xiomara's head with his long fingers, nimbly detangling the scrunchie from her hair. He leaned her head back under the stream of water, his lips turning up as her fingers gripped his hips for balance.

They remained in comfortable silence while Calehan washed Xiomara's hair. Fingers rubbing vanilla scented conditioner over her scalp, Calehan was gentle as he combed the knots out; one of the many benefits of dating a long haired man. Mutual understanding.

She smiled up at him with her eyes still closed, "You spoil me."

"I want to spoil you." Calehan said simply, finger combing her hair as he rinsed the conditioner out. Squeezing out the excess water he wrapped her hair up in a towel and tucked it into itself, securing it atop her head. Turning off the shower, he wrapped her fluffy pink towel around her before wrapping the extra around himself.

They slept under one thin sheet, Anubis spread out on the wooden floor to keep cool. She dreamed of the site, the people who lived there, who made that place their home. Though they would never be able to retrieve and save what was left of them, she was confident they were happy to be lost to the waters that had fed and cared for their descendants eternally.

← metate

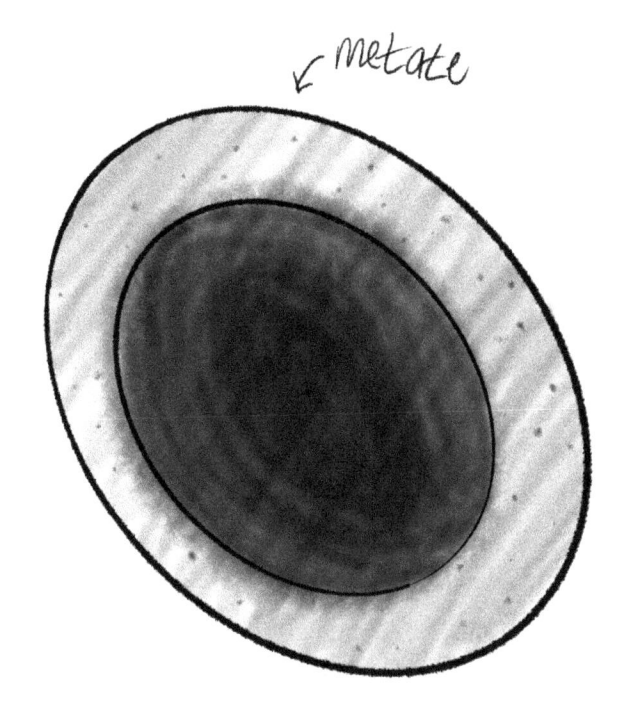

Chapter 13

Sunlight pulled her from a dreamless sleep an hour before her alarm. The week had gone too quickly, work arriving to tear them from each other's arms. Calehan was already awake, having tucked her into his body while he checked emails on his phone. Clover was covering the construction site today, the duties of a best friend and brother still in effect well into their thirties.

Calehan smiled when she stretched against him, dropping his phone to face her.

"Good morning," she whispered, rubbing her nose back and forth across his.

"You're up early." He matched her soft voice.

"So are you." Xiomara kept her eyes closed, lips swollen dark pink with sleep. Finally opening her eyes, she looked at him as though she could swallow him whole.

He nosed her cheek. "Ranchers don't sleep in." His lips moved over hers.

Time stopped again. Funny how he kept doing that.

Eventually, time restarted, when Calehan accompanied Anubis to the backyard, the dew of the morning blurring their forms in front of her. Anubis ran past Calehan to show her the stick he had retrieved, tapping his puppy toes in excitement. She took the stick from his mouth as he ran inside, replacing it with a chew toy instead.

"You look nice." Calehan dragged his eyes over her, stopping on the coffee mug in her hand.

"Your coffee is on the counter." She stood on the top step, tall enough to pull his face down to hers. "I have to go."

"Don't," he said against her mouth, kissing the protest from her lips.

"You've got a museum to build." She laughed, letting him steal a swig of her coffee.

"I don't know." He turned his head side to side in thought. "I am sleeping with the boss. Think I could get an extension?"

"Well, in that case, I think you should be done a week early." She patted his chest and turned inside, gathering her things to head into the office.

She would've brought Anubis to the lab, but David was on site with the interns, and she didn't like leaving him in her office unattended. Setting a frozen lick mat across the room from his food bowl, she hoped it would occupy him long enough to tire him out.

Calehan shouldered their bags while she locked the door behind them. He threw his bag into the bed of his truck, placing hers gently in the passenger seat of her Jeep.

"I'll see you soon." Xiomara buckled the seatbelt and turned to him.

He grumbled in his chest and frowned. She pressed her lips to his downturned lips and teased a smile to his mouth. Hands roamed over her thighs in the seat.

Calehan gripped the sleek ponytail on the back of her head. "I like your hair like this."

"Basta," she said, wrapping her arms around his neck, kissing him again. He closed the door for her, kissing her one last time through the open window. Calehan waved goodbye before climbing in the truck and heading in the opposite direction.

Xiomara wrung her hands as she waited for the elevator. She was not looking forward to this meeting. While the survey had gone fine and she had multiple findings to present to the Chief, she knew he would try to investigate her and Calehan's relationship as well.

Chief Thomas asked her to meet in the lounge of City Hall. Historically a cigar room, the lounge was filled with lush leather furniture and historic images of Bunchberry. Xiomara beat him there, taking her time to examine the photos on the walls. She stopped on an image of a man wearing a large feathered headdress. He bore a striking resemblance to Calehan despite the age of the photo.

He had Calehan's soft, rounded nose and his hauntingly high cheekbones. His eyes were darker and deep set, almost as if he had caves on his face. The image had a plaque beside it, *Chief Yellowbird, 1892.* Calehan's great grandfather, the last hereditary chief of Bunchberry. Xiomara read further.

Bunchberry's hereditary chiefdom was dissolved at the end of the 19th century. Chief Küpeyakwüskonam stepped down as Chief of Bunchberry at the end of 1917, at age 62. He died four years later, aged 66. He is survived by two children; Pakihtakonakâw and Delphine, two grandchildren; James and John, two great-grandchildren; Muskwa and Mahikan; along with four great-great-grandchildren; twins Calehan and Juniper, Buffy, and Clyde. None of his descendants have ever run for chiefdom.

Xiomara imagined a young Calehan. The harder lines of his face gentle with baby fat, his stature still growing, she might've been able to overpower him a time or two. With mostly male cousins, Xiomara had grown up quite scrappy. She imagined she could've taken him before he got too tall.

The image beside Chief Yellowbird yanked her attention. It looked oddly familiar, and she was certain it was taken in Mexico. The mountains in the back were rounded where they touched the sky, their tips taken by centuries of wind. Xiomara moved closer to the wall to inspect the image. Familiar was certainly the correct word.

Xiomara recognized the church in front of those mountains; it was a few towns from hers, and she had been many times. She leaned closer to the image, attempting to make out the faces staring back at her. The photo was old, two women standing beside each other, unsmiling. A white church split the mountain behind the women. One carried a jug atop her braided hair, the other's arms overflowing with nopales.

"Sorry I'm late," Chief Thomas said as he strode into the room.

Xiomara didn't jump this time, finally getting used to the way Chief Thomas barreled into rooms. He placed a folder and coffee on the table before looking at her.

"Do you know anything about this image?" Xiomara asked.

He removed his suit jacket and draped it across the arm of a leather chair before joining her. Chief Thomas leaned down, examining the picture.

"You would find an image from Mexico." He grasped the wood edges of the frame and removed it from the wall.

"Do you know the women in the photo?" Xiomara craned her neck.

"Why? Do you recognize one of them?" Chief Thomas was staring at her intently, his green eyes bright.

She shook her head. "I'm not sure. I know the church, though."

Chief Thomas pointed to the taller woman. "This is my great-grandmother and her sister at their village in Mexico."

"What was her name?" Xiomara took the frame from his hands, squinting at the faces staring at her.

"Guadalupe Gonzalez," he told her.

Guadalupe Gonzalez. The name rolled around in her brain, pulling at memory chords. She nodded as one wove itself together in her head. Problem solved. She hoped, at least. A laugh bubbled to the surface.

"What are you laughing at?" Chief Thomas had returned to the sitting area, sipping his coffee.

"Well, Chief." She took a seat in the leather chair opposite his. "We are cousins."

The Chief's eyebrows furrowed. "What do you mean, cousins? Like distant cousins?"

"Our great-grandmothers were sisters. I'm pretty sure that makes us siblings in the old ways." Xiomara watched as the Chief absorbed the information, a myriad of emotions dancing across his face. A relaxed smile settled on her face. This was *perfect*. She sent a quick prayer of thank you. Her ancestors had intervened in the nick of time and in the most ironclad way.

Chief Thomas blanched, a gray cast settling into his skin. "There's no way. I ran a background check on you."

"Things are different in Mexico. My father didn't have a birth-certificate, much less the matriarchs before him. Your grandmother had it differently. Their land became the largest city in Sonora. Modern life was forced on them."

"I just can't believe this." Chief Thomas sat in the leather chair across from her. He leaned forward, resting his elbows on his knees. Fingers worrying together, he twisted his palms around each other. "How did I hire a cousin for this project?"

"Creator works in mysterious ways." Xiomara smiled, fully enjoying the emotions flashing across his face. Confusion, regret, disbelief, shock. "Do you have any more photos?" Xiomara didn't mask the hope in her voice. "I would love to see what their life was like."

"Of course." Chief Thomas nodded, scrubbing his palm along his chin. "I should call my dad."

"I need to call my mom."

They shared a laugh, Chief Thomas reaching for her hand. She let him take it, holding his with a firm grip. Grounding them together. "Since we're family, do you think you could teach me Spanish now?"

Xiomara leaned back in the chair, laughing as Chief Thomas moonwalked to the storage room. Rummaging around for a while, she ate a muffin while she waited. He exited with five binders stuffed into his arm and two tucked into his armpit.

Chief Joseph arrived with salmon jerky and honeyed bannock. They fell into the memories together.

Xiomara's eyes widened when she pulled up to the construction site. Things had changed in the few weeks since she had last visited. There were concrete stairs connecting the doorway to the ground, and a metal railing in the center. Exterior walls had been stuccoed, the top half painted a stunning deep purple to match the casino.

She could see people moving inside, the glass windows and doors installed but not yet framed in. Looking for Calehan, she climbed from the Jeep and headed up the stairs. Walls were erected and framed out; the farthest were finished, while the interior was still open to the electric wires hanging from the ceiling.

Calehan found her quickly, his hair wrapped in a bun, a pencil tucked between his ear and baseball hat. She chewed the edge of her thumb while she watched him cross the room. His jeans were dirty with white drywall dust, his boots and arms splattered with paint. He was downright edible.

"Hey you." Calehan toyed with the tools in his hands.

"You've done so much!" Xiomara gripped his arm.

Calehan shrugged her comment off, brushing her hand gently when she released him. "How was your meeting?"

"I went really well, actually." She leaned in. "Chief and I are related."

"You're shitting me?" Calehan hid a laugh behind his closed lips. "Come on." He nodded toward her office. This smaller room was completely framed out, missing only a door.

Calehan had chosen a beautiful wallpaper covering the top half of the room, the bottom half a cream painted board and batten. The wallpaper was the color of the mountains outside her home at sunset. A shade of rust similar to the red ochre found here in Bunchberry. Palm-sized creamy suns rose over each other, patterning the wall. The matching ivory bottom half kept the room bright even in the late afternoon light.

The floors were polished concrete, a single folding table in the room beneath a bare lightbulb.

Calehan watched her expression carefully. "The furniture hasn't come in yet...well, Joy and I haven't gone thrifting yet."

Xiomara tilted her head just a few centimeters.

"You love it?" he whispered.

"I would love it more if it had a door." Xiomara's eyes glazed over while she admired his figure.

"It's on the way, darling." Calehan toyed with his lip, catching it with the point of his turned tooth.

Darling.

He was going to be the death of her.

Xiomara loved the way she made him blush, watching him attempt to collect himself. His stare draped over her like a heavy cloak, settling into the dips and curves of her body.

"Care to choose some paint colors?" Clover entered the room, oblivious to the tension he had cut through. Calehan and Xiomara shared a grimace, joining Clover at the cluttered table.

Paint strips covered the table, showcasing the shades of the rainbow. Xiomara thumbed through a stack of printed artifact photos, each stapled to a corresponding paint chip. A black number was scratched on each tag, assigning it to an exhibit.

"The walls will be curved." Clover pulled an illustrated blueprint on top of the items. "They can be different lengths, but it would be ideal if each section was one paint color."

"I have to decide today?"

"No," Calehan told her.

"Yes," Clover contradicted.

"Okay..." Xiomara laughed. "Can I have until the end of the day?"

Clover nodded, picking up his tools and heading to the main room. Choosing a paint color might feel inconsequential, but the color of the walls affected the color of the light reflected onto the artifacts. Paint mattered significantly.

"You hungry?" Calehan asked Xiomara. The scent of elk and wild rice drifted from the casino kitchens.

"Starving." Together they walked to the casino entrance, slipping in amongst the snowbirds who carved the seats of their slot machines like marble statues.

"Can I tell you something?" Xiomara drummed her fingers against the tabletop, a pensive look on her face.

"Anything." Calehan relaxed into the booth, stretching his legs wide and long as he trapped Xiomara's feet between his.

"I knew you'd all be tall up here." She leaned forward and dropped her voice to a whisper. "But I did not expect you to be *this* tall."

Calehan laughed heartily, his voice wrapping the rafters.

"We used to be taller."

"I'm aware." Xiomara stated exaggeratedly. "But after the buffalo and then the oil…" She trailed off with a shrug.

"Some things are woven into our DNA." Calehan looked at her in earnest. "There were some things that were destiny, fate, Creator's will. No matter what they do to us, they cannot stop us from growing taller than the trees. Are your people typically as short as you?"

Xiomara furrowed her brow. "I am tall."

"You're literally tiny." Calehan furrowed his eyebrows and squeezed her feet between his.

"I am not!" Her face wrinkled. "Everyone is like five feet back home, and I am five foot five, okay? That's five extra inches."

"I mean, if you need a few extra inches, I can probably arrange that for you."

Xiomara fought the smile that rose on her lips.

"Tell me how you found out you're related to Kenny." Calehan circled back to the elephant in the room.

Xiomara sipped her drink. "We're cousins."

"You're kidding."

Xiomara shook her head, laughing at the pure shock on his face. She detailed their shared lineage, watching Calehan's mouth drop open in shock. Their pizza was made on bannock, tomato and butternut squash sauce tucked under mozzarella, and a plethora of seasonal veggies.

"Can I have your mushrooms?"

"Of course." Calehan had told her that mushrooms did not belong on pizza, and her love for the roasted, squishy, rubber-skinned vegetable on said pizza was a crime. Still, she asked before picking the mushrooms from his slices.

Calehan watched her silently. She separated two pieces from the whole pie and placed them on his plate, then slid the parmesan and red pepper flakes in front of him, followed by extra napkins. She served herself last, dropping the extra mushrooms onto her slices and dousing them in a healthy amount of parmesan.

He was so used to taking care of everyone else that it felt disorienting to have someone do menial tasks for him. This morning, she had poured his coffee and even mixed it with milk and piloncillo—which she insisted he would like more than white sugar. Xiomara had tucked herself behind him last night and braided his long hair. No questions, no hesitation.

Xiomara Chavez had her hooks embedded deep into his heart, twisting with his spirit. She was halfway through her second slice before he spoke.

"Do you have plans this weekend?" Calehan asked.

"Not yet."

"Spend the day with me?"

"I could be convinced." Xiomara licked tomato sauce from the corner of her mouth. "Perhaps with those few extra inches you mentioned earlier?"

Calehan put his hand up in front of him. "It's more than just a few, okay? We don't need to crush my soul."

"I have measuring tape in the car." She hooked her thumb behind her. "Should we check?"

"I can think of a few ways to use that measuring tape." He threw cash on the table and led her outside.

Calehan held the Jeep door open, catching her as she moved in front of him. Covering her face with his broad shoulders and the car door, he melted his lips into hers. Fleetingly, his lips were gone before she had fully closed her eyes. He squeezed her thigh, leaving a kiss on her knuckles before climbing in his own truck.

It was too hot inside the Jeep. She could see him in the rearview mirror, following her all the way home. Her heart was close to exploding as she finally reached her driveway.

Xiomara couldn't remember how to breathe. Calehan was hauling her from the car instantly, her back pressed into the warm white metal as his mouth closed over hers. Xiomara kissed him back, pulling at the hair tie securing his bun. She smiled against his mouth when she finally freed his long hair, running her fingers through it as it fell down his back.

"Hey, that takes a long time, you know." Calehan pulled back slightly, watching her heavy-lidded smile. She twined his hair around her finger, bringing it forward over his shoulder.

"I like your hair down," she whispered. She pulled back to admire his loose locks. "I picked my paint colors."

"Yeah?"

"I want the first room to be the color of dusk." Her lips found the hinge of his jaw. "The middle should be black as midnight." The edge of his mouth tasted like chokecherries. "The blue of the dawn for the next room." Her lips met the skin of his throat, his heartbeat racing within. "And at the center"—she leaned back to meet his eyes— "I want you to paint the color of the sunrise."

His breath caught in his chest, giving her the distraction she was hoping for. She ducked under his arm and ran up the porch stairs before he registered her absence.

Calehan blinked before taking off after her, catching her around the waist as she stepped through the doorway.

His arm was iron-locked around her waist, his lips making a mess of the exposed skin at her shoulder. He kicked the door shut behind them. Calehan wrapped her ponytail around his hand, pulling her head to the side and exposing her neck. "I'll get you back for that." He kissed wetly along her neck.

"I'm counting on it."

← scortch marks

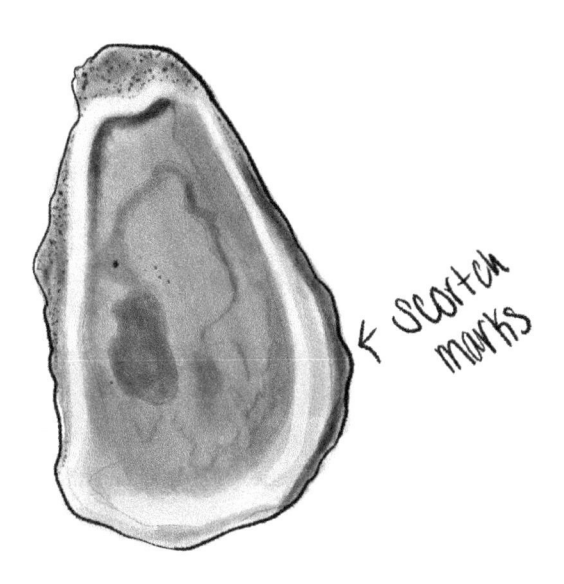

Chapter 14

Calehan woke before her again. Xiomara faced away from him, her back exposed to the sun. She was laid out like a lizard, stretched across a sunbaked rock to warm her spirit. Would she consider moving to Spain if he asked? It was sunny there almost year round and though it wasn't as warm as Mexico, it was certainly hotter than Bunchberry. Could he convince her to come with him? To give up her career for three years and join him halfway across the world?

Calehan couldn't answer that.

He ached to touch her, running his fingers over the vertebrae of her back, tracing the legs of the lizard petroglyph tattoo at the base of her neck. Xiomara stirred at his touch, pushing into his hand.

"Good morning," Calehan whispered, wrapping an arm around her and dragging her to his chest.

He had spent enough early mornings with her over the last few days that he didn't expect a response, her groaning stretch answer enough. Xiomara kept her eyes shut while he worshiped her, dropping gentle kisses across her neck and shoulder while he massaged her back with his thumbs. Xiomara turned in his arms, pulling his mouth to hers.

She mewled, pressing against his warm body, nuzzling her nose into his. A grumble ran through her stomach, and Calehan could feel it in his own. He laughed into her mouth, pecking her lips quickly three times.

"Desayuno?" he asked, showing off the vocabulary he had picked up from her.

"Claro que sí." She smiled, using her knees as leverage to perch above him as she pushed him on the shoulder. He complied and laid flat on his back, allowing her to climb on top of him.

Leaning down, she kissed the center of his forehead, pulling back to sit up straight before him. His hands wandered her body with his eyes, admiring the stunning woman who had chosen him.

"You're so beautiful." His thumb stroked across her cheek as he gazed lovingly at her.

A soft blush crept over her cheeks. She grabbed his other hand, tugging on it until he sat up, dropping his hands to wrap around her waist.

Rubbing her nose against his, Xiomara fit her lips to his. He sighed into her mouth, tongue dipping in to taste her. She lavished him in kisses and touches, her hands all over his back, his hair, and his face. Breaking the kiss, she held his cheeks between her palms, their foreheads pressed together.

"We have to get out of this bed before I eat you out of starvation." Xiomara's face was serious.

"I can get down with that." His voice was rusted and rocky with awoken desire. His lips attached to her neck when she threw her head back in laughter.

Escaping his grasp, she slipped on a robe and beelined for the kitchen. Anubis gobbled his food beside the open back door. Xiomara directed Calehan to slice the cold leftover carne asada into small pieces and warm it with the cooking vegetables. He watched while she mixed flour and water in a deep bowl.

Xiomara flattened the dough in a press three times, then thinned it again with her fingers before placing it on the hot stove. He repeated her motions with one of the balls, ripping a hole into the thin dough when he placed it on the stove.

Xiomara giggled, shooing him so she could quickly press the hole shut. Her fingers moved quickly on the hot metal, squishing the hole shut with bare hands. Calehan gripped her stove-touched hand in his and brought her fingers to his eyes.

"I didn't burn myself." She laughed as he placed a gentle kiss to her fingers.

"They're warm." He glared at her.

She clicked her tongue against the roof of her mouth and ignored him, flipping their tortillas to finish cooking. Calehan poured the egg mixture over the vegetables, adding salt and cumin to the pan. Xiomara leaned against the fridge and watched him stir the eggs, folding them gently.

"Oh!" She turned to the fridge and pulled it open, grabbing a bag of white shredded cheese. "I almost forgot the cheese." She grabbed a handful and pinched it over the pan, watching while he folded it in with the eggs and chiles.

She offered Calehan a taste of the cheese, pushing a few shredded pieces into his open mouth.

"What kind of cheese is that?" Calehan asked.

"Queso Chihuahua." Xiomara smiled over the door of the fridge. Her mom had sent her with three bags full. She had already finished one and was halfway into the second. The third was stowed safely in the freezer. "I've been wondering, how many people live here on rez?"

Calehan pulled the tortillas off the hot pan and packed them between two towels. He spooned their eggs into their bowls, setting them on the breakfast top.

"There are a few hundred of us on reserve." They sat together on the cushioned bar chairs. "A few hundred more off the reserve. And something like twenty non-tribal members living on tribal land."

"How do people end up here if they aren't a member of the community?" Xiomara ripped off a piece of tortilla and held it between three fingers. She spooned the eggs and meat into the center and rolled it, sticking the entire bite in her mouth.

"Who do you mean?" Calehan pulled her legs into his lap. "Everyone living here now was born to one of us or married someone from here."

"Chief Joseph married a woman from Mexico?"

"Yep. They went to Mexico every few years too, so Kenny and Kate always came back extra tan and toting far away treasures." Calehan scoffed, meeting Xiomara's eyes, "That's part of why Chief was so enamored with you."

"He looks so different from us." Xiomara sipped at her steaming cup of coffee.

"His mom was born in Sonora and her dad was Native and Black. They moved to Canada when she was little. I think Kate and Kenny always struggled a little with that...looking different." Calehan sighed. "I remember a few years ago everyone found out Kyrie Irving was Native and Ken's whole world changed. He decided to run for Chief not long after that. He ran uncontested, of course." Calehan held his tortillas like tacos, overstuffed with meat and eggs falling out of the bottom. He topped it with green hot sauce.

"Who's Kyrie Irving?" She took the hot sauce from him and dashed some across her last piece of meat.

"He's a famous NBA player in the US. There aren't a lot of famous Black Natives up here... there are some people who still believe wrong things. They were both teased for being dark-skinned, and once their mother passed... I don't know." Calehan shrugged, empathy clear on his face. "I'll never understand it, but I think when he saw someone like Kyrie Irving be successful while uplifting Black and Native culture, it empowered him."

"Is he the first Black Chief in Canada?" Tortillas eaten, she spooned the remaining bits into her mouth.

"That's a good question." Calehan tickled her ankle. "I don't know, actually. But I can find out."

"So how do you date?" Xiomara elaborated at his confused expression. "If everyone here is related, how do you date people? Town is mad far away."

Calehan shrugged. "Mostly Natives from nearby. We see them like once a month for whoever has ceremony."

"There used to be thousands of us." Her smile faded. "But now, it's just me and a few cousins. We are all that's left."

"I'm sorry." Calehan took their empty dishes to the sink, washing and laying them out to dry. Xiomara sat on the countertop.

"I know." She sighed, watching as he finished the dishes. He dried his hands on a dish towel before walking to her. She leaned her head on his shoulder. "You know the pain just the same."

Calehan rubbed at her thighs with his thumbs, his touch soothing. He pressed his lips to her forehead, lingering there in an attempt to draw some of her pain into him.

"Come on." Calehan gripped her waist and lifted her off the countertop. "Let me drive you to work."

Rosebud was waiting in the lab when Xiomara arrived. She sat in front of one of the microscopes, examining the slide underneath. Her blue hair was tied up into small buns on the top of her head, like bear's ears.

"Good morning," Xiomara greeted. "You're here early."

"Well, I slept at my house." Rosebud winked. "Where I have all my clothes."

"I did sleep at my place." Xiomara dropped her bag onto the desk. She thumbed over a few of the sticky notes David left for her.

"Alone?" Rosebud narrowed her eyes at her friend.

"Of course not." Xiomara burst into laughter. Rosebud covered her mouth in mock shame.

"You naughty woman." Rosebud fist bumped her and sat in the chair in front of the desk. "Have you even spent a night alone lately?"

Xiomara pinched her eyebrows in thought. "I don't think so." She gnawed on the side of her thumb to hide the smile creeping up her cheeks.

"Don't get pregnant." Rosebud snickered, laughing harder when Xiomara turned red. "Everyone is staying at Juni's after the club, promise you two will stay?"

"Anything for you, Rosa." Xiomara opened her laptop and set it to the side, securing a pen and notepad so she wouldn't forget the details. "I told Calehan I was working late for the dinner, anyway."

"Perfect." Rosebud wiggled her eyebrows suggestively. "You can ride with me then and meet Calehan at Juniper's later."

"Works for me."

"Call your boyfriend and tell him you're doing dinner with the girls tonight." Rosebud clapped her hands excitedly and bounded up the stairs, pink Doc Martens shining under the cool laboratory light.

"He's not my boyfriend," she called after her cackling friend. "It's *casual*."

Squishing her earbuds in, she forced her thoughts to focus on cataloguing rather than dreaming of Calehan's thickly muscled body grinding against her in the dark lights of a club.

Xiomara crossed her legs and squeezed her thighs together.

Calehan wandered into the lab at lunchtime, dropping their lunch onto her desk between them.

"We're going out tonight?" He said, wiggling his phone at her.

"I guess so." Xiomara smiled at the heat in his gaze. "Think you can keep your hands to yourself?"

"Absolutely not." Calehan slid his hand gently over her jaw, kissing her sweetly. Clouds filled her head before she remembered where they were.

Pushing him off her gently, she stepped back. "Not at work."

"No one is down here."

"Still." Xiomara fought the smile threatening her lips and led him to the porch.

"Chief won't fire his own cousin." Calehan argued, kissing the back of her hand.

They sat together outside, Calehan taking the shaded seat while Xiomara happily stretched in her patch of light. Her eyes were closed, head leaned against the chair, warming herself with the sun's orange rays.

Handing her the hot sauce, he caught her ankle beneath the table and settled her feet into his lap. "We can keep Anubis at my place tonight. I'll feed him while you're at the church."

"Are you sure?" Xiomara kneaded her toes into his soft stomach. "You ready for daddy duties?"

Rosebud's voice echoed the word *boyfriend* through her skull.

"For you?" Calehan squeezed her foot with his free hand. "I'm ready for anything."

"Yeah?" She narrowed her eyes, ready to see how far she could push him. "Are you ready to go to Mexico and see what the desert is really like?"

"Are you going to stay through winter and see what it feels like to fuck on the ice?"

Her eyes went wide, toes curling against his flesh. She blinked a few more times before leaning forward, resting her chin on her fist. "I was thinking of staying for the holidays."

"Yeah?" Calehan grinned.

She nodded, biting her lips to keep the smile from her face. Calehan massaged the muscles of her calf resting in his lap.

"I would like that." Calehan smiled even wider. "Don't mind keeping you around."

"What are you getting me for Christmas?" Xiomara quirked one eyebrow up at him.

"Whatever you want."

"Anything?"

"Anything at all."

Calehan left her with his scent and taste stuck to her skin. When the door closed behind him, she saw her reflection in the glass. Xiomara's eyes went wide at the lovesick expression and attempted to snap herself out of it.

Xiomara spoke to herself. "Get it together, pendeja."

Now that Chief Thomas and Xiomara had discovered their shared lineage, her work days flew by without distractions. Except for Rosebud, who would take a walk to the lab anytime she was bored. Which was often. Now that it was close to four, Xiomara packed her bag as soon as she heard the footsteps.

Rosebud waited for her at the top of the stairs, a clipboard tucked under her arm. "Ready?"

Xiomara nodded.

Rosebud clapped her hands and ushered them quickly out of the building, barely allowing anyone a goodbye.

Their first stop was the café, where the staff graciously donated meals for one hundred tribal members once a month. Rosebud borrowed her brother's truck, loading the back with crates of food and other donations. Together, they strapped the boxes into the truck bed.

Nataani waited for them outside the church. Standing with a few other teenagers from Bunchberry and Junebug Crossing, they backed the truck up to the loading dock and supervised as the teens quickly unloaded the truck bed.

"It smells spicy," Nataani noted, opening one of the boxes to get a better whiff.

"Ashley made half with green chile." Rosebud closed the truck bed once the last box was unloaded. "Half without."

Xiomara itched to fill her belly with green chile stew, though she knew this food was not for her. People of all ages moved around the church, the pile of children's coats growing ever larger. Rosebud handed Xiomara a pair of clean gloves and directed her to the vegetables.

"Ready?"

"Yes, ma'am." Xiomara faked a salute and pivoted to face forward.

"You're the worst." Rosebud kicked at her calf before turning to greet the head of the line.

The Elders moved swiftly, spurred into excitement with the tangy scent in the air. Nataani was in charge of handing out dessert, stationed next to Xiomara where he spent the evening teasing her about her lack of Manitoba foods knowledge. He offered her a bite-sized piece of bannock, green chile and deer meat spooned on top. Xiomara took the piece happily, closing her eyes as the familiar taste washed over her. An elbow in her side pulled her to the present, where she spooned steamed wild rice onto the plate in front of her. Dessert was a bowl of freshly picked berries or a chocolate brownie that captured every diner's attention.

Xiomara sat with Rosebud on the floor, their bannock slices topped with leftover meat and chile. They had been able to serve everyone seconds, except for dessert. The berries had disappeared before the line did. Xiomara had hoped to be able to taste some of them, but she didn't feel right about stealing a cup when they were so highly coveted.

Rosebud bumped into her shoulder. "Calehan is going to take you berry picking, don't worry." She tore through another bannock tostada. "The Yellowbirds have the *best* berries, I swear."

Xiomara saw Joy across the room and waved to her. Joy turned her nose at the sight.

"What's up with her?" Xiomara quirked her chin towards the younger Yellowbird.

Rosebud shrugged. Joy conveniently avoided Xiomara for the remainder of the dinner, disappearing with the crowd.

"Do you need help at the site next week?" Rosebud turned hopeful eyes to Xiomara.

"Actually, I could probably use your help in the lab." Xiomara said.

"Oh, with what?" Rosebud tried to veil her disappointment.

"I have a group of artifacts all carved with the same symbol." Ximara smiled when Rosebud's eyes relit with excitement. "I was thinking we could go through them all together and work on an analysis. Am I dreaming to think you might have access to old records, photos, journals?"

"Yes, you are a dreamer." Rosebud bumped their knees together. "But we do have some archives. What time period is it from?"

"That's the thing." Xiomara's eyes glazed over in thought. "I've found it in multiple strata, along with some surface artifacts too. It's impossible to say until we do carbon dating, but I think it might be a clan symbol that was passed down through generations."

"Do you think we could find the descendants?"

"I think it would be a stretch, but nothing is impossible."

Xiomara and Rosebud shared stories of this mystery clan through the rest of the dinner, imagining if they were small in number or vast. Did they belong to the summer? The fall? Winter or spring? They had more questions than they would ever have answers.

Rosebud took a back road to the Lavoie ranch, the inky black night stubborn against her high beams. Xiomara tapped her foot against the rubber flooring. Nerves tugged at her stomach. Joy didn't seem too receptive to her since she and Calehan had started spending more time together, and she hoped tonight would go well. There was nothing worse than being the one unwanted person at the gathering. Calehan would save her if that was the case, right?

No, she couldn't tattle to big brother. She would have to suffer through the night, no matter what happened. Joy was still young. It really wasn't that out of character for her to be so hot and cold toward a new person.

Pizza was coming out of the oven when they arrived. Joy took the seat to Xiomara's right, taking the last slice of mushrooms and olives. Juniper quirked an eyebrow at her youngest sister.

"Mushrooms are my favorite," Joy lied, holding her breath as she put the slice in her mouth and bit down. Xiomara watched her chew quickly, swallowing the bite while it was still whole.

"Me too." Xiomara specifically asked for it tonight. But if Joy wanted to tease her, then she would let her. Traps made of honey caught more bees than traps made of poison. "Jalapeños are one of my other favorites, though." Xiomara took two slices of jalapeño and onion pizza. She wished there was cilantro to top it with, but she could do without.

"So, you're fucking my brother?"

"Joy!" Juniper screeched, her words coming out garbled around the pizza still in her mouth.

Silence settled around the kitchen table.

"I told you everyone knew he was hot for you." Rosebud scoffed, popping the cork from a red wine and drinking some straight from the bottle.

"That's true." Juniper spoke behind a napkin this time. "No subtlety with him anymore."

"I just want to know if you're going to break his heart." Joy glared. "He's done the distance thing before. We all have. It doesn't work."

"Then I guess it's a good thing migration is in *our* nature." Xiomara said.

Joy's jaw ticked. "I get that you make him happy, but you're just a tourist. You're just going to break his heart and leave."

"I don't have any plans to leave your brother." Xiomara looked her in the eye. "When my contract ends, we will make a decision together." She shrugged softly.

Xiomara didn't have these answers, but she wouldn't lie. Not to Joy. She could see herself with Calehan, many moons passing between them. But that didn't mean he saw the same. They would make it work or they wouldn't. It was that simple.

"What about his career?" Joy crossed her arms.

"Joy, we just started dating." Xiomara said, facing the young woman. "These are all things that he and I will figure out when the time comes, okay? There's no sense in worrying about things that haven't happened yet."

"What if he gets a job offer somewhere?" Joy questioned further.

"Then maybe I follow him and find a job there." Xiomara shrugged. "Or maybe I find a new job and he follows me. There is archaeology everywhere. I'm not here to break your brother's heart."

Joy softened finally, trading plates of pizza with Xiomara. "He really likes you."

Xiomara blushed and attempted to brush off the comment.

"Are you blind?" Rosebud shoved her in the shoulder.

"Calehan looks at you like a house made of dawn." Juniper said.

Xiomara couldn't meet Juniper's eyes, *his* eyes. Juniper would certainly see the shame in her face, the secrets holding her beneath the surface. She felt like she was drowning, panic rising easily in her throat.

She hated to admit it but she had strong feelings for Calehan already too. He didn't even know about her past yet, the baggage she carried, the spirit she was responsible for keeping alive. Would he still want her when he knew the whole truth?

The women got ready in the living room, the heat too stifling in the smaller rooms of the house. She sent a silent thank you to past Xiomara for packing a few in-case-of-emergency dresses. Xiomara selected a red dress with mesh long sleeves, hoping they would prevent the spring chill. Her black hair was pulled back in a slick high ponytail, large, beaded earrings warm against her russet skin.

She smeared on matching lipstick and fine gold body glitter, hoping to torture him all night.

A low whistle announced his arrival. Calehan took her hand, spinning her around for a better look. Red painted toenails peeked out of her heeled sandals.

"I like you in these shoes." He held her at arm's length, admiring her from a new angle. "Deadly."

Calehan wore his damp hair in a long braid, a button-down straining around his barrel chest. Her eyes roved over his hands, trailing over the hard worked skin. Metal shone in the light, his fingers clad in silver and turquoise rings. A small white circle hung from each of his ears, glinting in the kitchen lights. Xiomara took a steadying breath at the sight. She hadn't seen him wear a lick of jewelry in all the months she'd been in Canada. Until tonight.

Did they have time to sneak away before they left?

"No." Calehan answered with a laugh, loading her into the van beside them.

Oops. Did she say that out loud?

They clamored out of the van in a mess of bodies antsy from the long drive. She let Rosebud link their arms as Kate pulled them through the crowd. Under the flashing lights, Xiomara was having trouble mustering the energy needed for a night at the club. She leaned on David's shoulder, yawning into his ear. The drive had nearly put her to sleep.

"You need a second wind," David shouted over the music at her. "Green tea shot?"

"Green tea shots!" Rosebud squealed, throwing her arms straight up in the air, her fingers jazzed out.

Xiomara headed to the bar. She and David had a long-standing agreement. Xiomara got drinks while David got tables. Getting drinks was for *girls only*. She smiled sweetly at a man with pale blue eyes while she tried to squeeze by him to reach the bar top. Letting her fingers trace over his arm, her grin widened as he stepped back to let her right up to the bar.

Xiomara's forearms crossed on the cold, but thankfully dry, wooden counter. A bartender nodded at her immediately, finishing the bright blue drinks he was pouring before taking her order.

"What's a green tea shot?" He furrowed his eyebrows.

"A shot..." Xiomara narrowed her eyes. "With green tea?" She had no idea what was in a green tea shot, but she was pretty certain it was not actually green tea.

"We don't have green tea." The bartender looked even more confused.

Xiomara bit her lip, trying to think of something equally as delicious and that would bring her back from the dream world.

"What do you like?" Suddenly, the club lights darkened further, the music growing even louder. Xiomara looked at the clock. It was eleven. The party had officially started. The bartender leaned closer to her, repeating his question directly into her ear, "What do you like to drink?"

Leaning over the counter, Xiomara gestured the bartender closer. Their cheeks rubbed together as she spoke, quickly rattling off a few liquors and mixes.

"Quantos?" He leaned back and looked down at her with heavy eyes.

Xiomara held up six fingers, looking up at the man from beneath her black lashes. She tucked her hands under her chin, still leaned on the bar—settling in to watch him.

"I got you." He winked and set out making her six shots. She watched him pour Red Bull and fruit punch over vodka. "Vegas bombs."

The bartender poured two extras, setting one in front of her and one in front of himself. He picked up his, gesturing to her with his lips. Xiomara lifted the plastic cup level with her mouth, waiting for him to lift his own.

"Salud." She held his eyes and tipped the shot into her mouth. It burned as it traveled down her throat, warming her from the inside out.

Xiomara was still smiling when she took the tray of shots and turned toward the table. Calehan was sitting at the edge of the booth, staring directly at her. She couldn't read his gaze in the dim light and wondered how much he had seen. What kind of idiot would she be to deny a free shot? Surely he'd understand the shameless flirt.

Placing the tray of shots in the middle of the table, the group passed out the red and gold liquids until everyone, save for Clover, had one in hand.

"Okay, vamos todos, repeat after us." Xiomara made eye contact with David, preparing their drinks. "Arriba." They raised their glasses up in the air. "Abajo." They tapped their glasses on the table, the group doing the same. "Al centro." The whole group pressed their glasses against each other in the center of the table.

"Pa' dentro!"

Xiomara lost her balance when she threw the shot back. Calehan's hand slid to her hip to steady her. She dropped her empty shot glass inside his, avoiding the look of fire in his eyes. A waitress delivered a round of drinks while Xiomara halfheartedly listened to Juniper implement the buddy system.

"¿Estás celoso?" she asked, tilting her head slightly to the side.

"Jealous?" Calehan leveled his gaze, his legs spreading wider when he dropped his hand from her hip. He shook his head with a shrug.

Xiomara leaned down, dragging her nose up his neck. His skin smelled of lies. "Mentiroso," she whispered.

Calehan finally slid over, leaving her just enough space to sit if she pressed against him. Xiomara was right. He dripped with envy. Xiomara reached over him, taking the orange slice off the top of his drink, then tracing it over her tongue before biting down.

She kissed him then, leaning her neck into his arm stretched across the back of their seat. His hand curled over her shoulder, enveloping her in his embrace. His mouth was claiming against hers and she had to fight the smirk of satisfaction from settling onto her lips.

David grabbed their attention from across the table and pointed to a small group of people watching them from across the room. The group got closer and had a whispered conversation. Blue and green eyes darted over their faces. A lone woman stepped forward. Xiomara tried to control her expression, but she guessed it was an unsuccessful attempt, considering the closest woman's apprehension.

"You're Indians, right?" The woman forced a tight smile as she came closer to the table, wide eyes blinking at them. "First Nations, I guess or whatever." The woman laughed. Xiomara didn't understand what was funny about calling them by the correct name.

"I studied you guys in college." The woman's blue eyes focused on the beaded medallion lying against Calehan's chest.

"I've studied your people, too." Xiomara smirked at the woman, her hand holding Calehan's arm tight across her chest.

"What?" The woman's smile dropped.

Chortles sounded around the table.

Clover leaned forward, his voice heavy. "Tell me, I've been wondering for *years*... What do you guys love so much about mayonnaise?"

The woman blinked a few more times and retreated back to her group.

Rosebud stood. "Xio! Let's go dance!"

The entire table rose at her command, filing out of the booth. She took a few steps away before noticing Calehan hadn't followed them. She stalked over to him.

"Baila conmigo," Xiomara breathed, crowding Calehan deeper into the booth. She slid her knee onto the seat between his legs, his face level with her sternum. Her fingers tickled under his chin, his nose running through the valley of her breasts to look up at her. "Dance with me."

Calehan gripped her hips, lifting her with him as he stood from the booth. She took his hand, leading him through the crowd behind her. Calehan towered over most of the clubgoers, parting them like a red sea.

Finding their friends in the middle of the floor, Xiomara turned around to face her behemoth of a man. He stole her breath when she saw the dark look on his face. Glazed over, his eyes were locked on her and she suspected he was seeing straight through her dress.

She smirked, knowing that despite the flashing lights and moving bodies, his attention belonged only to her. Xiomara invaded his space, scratching along his neck to slide her hand under his braid. Calehan gripped her flesh, raising goosebumps along her spine. Smoothing his hand up her back, he twisted his hand into the end of her ponytail. He tugged her hair until she looked up at him.

Finding the edge of the fabric at her back, his fingers curled around the hem, pulling it to the side slightly to dip inside. He slipped his thumb under the hem leaving his entire palm against the bare skin of her waist. Xiomara sucked in a breath at the intimate touch. Sparks sizzled against her skin. Xiomara felt like she was on fire and they hadn't even started dancing yet.

"I can't dance." Calehan teased the side of her head with his nose, sliding his thumb up and down where it rested inside her dress.

Xiomara warmed at his shy admission, wrapping her arms all the way around his neck to bring him closer. Thank Creator she had worn heels.

"You're a dance champion," she challenged.

"That was not dancing. It was stepping at best."

"Then step to the beat, but with your hips." A devilish grin spread across her face. "Es nada, yo te prometo."

Xiomara turned in his arms, pressing her back into his front. She knew he could dance. It was evident in the way he walked, the silent grace he took his steps with. Calehan ran his hands over her hips as she moved against him.

The club melted away when she dropped her head onto his shoulder. His warm breath ghosted along her neck. Calehan bit the edge of her earlobe, tugging it until she squirmed away from the tickle. Xiomara let him kiss down her neck and across her chest, before bringing his lips to hers.

She would've kissed him while they danced forever if not for her squirrel bladder. Holding it for as long as she could, she whispered in Calehan's ear.

"Where's the bathroom?"

He ran his nose up her neck, biting gently on the corner of her jaw. Taking her hand in his, he brought her close, leading her through the crowd. The music pounded in her ears as she clung to his hand, her other fisted in his shirt.

Calehan guided her down the hallway, heading toward the bathrooms. The line was out the door, so he turned, flipping Xiomara around with him. Gripping her by the hips, he guided her toward a dark hallway.

"Where are you taking me?" Xiomara chewed her lip.

"Don't you trust me?" Calehan put his hand against his chest, stopping short and allowing her to slam into him. "There's another bathroom down here." He gestured to the hall with a nod of his head.

The hallway was empty and dark, a neon pink toilet-shaped light hanging at the end. Set far from the crowd, the walls shook with the bass, though the lyrics were indistinguishable from the drums. Xiomara whirled around to face him, walking backward in front of him.

Calehan peered at her unabashedly, holding tight to her hand. Xiomara's back hit the cool brick wall, stopping her retreat. She waited for him, body thrumming, skin tingling. He was so close to her, eyes dark, mouth slightly open. Xiomara gulped, her mouth suddenly dry.

"Stop looking at me like that," she whispered, toying with the chain of the medallion around his neck.

"How am I looking at you?" His voice dripped like molasses.

"I don't know." She shrugged.

"Tell me." He touched her jaw, forcing her eyes to his. "Tell me how I look at you." His voice was gruff and impossibly deep.

Xiomara slipped her fingers through his beltloops. "Like you want to see me on my knees."

Calehan's lips parted just the slightest amount. Xiomara watched as his pink tongue wet his lips before he gulped.

"You're killing me." Calehan's voice rumbled through her bones.

The smell of rum carried on his breath. Calehan dropped his head to hers, lips inches away, when the bathroom door finally opened. Light poured into the hallway, both of them squinting away from the neon pink light. Calehan caught the door, holding it open for her. She walked under his outstretched arm into the minuscule room.

"You can come in with me." Xiomara spoke clearly, her voice even and pure over the noise of the club.

Locking the door behind him, Calehan stood awkwardly in front of the sink, looking anywhere but at her. Xiomara laughed.

Adjusting her dress, she washed her hands under the hot water. The bathroom was dark, casting both of their skin into a purply pink hue. Reaching a hand behind her, Xiomara brought Calehan close. Surveying him in the mirror, Xiomara sucked in a breath when Calehan trailed a hand over her bare thigh. Feather-light she could barely feel him on her skin but her flesh rose to meet him instantly, her nipples pebbling in anticipation.

Pushing her hips back into his, Xiomara encouraged his touch. Calehan snapped.

Manhandling her skirt to her waist, he dropped to his knees behind her and pulled her thong to the side. Xiomara bit the thick muscle of her palm to muffle her groans when he dove his tongue into her. Calehan devoured her as though he was pussy-starved and only she could alleviate his pain.

Reaching around her, his fingers found her center and sent her careening over the edge. Bent over, Xiomara was flat against the cold bathroom counter. Their eyes met in the mirror as he pushed into her.

She couldn't hold back the moan this time, her oversensitive clit spasming from the friction. A smack split the air as she steadied herself against the mirror, propping up enough for Calehan to take the end of her ponytail in his hand. He hoisted her from the countertop and into his arms.

His lips met hers, crashing into her in time with his movements. Pinching her nipple through the fabric of her dress at the same time he yanked her ponytail back was a finishing move he hadn't used before and shot sparks through her veins.

Xiomara came in surprise, holding tightly to Calehan's hand when it covered her mouth. Muffling her screams of pleasure, her thighs squeezed tightly together and brought Calehan along with her. Their eyes remained locked on their reflections, binding themselves together another notch tighter.

Panting and a deadweight, Xiomara was limp in his while they struggled to come to their senses. A knock rattled on the door, startling them apart.

"Xio! Let me in!" Juniper shouted through the door.

Wide-eyed Calehan cleaned her up quickly, stuffing himself back into his pants while she held back a laugh. Xiomara pulled the door open as soon as his belt was through the last loop, pulling Juniper in while Calehan crouched to slide out. Despite their efforts, Juniper saw him and flicked his ear as he joined Clover in the hall.

"It smells like sex in here." Juniper laughed as she used the restroom, ignoring Xiomara's repeated denials. "You're like horny little teenagers."

Blushing, Xiomara patted cool water on her steaming red cheeks.

"Do you think it'll be a boy or a girl first?"

"No mames." Xiomara shook her head in exasperation and led Juniper back into the hall.

"You'll have to teach me some of those moves one day." Juniper linked her arm with Xiomara's. "Clover would shit himself."

Feet tired and in need of a bar snack, they wound their way through the crowd and back to their friends. They slid into the booth on opposite sides, resting their feet in the laps of their tall companions.

Clover pulled the van up to the curb when it was time to head out, saving them from walking through the freezing cold air. Her lustful drunken haze dissipated when they arrived back on Bunchberry. The wind was howling across the island, bringing the temperature of the air even lower than it had been when they left. Juniper linked arms with her, welcoming her inside. The home was large, a porch wrapped around at least the three sides she could see, and there was a deck upstairs, too.

Calehan and Clover traded their dress shoes for rubber wellies and headed out to check on the animals before they went to bed. Juniper pulled *Mamma Mia* up on the TV and somehow convinced the half-asleep Joy to join them in a sing-along of her favorite songs.

Heels discarded one by one, the boys returned to find all of the women spread on the floor, screaming along to Dancing Queen. Their hair overlapped in a pile, shades of brown mixing with blue. Kate wore a piece of Rosebud's hair over her forehead like side bangs, Juniper screaming that she was going to pee any minute from laughing too hard.

Clover snapped a photo of them on his phone. The women were a tangled mess of legs and hair, their faces frozen into squeals of joy. Calehan set the image as his home screen, moving one lone app to its own page so he could see the entire photo. He loved the way Xiomara looked with his sisters.

He loved *her*.

← incised

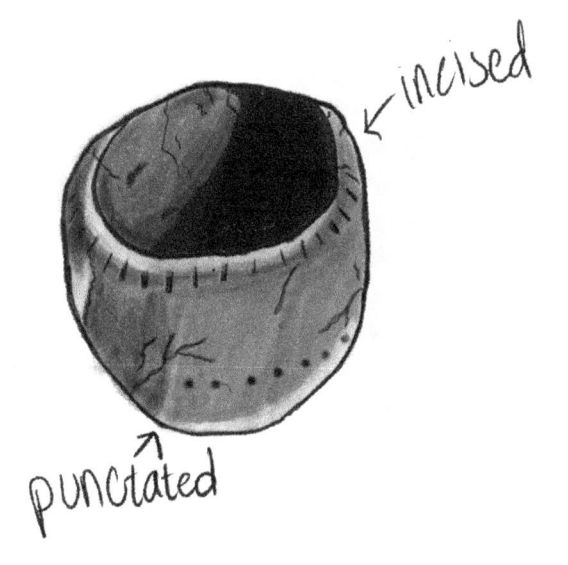

punctated

Chapter 15

Calehan was already gone when she woke. The sun hadn't yet reached the sky, just her warm yellow shadow visible at the top of the mountains. Xiomara's feet *ached* through her muscles and into her bones. Her head throbbed gently. The water they chugged in the car the night before was really paying off. She scrubbed her eyes, blinking a few times before standing. As quietly as she could, she crept into the ensuite bathroom to pee and emergency finger-brush her teeth.

Rinsing her mouth out, she borrowed some of Juniper's face wash sitting on the counter. Scrubbing off her day-old makeup, she looked normal—minus the bare feet and fancy dress—for six in the morning. She worked her hair free of the ponytail, shaking it out before wrapping it into a loose bun at the nape of her neck. The skin of her scalp was sore. She rubbed her fingers into the relaxing skin.

She crept out of the bedroom in search of coffee and her hopefully-not-left-at-the-club purse. The kitchen was flooded with pale pink morning light. Large bay windows full of herbs overlooked the eastern shore of Bunchberry. Xiomara took a deep breath, admiring the clouds as they moved languidly across the sky.

The smell of coffee brought her out of her thoughts. Joy sat perched silently on the counter in the corner of the kitchen.

"Good morning." Her voice echoed through Xiomara's aching head.

"Morning, house cat." Xiomara took the mug from Joy's outstretched hand and filled it with coffee.

"You look nice for six in the morning." Joy snickered.

Teasing seemed like a good sign from the young woman.

Xiomara blushed and poured milk into her coffee.

"Would you like a change of clothes?" Joy relented.

"That would be nice." Xiomara said.

Joy disappeared down the hall for a few minutes then emerged with a stack of clothes in her arm.

"Bathroom is right here." Joy opened the door and waved Xiomara inside with an over the top flourish.

Xiomara dressed quickly in the borrowed clothes. She looked straight out of the 90s, a la Princess Di. She rolled the sleeves so they wouldn't cover her hands and exited the bathroom.

She followed Joy outside to the porch. The women stood shoulder to shoulder. Silence stretched between them, the birds talking enough for the both of them.

Calehan was sweaty when he drew her into his arms. His lips were hungry when they claimed her mouth, the scent of grass and tobacco flooding her senses. Taking advantage of her laughter, Calehan plunged his tongue into her mouth. He held her like she was fragile, breakable, but in a grip that one could not pry open no matter how hard they tried. Calehan kissed her like she belonged to him.

With a heavy sigh, he detached his mouth from hers, keeping their foreheads pressed together. Xiomara reached for his lips again, and he gave in, unable to deny her. Calehan was in too deep to let her go now.

"You're sweaty." Xiomara trailed the tips of her fingers along his shoulders and back.

"Is that a complaint?"

Xiomara bit her lip and shook her head, gripping the center of his shirt and pulling him close, her lips brushing his ear. "Claro que no." She dragged her nose down his neck, pulling the collar of his shirt when she reached his chest. Her tongue dipped into the dimple between his collarbones, dragging over his shoulder and back up his neck. She kissed the soft spot of his jaw just in front of his ear. "Sweaty Calehan is in my top five favorite Calehans."

He groaned into her neck, biting playfully where it met her shoulder.

"Oh my God." A disgusted voice broke the bubble surrounding them. "You were gone for a few hours, Cally. You're not a warrior home from battle." Joy gagged at them.

"Go feed your horses or something," Calehan called back, pulling Xiomara in for another exaggerated kiss.

"You're cleaning up my vomit." Joy sneered.

Xiomara scrunched her face at the noise, pushing on Calehan's chest.

"You're ruining it!" he yelled at his sister.

"Good!" Joy started up the four-wheeler stacked with hay and took off in a cloud of dirt.

"Come on." He tipped his head back, pulling her with him toward the truck.

"Adónde vamos?" Xiomara followed Calehan. His gaze was consuming, as though he had shrouded the two of them away from the rest of the planet.

"I want to show you my favorite place in the world." He smacked her bottom and pushed her toward the truck.

After a quick pit stop at his place to feed Anubis and change their clothes, they were climbing back in the truck.

Calehan held the truck door open for Xiomara and Anubis to climb inside. Before he could close her door, she reached for him, her fingers sliding beneath his braid and gripping his neck to pull his face to hers. He went enthusiastically, attempting in vain to close his lips, the smile she brought out of him too wide to contain. Their lips met in an open mouthed kiss, Calehan catching her bottom lip between his smiling teeth, his hand squeezing her thigh.

"We've got to pick up the boat on the way." Calehan pecked her once more before walking around to the driver's side.

"The boat?" Xiomara exclaimed. "Where the heck are we going?"

"Somewhere special." Calehan said. "You'll love it, I promise."

Stopping at the main house briefly, he hooked up the boat for towing and packed them a picnic basket. Xiomara pestered him with questions, but he was as impenetrable as granite.

"Where are you taking me?" Xiomara peered out the window.

"You'll see." Holding Anubis' leash, Calehan grabbed the picnic basket and led them to the wooden dock.

Xiomara followed slowly behind him, watching as he climbed inside the boat and turned, arms open. She swore Anubis had a smile on his snout as he leapt into Calehan's waiting arms.

Calehan held a hand out to Xiomara. He wrapped his arm around her waist as her bare feet traversed the leather seats. Reaching the bottom, he pulled her with him, holding her against his side as he flipped switches and pressed buttons on the dash. The boat rumbled to life, noises buzzing from every side. He leaned against the seat, easily maneuvering the boat into the waterway.

Xiomara stepped in between his spread legs, facing him. She rubbed her palms up and down his thick arms.

"You have no body hair." She glared at him accusingly. Xiomara fought to keep her fingers from brushing over her top lip. Calehan didn't grow one hair in a place he didn't want it.

"You seem to have a thing for hairless men." His hand snaked under her white skirt and pinched her bottom. He nuzzled his cool nose against her neck, pulling laughter from her chest.

"Anubito is just a baby." She stuck her tongue out at him, earning another smack to her ass cheek. Xiomara corralled Anubis on the seat beside her. She held onto his harness while Calehan drove the boat through the narrow passages.

Salt sprayed the exposed skin of her back, chilling her spine with each splash. The wind was biting against her face, wooded green islands passing them. Too cold in the wind, Anubis settled into his bed on the floor. Xiomara turned her attention to their chauffeur.

Calehan stood confidently in front of the controls, his long braid centered between his muscled shoulders. He wore a soft smile—one Xiomara was certain he wasn't conscious of. It was a relaxed grin, the face of an unguarded Calehan. She blushed. He had let her in completely. She made a promise with herself to do the same for him. Javier had been asking her to tell Calehan about him for days now. Maybe she should listen to Javier, for once.

Hands slid around his waist, her body molding to his back. Calehan squealed when she tucked her frigid nose into the center of his back, the chill seeping quickly through his shirt. His abdominal muscles flinched when she lifted the hem of his shirt, tucking her hands against his warm skin. Xiomara hummed contentedly.

"There's a blanket in the bag," he said through a hiss at her shivering fingers.

Xiomara returned to him wrapped in a fuzzy blanket, her nose tucked into the bundle of fabric. Her bare toes wiggled over his feet as she stood in front of him, her back against his broad chest. Calehan wrapped his arms around her, resting his chin on the top of her head. She sighed dreamily.

A weathered dock appeared on the edge of a long piece of green land. Calehan slid the boat through the rocking water, tossing a line as he hopped out to tie them to the side. She handed him the picnic basket and Anubis before climbing out herself.

"Shit, I forgot my shoes." She turned around to climb back inside.

"Don't worry about it." He was barefoot, too. Threading his fingers through hers, he led her deeper into the island.

Grass poked between her toes, the forest floor still damp with morning dew. Sweetness hung in the air like rain. Drops of sugar coated each breath she took. Berries surrounded her from every angle.

Clumps of orange and pink berries were tucked close to the ground. Anubis nearly sucked them up his nose with his vigor. Blueberries reached her knees, growing close to the trees surrounding them. Huckleberries tucked themselves around their blue cousins, teasing the darkness from their skin and into their own deep shine. Patches of berries stretched as far as she could see. Xiomara's chest felt tight. She had never seen anything like this before.

Calehan led her to a grassy clearing, laying a blanket down for them. He took her hand in his and placed a pinch of tobacco in her palm. He whispered thanks for both of them, and they let the tobacco fall from their hands at the edge of the berry bushes. His fingers closed over a vibrant coral pink colored berry, pulling a handful quickly from the bush. Xiomara held his eyes as he popped a few in his mouth. He offered her one, holding it up to her face between his thumb and forefinger.

Xiomara grabbed his wrist, bringing his hand close to her face. Without touching his fingers, she wiggled the tip of her tongue over the skin of the berry and pulled it into her open mouth. The berry was firm under her teeth, sweet as she crushed it with her molars. Tongues stained red, they stood shoulder to shoulder and pulled berries from the thicket, dropping them into a small wicker basket. Anubis made himself at home in a pocket of sun, chomping down on a piece of bread Xiomara threw to him.

By the time they made it to the blanket, she had eaten at least half her weight in berries. Xiomara grabbed the bottle of wine and unscrewed the top, washing the fresh berry juice from her mouth with aged berry juice. Fingering a piece of cheese, she popped it into her mouth while Calehan poured glasses of wine for them.

"Que romántico." Xiomara shook her shoulders at him, sipping from her glass this time. "Want to tell me where we are?"

"My family has been coming here forever." He rolled a slice of salami and placed it on her tongue. "There are always plenty of berries and small game here." He chewed a grape and washed it down with some cheese. "There's fish here, too. You'll see."

"We should bring some berries back for your dad," she told him absentmindedly, eyes closed to the sun. Xiomara reclined on her arms, stretching her neck leisurely.

"We can," Calehan said, watching her with a grin.

Stretching out on the blanket, Xiomara relaxed under the sunlight. She could feel her body warm from the sun's rays, her heart filling quickly. Happy.

She was happy.

Xiomara opened her eyes to find Calehan drooling at the dip of her chest. Xiomara reached forward and trailed the back of her fingers tenderly over his face.

Calehan caught her hand and pressed his lips to her open palm. "You're so beautiful." He kissed the inside of her elbow. "I love the way your mind works." His lips found the curve of her shoulder, the edge of her jaw, the shell of her ear. "I'm addicted to you."

"Addictions can be dangerous," she warned.

He crawled over her. "Good thing you're a renewable resource."

Xiomara let her lips ghost over his, teasing a groan from his throat she kissed the center of his vibrating neck. She nipped gently at his Adam's apple, a hiss falling from between his lips. Kissing over his reddened skin, she let him press her flat to their blanket.

Xiomara accepted his lips then, laying together beneath the sun. He tasted of berries, tongue stained red where it danced with hers. She grabbed a handful of berries from the basket beside them, pulling back enough to set a few in his open mouth.

Calehan looked confused. Apparently, this was new for him. He blinked at her.

Placing a few on her tongue, Xiomara crunched the berries between her teeth. Warm sweet juice squirted through the burst flesh and filled her mouth, dripping from the corners. She could feel his hardness grow against her. Calehan surged forward, locking her into a messy, juicy kiss. His hands pulled through her hair. Pink and purple berry juice dripped from their lips, leaving a sticky, wine colored trail between her breasts. Stains bloomed where it reached the white fabric of her dress.

Calehan dragged his open mouth over the berry drip, mouthing the tops of her breasts.

"Your dress." He pulled back, worry etched into his face.

"I don't care." Xiomara brought him back to her, locking her ankles around his waist.

They slowly shed each other's clothes, lips following each inch of skin as it was exposed to their shared sun. Calehan sat back on his heels, bringing one of her feet to rest on his shoulder. He kissed the inside of her ankle, nipping the skin softly. He leaned lower, kissing the inside of her knee sloppily, biting into her thigh and licking over the marks his teeth left behind.

Xiomara hooked her knee around his neck and pulled, bringing his face to hers. She kissed him, drinking him in. Her tongue moved against his, the moans falling from her mouth downright filthy.

Words were begging to fall from her lips, and she didn't know how else to block their flow. Calehan accepted everything she gave him, clutching her tighter. It lit her on fire. His hands were greedy against her, fingers flexing into her dimpled flesh while he held her tightly against him.

A smile played at the edge of her mouth as Xiomara rutted against him. The friction was almost painful. Calehan dropped his weight onto her, stalling her movements. His hands were gentle on her face, tracing her features while she panted beneath him. He pressed himself against her entrance. She shut her eyes in anticipation.

"Look at me," Calehan whispered against her mouth.

Xiomara opened her eyes. It felt too vulnerable to look at him in this moment. She could practically hear him screaming his declaration of love in the way he touched her. She swallowed. He had been inside her multiple times, tasted every piece of her, yet she still danced outside his grasp. Calehan deserved all of her.

"Cal?" Her eyes searched his face, open wide. "Make love to me."

Calehan placed his still-beating heart in her hands, joining himself with her fully, feeling as though there was nothing between them any longer. She pushed him to his back, seating herself atop him. Calehan couldn't stand being so far from her and sat up, wrapping his arms around her bare back. She pressed her forehead to his, his name falling heavy from her lips. Her nails cut crescent moons against his shoulders when his hands gripped her hips and began to move. Calehan couldn't restrain himself any longer and let himself pour into her. They swallowed each other's screams, the flowers blooming brighter with each shout.

The sun was starting to set when Calehan finally roused Xiomara from the blanket. Anubis had spent the last hour chasing squirrels up the trees and was starting to get restless. Xiomara didn't want to move, trying in vain to soak up the last of the sun's rays.

Calehan kissed her closed eyelids. "Ready to go?"

"No." She kept her eyes closed and covered his mouth with her hand. "I want to stay here forever."

He licked the palm of her hand, catching it in his when she pulled away. "I'll bring you back. I promise."

They gathered their things and chased Anubis to the water.

"Come here, berry picker." Calehan reached for her where she waited on the dock, kissing her sweetly, the taste of bunchberries on their wine-stained lips.

She giggled into their kiss. The boat rocked side to side with their weight. Xiomara wrapped herself and Anubis into the blanket while Calehan chased the sun. Sneaking his phone from her bag, he snapped a few photos of Xiomara and Anubis snuggled up in his jacket, under his blanket, on his boat. He wanted to keep them his forever.

The sky was dark by the time he was docking at Bunchberry.

"Your place or mine?" Xiomara toyed with the end of his braid.

"Mine is closer." Calehan felt himself flush under her heated gaze.

"Yours it is then." She tugged his braid gently to turn his attention to her, leaning to mouth his thumb from where it lay on her collarbone. Her tongue reached out to slide it between her lips, twirling around it as she sucked it deeper. Calehan gulped as he felt his thumb touch the back of her throat. His dick strained against the denim of his jeans.

Xiomara released his thumb slowly, an audible pop when it fell from her lips. He dragged a wet line across her chin as he cupped her throat and brought her face to his. He let the truck slow to a stop on the private road, devoting his attention to devouring her mouth.

Xiomara's voice was breathy when she broke the silence, "Drive faster."

His fingers flexed against the sides of her throat, lips pressing a wet kiss to her mouth.

Calehan dropped his hand to her lap, wedging his fingers between her closed thighs, foot pressing down on the gas. The summer air outside was cooler than the truck cab, the windows frosting as Calehan zipped through a back road to his house.

← Carved gourd

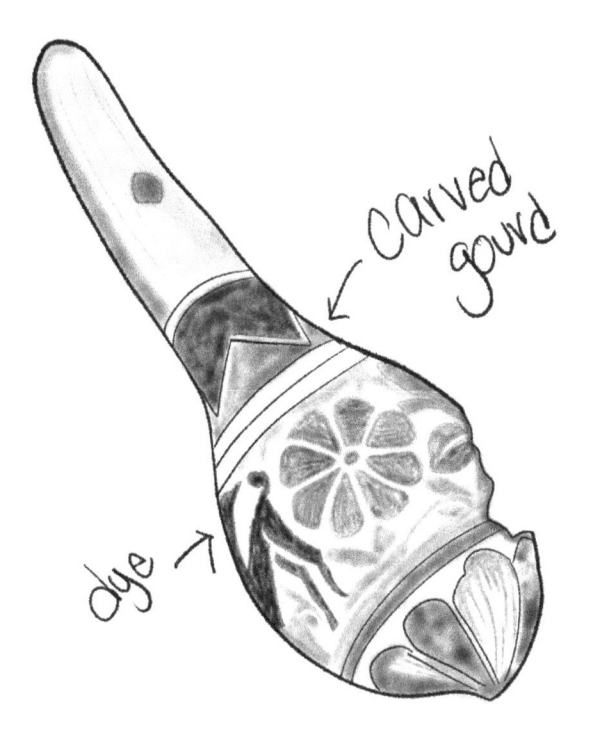

dye →

Chapter 16

The bed was cold beneath her hand. Anubis, ever loyal, remained at her feet, but the handsome man who had fallen asleep still seated inside her was missing. She felt the pout overtake her face in his absence, somehow already accustomed to waking with him by her side.

A receipt was resting on his nightstand. She stared at it without moving for a few minutes, willing Calehan to return before she had to read the note. He didn't.

Xiomara rolled to his side of the bed, cuddling into his pillow as she took the note. The fabric threatened to pull her eyes shut. The scent of sweetgrass stuck to his pillow.

Mouths to feed.
Be home as soon as I can.
Wait for me.

Her fingers brushed over the letters, feeling the depression his pen made in the slick paper. Xiomara pressed her face into his pillow. She missed him. If she wasn't afraid of running into a Yellowbird sibling, she would go outside in search of him. It felt like a rope tethered them together, and it was tugging on her every second they spent apart.

His room looked different in the daylight. It reminded her of the cabin she was staying in. It seemed like they had the same floorplan. The walls were painted a deep forest green, bare of decoration other than books and a few landscape photos.

Xiomara rose from the bed and pulled his t-shirt from the day before over her naked body. It smelled like smoke. Standing, she looked around his room, examining the images and books he kept beside him while he slept. She didn't recognize many of the titles on his shelves, save for a few classic authors like Louise Erdrich and Stephen Graham Jones.

The photos on the walls were aged, maybe from the nineties or early two thousands. It looked like photos of Bunchberry, slightly less developed, slightly wilder. One image was of a woman, two children on either side of her. They faced away from the camera, admiring the mountains in front of them. They were nestled into a field of wildflowers, pinks and purples vibrant against the lushly forested mountains.

Xiomara examined the image intently, certain it was Calehan with his mother and twin. None of the other photos in his room had people in them. She peeked inside his dresser drawers, unsurprised at the organization and cleanliness of his things. Thirty years old and Calehan still had superhero socks in his drawer.

"Boys will be boys," Xiomara whispered, endearment forcing her heart ever bigger.

Stepping through the doorway, she hesitated. Her eyes roved over the small house, listening for any movement. Greeted with silence, she ventured on. The rest of his home was like his bedroom—bright walls with simple wood and gray furniture. The house would have been sterile if not for the dozens of family photographs. Mixed in with the photos, there were art pieces and children's drawings. She looked closer and recognized the name Joy scribbled into the corner of one drawing. Of course he kept his little sister's childhood drawings. That was exactly the kind of thing she expected from Calehan. His love for those around him was immense and never-ending.

Xiomara spent the longest amount of time in his kitchen. Her mother always said she could learn as much about a man from his kitchen as his bedroom. Calehan was organized here, too. His attention to detail and cleanliness delighted her.

Calehan's kitchen tools were few, but quality. The pans were all cast iron, stored inside the oven beside a cookie sheet and pie pan. He had four of every dish, a ceramic dark green with a few personalized mugs. One of the mugs was bright red, *Bunchberry High School* etched in white on the front. Pushing on her tippy toes, she reached for it, her fingers just barely touching the handle.

"Looking for something?"

Xiomara nearly jumped out of her skin and put a hand to her thrumming heart, realizing she had left all the drawers and cabinets open in the kitchen during her snooping. Anubis hadn't even had the decency to bark upon hearing Calehan return. She needed to double-check where his loyalties lay; he was *her* dog after all.

"No," she said, flicking her bangs out of her face.

"What were you doing, then?" Calehan trapped her between his arms and the counter. He kissed her on the nose. "Snooping?"

She shrugged, holding his eyeline. "I guess."

"Find anything noteworthy?" Calehan rested his forehead on hers, rubbing their noses together.

"I'm not prepared to discuss my findings at this time." Xiomara hooked her fingers in his belt loops. "I'm still gathering data."

"I love it when you talk science to me," Calehan groaned into her lips and kissed her.

Xiomara leaned into his kiss, gliding her arms up his sweaty back. Anubis came bounding out of the bedroom, jumping onto their legs. Calehan kept his arm around her waist while he scratched Anubis on the head.

"Are you hungry?" Xiomara batted her eyes at him.

"Starving," he told her. A wicked gleam sharpened his eye as his hands crept beneath her shirt. He palmed her bare ass, squatting to lift her onto the countertop. Xiomara squealed at the cold stone against her skin. Calehan lifted her shirt, kissing across her torso and chest.

A groan tumbled from her mouth when he kneeled before her, gripping her thighs to pull her to his lips. His nose drew shapes into her thighs, breath warm as it passed her center. Her feet flexed on his shoulders in anticipation. She tugged at his damp shirt, begging to dispel the tension somewhere.

Xiomara cried out when his lips kissed her wetness. Her hands threaded into his hair, holding him close while he devoured her. Calehan stayed connected to her even when she tried to push him away, legs shaking. He lifted his head to meet her eyes. Open-mouthed, Xiomara breathed heavily, the grip on his hair bordering on painful.

Light reflected off the shine of his wet chin as Calehan kissed up her spent body, lips pressing over her blissed out face. Xiomara could hardly move enough to kiss him back. He laughed into her mouth when she sloppily pushed her lips against his.

"Ahora no puedo caminar." Xiomara closed her eyes and wrapped her arm around Calehan's neck.

"I got you, baby." He kissed along her shoulder and gathered her in his arms.

Depositing her on the cold shower floor, she leaned against him under the warming water, spent from their hours together. Calehan lathered her hair with his shampoo.

Finished with her hair, Xiomara demanded to wash his. He refused, arguing that the back pain from bending wasn't worth the massage. While he washed his hair, Xiomara set to work with a rag, pulling the dirt from his skin. She could feel the roped muscles, some more knotted than others. Nothing a little knuckle work couldn't fix.

Calehan hissed in pain and tried to move away, but she followed him, working his muscles until he relaxed into it, the pressure of her fingers untying the knots. They stood together beneath the stream of water, Xiomara kissing the skin of his back through the falling rain.

Anubis whined, pushing the shower curtain with his nose.

"Guess we should get out of here." Calehan washed her body quickly, spending most of his time on the curves of her breasts and the thickness of her hips. He palmed her ass, gathering her flesh and working it like a stress ball. She squirmed out of his arms and shut off the water. Handing her a towel for her hair, Calehan mirrored Xiomara as they bent over and twisted the towels over their dripping wet hair, securing them on top of their heads.

Anubis puttered happily in circles around Xiomara's feet while she prepared his meal. Using some of Calehan's leftover rabbit meat, she stirred it with fresh wild rice and carrots.

Xiomara caught Calehan watching her when she bent over to set his bowl on the floor. Anubis dove in, slobbering over his unique breakfast.

She approached Calehan, her stare locked on the wet strands of hair stuck to his chest.

"You'll leave it down?" She bit her lip in anticipation.

"Anything for you." He kissed her forehead and drew the towel from her damp hair.

Xiomara dressed quickly in a pair of Joy's shorts and one of Calehan's hoodies. "What do you want for breakfast?" She asked.

"It's Sunday." Calehan gripped her hip. "Breakfast is at my dad's place."

Xiomara blanched.

"My dad loves you." He held her close in comfort. "And he knows."

Xiomara gasped, eyes wide.

"How was I supposed to keep you a secret?" Calehan wrapped his hands around the base of her head, then pressed his lips to hers. Her mind blanked, vision white and fuzzy. "Besides, he saw us kissing in the truck."

Xiomara stared at him, annoyance plain on her face. Pinching him in the tummy, she pushed out of his arms.

"Come on." He took her hand and led her from the house. Anubis following close behind them.

Ghost came barreling down the hill toward them, barking excitedly. Anubis immediately lept to attention, his ears pointed straight to the sun while the dogs wrestled. The house sounded noisy this morning, as though it was full of people. Stepping through the open door, Xiomara stopped in the entryway.

Calehan bumped into her. "What are you—?"

"Grumpy Cal finally caught himself a snag, eh?" A man bearing a striking similarity to Calehan, save for the blue eyes, peered at her.

Calehan wore a wide grin as he stepped around her to hug the man. The stranger was the same height, though he was significantly leaner, a true runner's build. Calehan reached for her, bringing her over to meet the stranger.

"This is my little brother, Clyde." He beamed as he showed her off to his brother. "This is Xiomara."

Clyde shook her hand. "You are way out of my brother's league. Tell me, how did he manage to trap you?"

"He kidnapped me." She smiled wide at Calehan's face, teeth on show.

"I didn't—"

"Walk with me." Clyde wrapped his arm around Xiomara, dragging her away from Calehan. "Did he threaten you with this scary hairless dog?"

"Wow." Xiomara mocked offense. "Xoloitzcuintle is the most ancient breed in the Americas."

"A what?" Clyde's eyebrows furrowed.

"Why are you bullying this sweet baby?" A woman with short red hair was in the kitchen beside Muskwa, leaning to scratch Anubis beneath the chin. She recognized her from their first bonfire, when she was still staying with Rosebud.

"Xiomara, meet Buffy." Clyde gestured toward the redhead.

Buffy pushed Clyde to the side and hugged Xiomara tightly. "We've met."

Calehan hugged the redhead, kissing her cheek. "Where's Winona?"

"She had tickets to a concert tonight." Buffy patted his arm. "Juni is meeting us at the dock?"

"Where are we going?" Calehan stole a few strips of bacon, pushing a piece between Xiomara's lips as he draped his arm around her shoulders.

"Berry picking, duh." Joy emerged from the hallway, smiling at Xiomara when she noted her outfit.

"Juni put it in the group chat like two months ago." Buffy huffed at Calehan, smacking Clyde on the hand when he tried the same.

"Clearly, you've been distracted," Clyde quipped, seating himself at the table.

"Where's Nataani?" Calehan pulled a seat out for Xiomara, standing behind her as Joy took the seat beside her.

"Still showering," Muskwa answered.

By the time Nataani emerged, they had finished breakfast and wrapped a piece of bannock with eggs in foil for him. Calehan ran Anubis to his cabin while Xiomara loaded the dishwasher.

Returning to the dishes loaded and the kitchen wiped down, Calehan took her in his arms and kissed her sweetly, holding her like she was unfired clay. Xiomara's blood sang, rushing to the edges of her skin, every cell on fire. Calehan pulled away, keeping hold of her cheek.

"You spoil me." Calehan spoke her words back to her.

"We should probably go," she whispered, the desire to stay tugging at her heart.

Calehan groaned and led her out the door. Joy and Buffy were waiting in the bed of the truck.

He stopped beside the bed. "Why are you two back here?"

"They called dibs." Joy said.

Calehan clicked his tongue and wrenched the passenger door open, pulling his younger brothers out one by one. He held the door open, gesturing for the women to enter. Xiomara hung back, expecting to ride in the bed with Calehan.

"Come on tiny, get in here." He nodded, beckoning her over.

"I can ride in the back with you. I don't mind."

Calehan stared down at her, a quirk to his lips. He didn't budge. She acquiesced and climbed into the cab of the truck, the door thudding shut behind her. Calehan leaned in the open window to kiss her cheek. When she turned toward the others, she found three copies of the same devilish smile staring at her.

"What?" Xiomara laughed nervously.

"He's in love with you," Buffy said, her smile growing wider.

"No." Xiomara blushed.

The trio simply laughed.

"I mean," Buffy said while Xiomara attempted to hide her vested interest, "he's never brought anyone to the house, much less to Mom's island." Joy rolled her eyes.

Xiomara had to take a deep breath. Sure, she had suspicions, but to hear it confirmed was all-encompassing.

No, he didn't love her. Not yet, at least. Right?

Did she love him?

Yes.

Fuck. She shouldn't have asked herself that.

There was a different boat at the dock when they arrived. Much larger, this boat was shiny and fancy—nothing like the Yellowbird boat. There were two levels, the top deck open to the sun. They filed onto the boat, joining Juniper and the other Lavoies in the sunshine.

Xiomara settled into Calehan's side, his arm warm across her back and down her arm. His hand wrapped around her hip, holding her tightly to him. Xiomara turned her cheek into his chest, the smell of salt mixing with his cedar scent. She felt her heartbeat slow, her breathing even with Calehan's. Peace lifted her shoulders.

Calehan looked down at her. "How ya doing?"

"Agradecida."

Calehan kissed the crown of her head.

"Buffy said we're going to your mom's island?" she asked.

"Yep. For some reason she loves this little rock the most and so our berry patch has been there since we were kids. You've already been anyway, it's the place we had our picnic." He wiggled his eyebrows at her instantly flushing face.

"Calehan..." She smacked his chest gently.

Laughing, he brought her closer, dragging her legs over his lap, Calehan leaned in for a kiss. Xiomara dodged his kiss, laughter falling from her lips when he caught her cheek instead. Calehan pressed his kisses to the skin of her chest.

Xiomara pushed his head away from her, squishing his cheeks in her hands. She smiled as he let her mess with his face, mushing his features in her fingertips. Meeting in the middle, they kissed slowly.

Frankie reminded them they could not, in fact, stop time. His tiny feet clapped against the wet wooden floor. They pulled apart just as he dove into his uncle's arms. Frankie curled himself in Calehan's embrace.

"You're like his uncle-dad," Xiomara teased.

"Juniper and I aren't identical." Calehan was holding Frankie upside down on his long legs.

"Are you sure?" Xiomara looked over to Juniper. "You have the same face."

Juniper cackled where she sat in her husband's arms. Clover was wrapped around her, his chin on her shoulder, legs over hers, arms keeping her tight against his chest. Xiomara smiled at them, admiring their intimacy after fifteen years together.

Would Javier have loved her for this long? If he was alive, if they were together now with children, would he still desire her like he did the last day she saw him? Would she and Javier steal kisses in the dark and fall asleep holding the souls they brought to life?

She didn't know.

Frankie was a welcome distraction for the majority of the boat ride, wobbling between family members on unsteady baby legs.

Hunger had settled into their stomachs by the time they docked at the island. They filed off the boat one by one. Xiomara carted a camping chair and a basket of cheese. Calehan helped her off the boat and took the chair from her shoulder.

Once Muskwa had the fire started, Xiomara crouched in front of him to take over stew-stirring duties. Joy and Nataani made plates for everyone, handing them out in order of oldest to youngest.

"Kate made frybread," Rosebud piped up and passed the basket around, a Blue Bird Flour towel keeping the fried dough warm.

Like a seasoned pro, Xiomara ripped a piece of frybread and dipped it into the stew. Using her spoon, she pushed a piece of meat and veggies into the pocket of the bread and tucked it in her mouth. Calehan's eyes widened at her actions, surprise evident on his face.

"You eat that like a sopapilla." Kate smiled, copying her motions.

Xiomara closed her eyes and smiled with her mouth full of stew, scrunching up her nose. Frankie chased bugs while they ate, occasionally running over for a bite of stew before taking off again. It was lovely to see a child playing and having fun without fear of snakes and coyotes. She couldn't remember a time they could run barefoot farther than a few feet from the house. Even that pushed her father's buttons. He had been bitten in the calf by a rattlesnake as a teen and found her desire to be barefoot outside increasingly irritating. She missed his stern command to cover her feet each time she stepped outside.

Calehan passed Xiomara a pinch of tobacco, saying a quick word of gratitude for both of them before they sprinkled it beneath the berry bushes. She caught his hand when he moved away, silently asking for his attention. She wrapped her arms around his waist, chin resting on his chest to gaze up at him. Calehan tucked a hair behind her ear.

"Your sister said you've never brought someone here before." Xiomara bit her lip in trepidation.

"That is true." He flicked their noses together. He laced his fingers through her hair, massaging her scalp with the pads of his fingers. "I want to bring you everywhere."

"Oh my God, can you get off of her for five seconds?" Joy pretended to puke behind a tree.

"Aw…" Rosebud put Joy in a headlock and ruffled her hair. "You want a snag, too, kid?"

Xiomara pushed Calehan from her and turned away. Locating Juniper across the open field, she set off to join her. The bush looked suspiciously like chokecherries, like she had at home.

"I figure you know these?" Juniper opened her hand, offering the cherries to her.

"No mames." Xiomara took a few of the deep red fruits and inspected them with wide eyes. She sighed happily when she tasted them, chokecherry juice filling her mouth. "I didn't know they could grow this far north."

Juniper smiled. "My mom planted these bushes when she moved here, some thirty-five years ago."

Xiomara stopped picking. She stepped back to admire the patch of chokecherry trees. They were lush, the tiny branches heavy with swollen fruit. Her mouth watered just looking at it. Warmth spread across her back as Calehan wrapped his arm around her shoulders. A prayer of thanks whispered into the land she stood on.

Realization dawned. Xiomara's eyes went wide, pulling Calehan level to her mouth. "You let us have sex in front of your mother," she hissed.

Calehan chuckled. "My house used to be her art studio, baby."

"Fuck." She closed her eyes and brought her palms together in front of her lips, saying a silent prayer for forgiveness to his mother.

Calehan laughed against her shoulder, chest rumbling against the bare skin of her back. He pulled her hands away and kissed her lips. "She wouldn't watch us have sex. She definitely saw us make those enchiladas last night, though." He snickered when she smacked his stomach. "Why don't you have any chokecherries?" Calehan palmed her empty bucket, shaking it dramatically.

She shrugged, twiddling with the strings of her hoodie. "They're for you guys, not me."

"I love your selflessness." Calehan kissed her cheek when she tried to squirm away. "My mom would want you to have them; if anyone understood these berries best, it would be you and her."

Xiomara relaxed, accepting a few cherries from his palm. He kissed her, chokecherry juice coating both of their tongues.

"There aren't going to be any berries left, you horndogs." Clover passed them with two full buckets in one hand. He grabbed Calehan's hair and yanked.

Calehan hissed and threw himself at his brother, wrapping his arm around his neck. Xiomara smiled, watching them wrestle like kids.

"Do not spill my berries, Clover!" Juniper shouted. "Come on, Rosebud and Kate are hoarding the cloudberries."

"What's a cloudberry?" Xiomara spoke the word slow, committing it to memory and deciphering a Spanish translation in her head. Indigenous food was incredibly diverse, and she found herself constantly discovering new berries, vegetables, even meats. The dictionary in her brain was ever expanding.

Juniper pointed her to a swatch of short green leaves, a small orange ball nestled atop white petals. The plants were growing in the gaps between tree roots. Xiomara reached down and picked one, rolling it between her fingers. It reminded her of a blackberry, but it was shorter and fat, like a pumpkin. The color was incredible, soft peaches and orange along the widest side, while the tip was a vibrant shade of coral pink. It was such a gorgeous item she didn't want to eat it.

Xiomara dropped it into her bucket and crouched to pick a few more.

Crouching beside her, Calehan leaned forward and kissed her cheek, dumping a handful of the orange berries into her bucket.

Frankie hid behind one of the bushes in front of them, preparing for a not-so-sneaky surprise.

"Get her, Frankie!" Calehan wrapped his arms around Xiomara, trapping her. Frankie latched himself to Calehan's leg instead. "Hey! You're not supposed to attack me. I'm your uncle."

"Francisquito! Ayúdame!" Xiomara giggled as the little boy jumped up and wrapped himself around her legs instead. Calehan let her go and lifted Frankie into his arms. He held him stretched out like a ferret and blew raspberries on his belly.

Xiomara smiled watching them, Frankie's baby laughs filling the air all around them. Everyone stopped to watch and absorb the joy. Xiomara slipped her phone from her pocket and took a few photos. Juniper and Muskwa lounged in the back. Buffy and Joy could be seen, laughing. Clover was crouched in front of his wife, holding her hand against his shoulder.

Time froze while they picked berries. Hours spent with family never aged. They walked together hand in hand back to Calehan's cabin, scratching Anubis when he jumped in happiness.

Xiomara watched Calehan feed Anubis from her seat on the couch, a glass of wine in her hand. "You wore your hair down today for me?"

"Just for you," he kissed the bashful smile on her face then, bringing her into his grasp when his weight dipped the cushions of the couch.

"You like me or something?"

Calehan shrugged. "I'd use a different word." His lips claimed hers again. Calehan removed the wine glass from her hands and placed it on the coffee table. He picked up her empty hand and brought it to his mouth for a sweet kiss. "I fell in love with you the moment we met."

Xiomara felt like her heart was going to explode. Nerves settled into her belly. Sure, his sisters had warned her, but she hadn't believed them.

"At the berry fest?" She recalled telling him not to "fuck up" her museum. No wonder he had been so nervous to show her his ideas.

Calehan nodded, thumb rubbing softly over her neck.

"I was mean to you." Xiomara whispered.

"I liked it."

missing tip →

↑ worked edges

CHAPTER 17

They left for Rosebud's in the nick of time, the Jeep rocking over back roads in an effort to make up for the time they lost in bed. Xiomara was anxious, her heel jiggling in the seat next to Calehan. The weight of his hand was heavy on her knee, switching her tapping heel for rubbing across his hand with hers.

Xiomara gripped him, irritated that he was driving the manual Jeep and couldn't hold her hand the entire ride. She felt better when David and Rosebud climbed in the car, Rosebud's infectious high energy and speed-talking a welcome distraction.

Anubis made himself at home in David's lap, looking out his cracked open window. Rosebud questioned Xiomara about the museum curation, offering to assist with cataloguing the artifacts. Parked on the ferry, Calehan turned the ignition off and set Xiomara's hand back in his lap.

Kate was waiting for them at the site, her father and brother beside her with shovels and digging sticks in their arms. Elders were taking the lead on the mound relocation. Armed with significant preparation from Xiomara and practice during the excavation, she felt confident today would go well. Knowing that fact did not temper the anxiety rolling around in her belly.

Calehan called her name from his seat atop the backhoe and waved her to him. He jumped from the seat as she came near, guiding her inside to sit in front of the controls. Calehan leaned in, demonstrating the process and how to push some of the dirt into the large open hole.

"I'm scared." Xiomara twisted her fingers in front of her, refusing to touch the controls.

"It's not hard, darling." He kissed the side of her head. "You've got it. I'm right here."

Xiomara groaned but finally reached for the controls, cautiously squeezing them. She repeated the movements Calehan had shown her, pushing the dirt from the top of the pile and into the empty hole. A smile of delight overtook her face at her successful use of the backhoe.

"Teach me how to scoop the dirt," she told him.

He smiled, his plan of distraction having worked, and demonstrated again how to use the backhoe.

They spent an hour filling the site in while the Elders worked on deconstructing the burial mound. They broke for lunch together, giving Xiomara time to inspect the mound for any weak spots before they continued. Her hands ran over the hard packed dirt, catching on the edge of a ceramic sticking out of the mound. Curious as to what treasures these ancestors held in the afterlife with them, she touched the piece again. A whispered prayer entered their ears through her fingers. Her thumb rubbed over the smooth edge. She turned, looking for Rosebud.

"There's our fearless leader!" Rosebud called out to Xiomara, waving a sandwich in her hand. Rosebud and Kate were seated on a boulder near the cliff edge, identical smiles on their faces.

Xiomara took the sandwich gratefully and sat beside her friends, picking at the crust. The nerves in her stomach had wound up again.

"How was your night?" Rosebud offered her a sip of lemonade. Kate stood and gathered their trash. Kate kissed Rosebud's cheek and offered a squeeze to Xiomara's shoulder before she walked away.

Xiomara was silent for a long time, staring out at the rushing water. Water was a tricky woman, hiding the shapes and animals beneath her, keeping constant secrets.

"He told me he is in love with me." Xiomara didn't look at Rosebud as she spoke, trying desperately to keep her tears at bay. The water was eerily still in front of them.

"I knew it!" Rosebud laughed and clapped, contrasting her friend's incredibly stiff posture. "What's wrong honey?" She patted Xiomara's hand twice then pulled away.

It felt like poison had entered her blood and was slowly taking her over. It felt like he was dying all over again. Memories flooded her mind. Javier Lopez Arellano had moved to their community at age seven. His hair was an inky silken onyx, with warm russet skin found only in the Yucatan. Javier stuck out like a sore thumb in their paler-toned desert landscape.

They had fallen in love as children. Then again, as teens. He asked her to marry him on her eighteenth birthday. She had said yes easily. Time moved differently in the desert, and they prepared to wed before her twenty-third birthday.

Xiomara turned twenty-three alone.

Unwed.

She never saw Javier again. She knew instantly when he was late. Javier had never been late to see her.

Motorcycles swallowed by semi-trucks pulverize the bone, evaporate the blood, rip the spirit from the body at first touch. Xiomara had felt him leave her and waited months to see him in her dreams. Xiomara had given up hope of seeing him before joining the spirit world herself, until she met Calehan.

Javier had visited her the night of the berry festival. The day she met Calehan. He had known long before her that she would love this man.

Rosebud rubbed her hand over Xiomara's cold arm. "I'm here for you."

"I love Cal."

"I know."

"I can't love him."

"Seems like it's too late, Xo." Rosebud leaned her head against Xiomara's. "We can't choose who we love."

"I can't survive losing him."

"You won't have to. He would do anything to make it home to you." Her voice was so gentle Xiomara almost didn't hear it.

"How do you know that?"

"I've known him as long as the spirits have." Rosebud bumped her shoulder. "I can see it in his eyes. He would do anything for you."

Xiomara looked back at the site. Calehan was standing beside his father, eyes roving the trees until they settled on hers. She offered him a closed smile before turning to the water.

"What do I do?" Xiomara sighed.

"Well, that's up to you. But if you're asking my opinion, I think you should tell him about your past. And that you love him." Rosebud squeezed her hand.

"What if he gets scared and doesn't want me anymore?" Xiomara squeezed her hands together until the knuckles turned white.

"Is that what you're afraid of? That he won't want to be with you anymore?"

Xiomara shrugged. "It's just a lot of baggage." She worried Calehan would feel second best, as though he were a convenient option rather than a choice.

She wouldn't be able to argue that with him. He was technically her second choice. None of this would've happened if Javier hadn't died. What if Calehan wasn't okay sharing her heart?

"Love is never baggage." Rosebud waited until Xiomara met her eyes to continue. "We are the first people. We are no strangers to lost love. There is nothing in this world that would turn that man from you."

Xiomara didn't respond, casting her eyes to the ground.

"He lets you braid his hair, Xio. He hasn't let anyone touch his hair since he cut it." Rosebud was whispering as though saying this out loud would disturb the world.

Xiomara filled in her unspoken words: *when his mother died*. Rosebud was right. She loved him, and she needed to tell him. Soon.

Xiomara needed to tell him before it was too late. Images of Calehan passed through her mind as she struggled to conjure an idea of what he would look like when she crushed his heart with her teeth. The worst part was that she couldn't imagine him angry with her. Her mind solely conjured images of him broken-hearted, grief in his eyes and grayness overtaking his face. How could she tell him about Javier?

Hey Cal, you've been the other man this whole time. Sorry.

Eyes trained on the sky, Xiomara searched the clouds for an answer, a sign, something to tell her what to do.

"Why are you torturing yourself?" Rosebud's voice moved across the sky, a window to another universe millions of light-years away.

"I'm a masochist, I guess."

"I did not have that on your bingo card." Rosebud laughed, finally drawing Xiomara's eyes away from the shimmering sky.

Xiomara sighed and shook her head.

"Trust him, Xiomara." Rosebud gripped her hands, the pressure grounding her. She nodded at Rosebud. She was right. "Great. Now, on to my problems."

Xiomara's laugh disturbed a sleeping crow, the caw splintering the air. "Dime." Xiomara offered the corner of her blanket to Rosebud, scooting closer so they could share body heat.

"I think I want to be an archeologist." Rosebud's words rushed out of her mouth on their own two feet.

"What?" Xiomara almost ripped the blanket from both of them in surprise. "Really?"

"It's just..." Rosebud sighed. "I always wanted to; you know that." Xiomara vaguely remembered Rosebud's introduction email nearly two years ago. "I didn't think it made sense as a job on a reservation. I wanted a job where I could work here... with the community. But now, I could be an archeologist at the museum. Like you."

Xiomara squealed, throwing her arms around Rosebud and squeezing the breath from her. "Yes!" Xiomara grabbed her friend by the shoulders to look her in the eyes. "That is the most perfect thing I've ever heard." She squeezed Rosebud closer again. "I may have already identified you as director."

"What?" Rosebud squealed, almost pulling Xiomara with her as she reared back in surprise.

"Who else would I choose?"

"Anyone but me?"

"Why?" Xiomara furrowed her eyebrows. "Rosebud, you are so fucking smart. There is no one else who would be able to do this job like you can. I'm going to train you over the winter, and you'll be ready before we open to the public." Now it was Xiomara's turn to grip Rosebud's hands, pulling them into her chest. "You can do this."

Rosebud didn't look convinced, but she finally let a smile creep across her lips.

Chief Thomas appeared in the trees behind them. "Apologies for the interruption, ladies, but I need to steal the doctor."

Xiomara took his hand and stood, gathering the trash with Rosebud. The mound was nearly excavated, the remains covered in a sheet.

"The remains are sort of stuck." Chief Joseph stepped closer and described the issue in detail to her.

"The earth is too dense around the bones," Xiomara explained. "You'll have to dig them out slowly, with a brush."

The father and son shared a stressed-out look.

"I can demonstrate." Xiomara twirled around, palming a small rock. "I can use this."

"No." Chief Thomas turned to her. "We cannot mess this up. You can demonstrate on the remains." Chief Thomas took her by the hand and pinched tobacco into her palm. Muskwa came next, wafting the smoke over her with an abalone shell.

Later, the remains were safely excavated with the entirety of their funerary ornaments. Xiomara leaned her head back with a smile, recalling the items in her memory. She rolled the window down and leaned her head outside, looking at the filled-in site and mound.

Thank you.

Yellowbird Island had gifted her not only with an incredible step in her career, but had filled her spirit. Opening her green field notebook, Xiomara flipped through her notes. The richness of their finds was insurmountable, something she had never seen in her time working in cultural preservation.

Xiomara was grateful the council had approved an expansion to the budget. They had found more than eight viable organic remains, including a pemmican. The one she had uncovered in the midden of the site looked to have dried berries as well. Rosebud would have to schedule their lab tests soon to discover exactly what was inside this ancient snack.

Her favorite find though, was a broken rattle. Rattles were not uncommon, but it was what she found inside the rattle that shocked her to her core. In ancient times, gourds were filled with seeds or nuts and then sealed at the end to provide a safe and engaging toy for children. This rattle was full of a rare nut, perfectly preserved thanks to the climate. Xiomara was certain it was one of the ancestors to the modern peanut, *arachis ipaensis*.

Arachis Ipaensis had never been sourced historically and was thought to be extinct. If this rattle really was filled with those nuts, not only would it be proof of trade routes from South America to Canada, but once sequenced, it could also prove the true ancestry of the modern peanut. This find alone was enough to rewrite history, and her fingers itched to sequence the genome and bring Rosebud fully into the world of archaeology.

The council had voted on a new burial space for the mound-dwellers, and the Elders would rebury the remains together, in private. She hoped Chief Thomas would eventually tell her where the new burial site was, so she could thank them one more time.

Calehan's touch pulled her back to the moment, his hand rubbing over her shoulder and neck. He massaged the muscles of her neck in time with the rocking of the ferry. Xiomara settled her eyes over his face, watching the thoughts twist in his head. Calehan gripped her knee and squeezed, tickling her. Xiomara squealed and grabbed his hand, pushing it from her leg. His hand tightened on her neck and he brought her in for a kiss.

"I missed you," he said against her mouth. They had spent the day on Yellowbird Island doing separate tasks, together but apart.

"Stop reading my mind." He growled in excitement and pulled her closer. "Cal, everyone can see us."

"I don't care." He flicked her nose with his three times, pulling her into another kiss. A knock on his window startled her, though Calehan simply looked out the window and set his mouth into a hard line.

His dad stared at him, an identical frown on his face. They stared at each other like that for what felt like an eternity. Likely less than thirty seconds later, his father turned around and climbed into his truck in front of them.

Xiomara snickered. "Te dije."

"Oh, that's how it's going to be?" He leveled her with an ominous stare. "You'll pay for that later."

"Prométeme?"

"Keep talking, and I'll take you right here."

"You wouldn't."

The horn bellowed from the ship, splitting their ears and distracting them from their love bubble.

Starting the car, Calehan leaned over and kissed her fleetingly. Leaving a tender bite on her bottom lip, he drove them to the museum. She let him wrap her hand around his forearm, patting her hand to keep it there while he drove. Xiomara felt the tendons move in his arm when he shifted gears. She couldn't resist dropping her hand on top of his. The next time he shifted, each of his muscles rolled under the skin of her palm.

Xiomara stared out her window, watching the trees and farmlands pass by. She was itching to see if they had finished painting the museum interior. Soil samples were stacked in the backseat. Once dry, they were an incredible shade of soft rust that was so similar to her desert. Calehan took her sample and matched it, so that the entirety of the artifacts would be nestled into a home reminiscent of the home they took breath in.

People often forget that artifacts have spirits, too. They yearned to be home, the same as she did. Designing this museum with the tribe and keeping it on traditional lands would keep them at rest. The dirt-colored artifact platforms were an added touch.

Calehan pulled up to an empty worksite. They had installed the doors and finished framing the windows, completing the exterior painting. Unlocking the double doors, she followed Calehan inside while he switched on the lights.

They had painted. More than painted. The walls were the varying shades of sunrise like she had requested. But they held a texture that looked as though Calehan had hung giant slabs of stone throughout the space.

"Whose idea was this?" Xiomara whispered.

"Mine."

"It looks like sandstone." Her eyes widened in awe.

"I know."

"Cal..."

He followed her as she walked around the half walls, winding her way to the center. The floor was clear plexiglass, still covered with protective plastic, but she could vaguely see the boxes below. It was her archives.

Xiomara stood in the middle of the floor. He had done everything she had asked, even going so far as to make the walls look like mud. She loved him.

"I need to tell you something." Her voice was so low Calehan barely heard her.

His face was stone.

"Come on, we can sort artifacts while you tell me." Calehan reached for her hand, pulling her toward him. He hesitated to kiss her.

Xiomara took his face and brought his lips to hers. She kissed him gently, opening her mouth to breathe him in. Pulling away, she wrapped his arm around her shoulders and let him guide her downstairs.

The boxes covered the room, stacked five boxes high; they were as tall as Xiomara.

"Ay dios mío." Xiomara couldn't breathe. How would she ever get through all of this? She needed to train Rosebud as soon as possible.

"Yep." Calehan sighed and crossed his arms, peering at the boxes. "You dug up a lot of stuff."

Xiomara rolled her eyes at him. "Did you guys stack them in order?"

"There's an order?"

"No mames." She scrubbed her hands over her face. Xiomara walked around the boxes, searching for each label. "This one..." She pointed to one in the middle of the stack at the far side of the basement.

Calehan removed the boxes on top and brought it over to the clean table. Xiomara dragged two rolling chairs over to the table, laying a soft towel on the hard surface. Opening the box, she dumped out the brown bags inside.

Xiomara took her seat and gently spread out the items from the first bag. It was lightweight, filled with thin flakes of chert. Calehan secured a couple empty drawers out of the farthest storage rack, depositing them beside her. She placed a palm-sized clay bowl on the table, cornmeal sprinkled inside.

"¿Tienes tobacco?" She tilted her head to the side, waiting for him to take the small leather pouch from his pocket and pinch some into the bowl.

They took their seats across from each other while Xiomara sorted through the flakes. Setting two to the side, Xiomara handed a drawer to Calehan and instructed him to place the remaining pile inside. He slid the drawer into the rack and grabbed another empty one, placing it at her elbow. Xiomara took another bag and carefully emptied it, laying each ceramic sherd out in a row.

Calehan observed her concentrated face, her eyes narrowed beneath scrunched brows. She turned the pieces over and over in her hand, before placing it in one of her piles. Calehan caught her hand.

Xiomara didn't meet his eyes when she spoke. "I was engaged, once."

Calehan was silent, rubbing his thumb over her knuckles. He peered at her, letting her know he was listening, but remaining silent so she could continue.

"His name was Javier." She took a deep breath, her eyes unfocused on the boxes. "He was my first love, and now he's gone."

Calehan attempted to process what she was saying. He had told her only days ago that he loved her. Was this her way of saying she didn't love him? Resisting the urge to wrench his hand away and protect himself from the embarrassment of heartbreak, he squeezed her hand in reassurance. Reminding her he was there for her, no matter what.

Xiomara grazed over his face. She reached over the table, placing her other hand on his, sandwiching him between her.

Calehan's eyes snapped up to meet hers. His heart hammered with anticipation.

Xiomara leaned on her fist as she told Calehan about the first man to possess her heart. She told him how Javier came to her the night they met, that he thought Calehan was good for her. Then she told him the truth.

"I feel like I am betraying him," she told him, biting into her lip to hold back her tears. "He died before our wedding. He is all alone in the afterlife and all I want to do is be with you forever." Xiomara's voice rose, tears scratching the smoothness from her words. "How wrong is that? What kind of person am I to leave him all alone?" The tears won, overflowing her eyelids.

Calehan bolted around the table to her side. He dropped to a knee in front of her, pulling her chair out so she faced him. Wrapping his hand around the back of her head, he tucked her into the crook of his neck. Xiomara fisted his shirt, yanking him closer to her while she cried quietly. His heart bled for her, the sorrow in her so palpable it stabbed through him as well. Calehan wanted to cry with her, gripped with pain just at the tears in her voice.

He waited to speak until her breathing slowed. "Xiomara, you've done nothing wrong." Calehan smoothed her hair with his palm. "You are the kindest person I have ever met. To even worry for his spirit, all these years later, shows how deeply you love him." He caressed her head back, wiping her tears with his thumbs as he held her face level with his. "Javier is too loved to be alone. A piece of you lives within him, no matter where you are. You carry a piece of him with you every day. Bonds like that do not break across worlds."

Xiomara stared at him, tears streaming, eyes exhausted. "How do you know? What if he is alone forever?"

"When we went to Arizona after my mom died…" Calehan wiped the tears flowing down her cheeks. "An uncle told me we each carried her spirit within us. That everywhere we went, the things we smelled, the foods we tasted, the emotions we felt—she felt them, too. Javier lives through you." Calehan tapped the skin over her heart. "He is with you every day. No matter what."

Calehan brought her face to his chest when the floodgates opened, and she sobbed. Xiomara nearly fell asleep in his arms with how long they sat there. Finally, her breathing slowed and Calehan relaxed. Sniffling subsided, her tears finally stopped.

The night was dark when they finally left, tucking the ceramics in their temporary homes. Calehan held her against him in the truck. Her eyes slid shut. His leg bounced as he drove to her house. She had bared her soul to him, told him she saw him in her forever. How was he ever going to tell her about Spain?

Winter loomed on the horizon. Clouds rolled in to settle the plants and animals to sleep. His departure date loomed. Dark fingers of guilt wrapped around his heart. Ice pressed against his neck, her nose dragging over his skin as she tucked closer to him in her sleep. His knuckles were white against the steering wheel the entire drive.

Sharpening Stone

Chapter 18

Calehan found his dad in the barn, a chicken under his arm. He tucked himself behind the tack room door, watching his dad explain the proper way to lay an egg to the young hen. His dad knew everything; he would know what to tell Xiomara.

Revealing himself, he joined his dad in talking to the chicken. Calehan wished the hen a good morning and gave her a head scratch. He could feel Muskwa's eyes on his face but chose to ignore it.

Muskwa set the hen down, her wings flapping in excitement at being reunited with her flock. Calehan was surprised to see two bridles appear in his father's hand, suiting up Angel and his father's horse, Áníínishní. Born the summer after his mother's passing, Áníínishní joined the world bathed in moonlight, eyes so blue they were nearly as white as her coat. She shined like the sun, and so his father named her for the sun of his own heart.

Calehan helped his father mount Áníínishní, before throwing his leg over Angel's bare back. They were in the trees before Calehan spoke.

"I don't know how to tell her." His hand flexed against Angel's neck. "I'm scared I will lose her. Three years is a long time, Dad."

His dad was silent beside him. Calehan wished his mother was here. She would've known exactly what to do.

"You need to tell her." Muskwa sighed, frustration tightening the muscles of his shoulders. "Tell her everything, tell her you want her to come, that you love her. Do not leave secrets between yourself and your iskwe."

"I don't know if she can come with me, Dad." Calehan rubbed his temples, tears building behind his eyes. "It took almost six months to get my work visa. Who knows how long it might take?"

"Find out." Muskwa robbed a tree of an overripe nectarine. "Show her how badly you want her there. Do the work so all she has to do is show up."

Calehan rolled his shoulders, slowly rocking his dangling feet. He didn't know anything about archaeology or how to get a visa to Spain. Would she even want to move to Spain? And work for the country who destroyed her community? He guessed not.

"The longer you wait, the more likely you will lose her forever." Muskwa patted Calehan on the shoulder, the hungry birds dipping into the water and returning with fish in their mouths.

"I almost lost your mother once." Muskwa spoke with his eyes closed, Calehan could tell in the way he sounded as if he was singing the story. "Before you two were born."

Thankfully, his father's eyes were closed, and he didn't see the way Calehan's jaw dropped open in shock.

"She disappeared with her father, back to Arizona. I didn't know what to do. I was paralyzed with fear that no matter what I did, she wouldn't return to me. I went after her. I bestowed her with gifts and begged for forgiveness." His father let silence stretch between them. "She was a sun, and I had been a darkness taking her over. It was right of her to leave me. I spent the farming season down there, sowing her family field the old way. When I brought her home, I became the man she deserved." Muskwa let the pride return to his face. "Xiomara is tied to you already. Anyone can see that."

Calehan met his father's eyes, worry clear in his eyes.

"Be the man she deserves."

Calehan remained on that hill for a length of time that he was too ashamed to calculate. His father was gone by the time he returned home, likely off to another *Elders Only* bingo night. Ghost was herding the goats away from the electric fence, barking whenever they would get too close.

The sun hung low in the sky, nearly ready to begin her descent. Calehan turned Angel out and fed him a few carrots, rushing to his truck to pick up Xiomara.

Calehan still hadn't made a decision as he idled outside City Hall, waiting for his sun to rise. Nerves wound so tightly in his stomach, it burned. Palms sweating, he wiped them on his jeans, hoping they would dry before Xiomara came outside.

Xiomara was talking to David when she exited, looking around for Calehan. Her smile was infectious when she saw him; she bounced on her feet and gave him a small wave. Turning back to David, she kissed his cheek and practically skipped over to Calehan.

He stood in front of her door, opening it for her to climb in. Instead, she threw her arms around his neck and worked her fingers into his hair. The burning in his stomach disappeared the moment she touched him.

"Te extrañé." Her eyes were hooded as she gazed at him, leaning her full weight into him. He wrapped his arms around her waist and leaned into the hood of his truck, lifting her feet from the ground.

Xiomara giggled when he lifted her. He sighed into her mouth, letting her attention infect his racing heart. Xiomara sidled up to Calehan's side for the drive home, tucking her shoulder under his. Anubis nosed Calehan's hand, demanding some attention. He scratched his mohawk and rubbed the dog's ears in circles with his thumb.

Xiomara was chattering about her day, sharing her every thought with a sense of urgency, as though he must know everything. He couldn't help but love that she needed to do a full meadow report when she saw him, clearly showing how safe she felt in his presence.

Calehan decided he couldn't tell her, not tonight. He couldn't ruin the elated mood she was in. The museum opened for community members tomorrow night, she didn't need to be stressed out professionally and personally. He would tell her after. That was a promise.

Rain started to fall as Calehan pulled up her lengthy driveway. Xiomara leaned forward, looking at the sky through the windshield. "The sky looks white. Is it snowing?"

Calehan opened his door and stepped out, offering Xiomara a hand as she followed him. Anubis barreled into the backyard, jumping to catch the falling ice.

"It's the first snow," Calehan whispered into the dusk, quick thoughts of gratitude warming the air around them.

"But it's only fall."

"Welcome to the north, baby." Calehan wrapped her in his arms, kissing her beneath the falling snow. He poured every ounce of love he had for her into their kiss, the first snow warning him of the little time they had left.

Her teeth chattered when he pulled away. "Get in the house." Calehan pointed to the door with his pursed lips. "I'll get Anubis and some firewood." Xiomara hesitated, watching him. Calehan smacked her ass, commanding her inside once again. She bit her lip and turned, running for the front door.

By the time Calehan found her in the kitchen, the room was warm with the hot oven, and she was washing pumpkin guts from her elbows. His hands found her hips, inhaling her scent from the crown of her head.

"What are you making?" He toweled her clean hands dry, her skin hot where his palms gripped her.

"Dulce de calabaza." Her voice came out like a whisper, the intimacy of this moment taking the breath from her lungs.

Calehan stoked the fire in the old black stove, leaving the door open so the heat would reach their pile of blankets on the floor. Twisted in blankets and each other, they ate the sweet pumpkin chunks in front of the roaring fire. Anubis made himself at home on the rug beside the stove, forcing Xiomara to scoot him back when he rolled too close to the roaring flames.

"Hey." Calehan jerked his chin at her. "You're almost done with the museum. What's next?" Xiomara stared at him blankly, her eyes reflecting the fire like glass. "What's in your future, huh?" He pushed her growing bangs toward her ear, though they couldn't quite catch.

"The future, huh?" Xiomara raised her eyebrows. "What do you see in the future?"

"You."

Xiomara blushed. "I can see the future, too."

"Oh yeah?" Calehan leaned forward, rubbing her calves beneath the blanket. "What do you see, *Wise One*?"

"I see you," she whispered. "And me." Her lips grazed his when she spoke. "In bed."

"Forever?" Calehan drew his fingers over her face, tracing her lips, nose, eyebrows. "I can't imagine my life without you beside me."

Tears filled her eyes. Calehan leaned on his knees and tore the blankets from between them, diving into her open arms.

"En la vida y la muerte," Xiomara traced his face this time, scratching over the stubble growing in. "Te quiero, Calehan."

"I love you, Xiomara."

Calehan leaned toward her, hovering just above her lips to rub her warm nose against his snow frosted nose. He kissed her, pressing his lips to hers as though he was trying to imprint it into his skin.

"I got you something." Calehan guided her head to the side, eyes pointing to a box on the top of the coffee table.

How had she not seen that? Hands shaking, Xiomara opened the white box, a long gold chain inside. The chain was thin between her fingers, glinting in the low light of the fire. The gold chain made a complete circle, long enough to stretch to her navel. There were pendants on each end to hang down her neck and back. Swinging lightly in her grip, Xiomara examined each charm. One, a shiny true gold hummingbird. The other was an oval piece of turquoise bezel set in gold.

"¿Por qué me haces llorar otra vez?" Xiomara covered her entire face with her hands to hide her welling tears.

Calehan pulled her hands free of her face, tucking them around his waist. He thumbed her tears away. "Happy tears or sad tears?"

"Happy." She let out a laugh that sounded like a sob.

Calehan kissed her, slowly, taking his time to memorize her lips, the warm cinnamon scent that stuck to her clean skin writing itself into every nerve. He claimed her lips until she was done crying, when she finally sighed into his mouth as though he were coaxing her to sleep. He smiled against her lips, stealing another quick kiss before swinging her into his arms.

Tucking her beneath the covers, he scratched Anubis behind the ears while he settled himself at her feet. Calehan slid under the blankets beside her.

Xiomara needed to know about Spain. Calehan should've told her months ago when they first kissed. He would tell her tomorrow night, after the museum gala. Calehan swore to himself that he would not lose the other half of his heart.

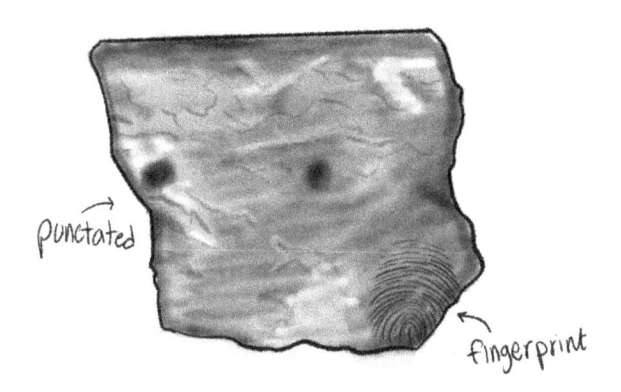

CHAPTER 19

"Listos?" Xiomara walked out of the bathroom, patting her hair. She had braided a red ribbon through the black strands, wrapping it into a crown around her head. Trimming her bangs, they sat just above her eyebrows. Her long-sleeve black dress hugged her skin, dipping low in the back. His golden bird was hanging in the center of her bare back, brushing against the sun-kissed skin.

"You look incredible." Calehan twirled her under his hand, admiring the red heels, silk laces wrapped around her calves.

"You look too good." Xiomara crossed her arms and walked around Calehan, scrutinizing the fit of his black suit. "I might need to bring a bat to fight off all the ladies." She fingered the beaded medallion laying against his chest. Tracing over the yellow hummingbird in the center, she met his eyes.

Xiomara tucked her hands inside his unbuttoned jacket, wrapping around his waist. She tipped onto the tips of her toes. "Te amo, Calehan Yellowbird."

If hearts could beat at the same time they were crushed to dust, Calehan would know the feeling. He kissed her like it was the last time. Mouth greedy against hers, his hands dimpled into the skin of her back as he demanded to feel her in his bones.

"Come on." Calehan rested against her forehead. "You can't be late to your own museum opening."

They entered the museum together, among the first few people to arrive. Chief Thomas spoke with his father in the center of the room.

"You've done a remarkable job." Chief Joseph pressed a kiss to her cheek, patting her shoulder. "I couldn't have imagined anything better than this."

Xiomara stood tall, but Calehan could see the blush settle into her brown skin. He couldn't help the proud smile that overtook his face, wrapping his arm around her waist and tucking her into his side. Calehan was lucky to stand beside her—a woman built of strength and intelligence and ferocity. Everything in this building was under her direction, and her expertise was plainly evident.

Chief Thomas shared a traditional greeting with Xiomara, exchanging their breath in trust and thankfulness. He gripped her upper arm, pride seeping from his pores.

The quiet moment was disrupted when Rosebud came barreling over, squealing in excitement. Rosebud's joy quickly infected Xiomara and together the women clapped and jumped up and down, their excitement bleeding through the room. Smiles rose on every face around them, even newcomers who had no idea the special relationship between the two women.

"Don't leave me alone with all of this." Rosebud had the most serious case of puppy dog eyes she'd ever seen.

Xiomara laughed, hugging Rosebud. "I am only a phone call away." She shrugged, making eye contact with Calehan. "I might stick around for a while, anyway."

Rosebud clapped her hands, grabbing onto Kate to share her excitement this time. "Obviously you're invited to spend Christmas with us."

"I think I got dibs on that one," Calehan interrupted, kissing Xiomara on the brow.

"Why don't we just have a big Christmas at our house?" Juniper shrugged as though hosting a four-family Christmas was no big deal.

Juniper wore her russet brown hair tied in a tsiiyéé. A turquoise squash blossom hung around her neck, matching blue bell earrings dangling from her ears. She congratulated Xiomara while they watched the Elders arrive, along with the tribal council. Muskwa kissed Xiomara's cheeks, a look of pride shining from his face. Xiomara fought the tears that rose when she thought of her own father, hopeful that the red ribbon in her hair allowed him to see her clearly across worlds.

With a hand on his shoulder, Xiomara kissed Calehan's cheek before joining Chief Thomas at the front of the room. Chief Thomas welcomed everyone, dramatizing the events that brought them here. Painted as the driving force behind the project, Xiomara fought to hold back laughter when Chief Thomas used incorrect descriptions and time markers. He finished by thanking Calehan and Clover for building the space and creating a beautiful home for their ancestors' lives.

Xiomara took the microphone from Chief Thomas, finding Calehan's eyes in the crowd to ground herself in preparation. Rosebud threw her two thumbs up, a quick whoop sounding through the room.

"I want to begin by thanking all of you. Each of you here made it possible to do every step of this project, and I am so grateful to have been chosen to do this for Bunchberry. I originally mapped this as a point-in-time site. I was way off." She blew air out of her cheek, the room laughing with her. "This site had single-time occupations across more than three thousand years. There are secrets that the earth will forever keep, but we are honored to have revealed some of those secrets through our excavation. We believe this was one family, or one clan, who came to the island for annual fishing. You might see the small pattern here on the floor tiles."

The crowd shuffled, people making space to examine the floor.

Xiomara smiled at the awe in their faces. "That pattern was found etched into multiple items recovered during excavation. We found three different axes, likely all from different occupations, each with the same symbol carved on the underside of the stone. Multiple ceramic sherds had the symbol pressed into it, along with more than twenty clay beads—all bearing the symbol. This museum tells more than the story of your ancestors; it tells the story of a family."

Xiomara spent the next two hours torn in a million different directions, answering questions, explaining design choices, and detailing stories from their time in the field over summer. Calehan kept her in his eyeline the entire night, smiling each time she paused and looked for him, bringing an instant rosy flush up her face.

Juniper cornered her brother at the back of the museum, not far from Xiomara's office. They leaned against the wall, shoulders joined together. Two of a kind. This was the type of image that ended up in museums like this or lining the hallways of tribal buildings. Two six-foot-plus Cree twins, dressed in their own matching jewelry sets.

Calehan kept his eyes on his toes, not wanting to see the scrutiny of his mother mirrored through her carbon-copy first-born.

"Have you asked her to come with you?" Juniper elbowed him in the side. "You could use the help. Your Spanish sucks."

Calehan didn't answer.

"Cally..." Juniper sighed his name, her disappointment dripping down the wall behind him. "What's holding you back?"

"She's going to say no."

"How do you know?"

"I just do."

Calehan flinched, Juniper's hand shooting out to thwack against his chest. She clicked her tongue at him, a sneer on her mouth. "You need to ask her. She loves you, give her the choice. Didn't she say she's thinking of sticking around? She wants to spend Christmas with you, you're flying her mom out as a surprise. Ask her to go with you."

Calehan shook his head, refusing to meet his sister's eyes. Staring at the floor, he whispered, "She won't see it that way."

"How is she going to see it?" Juniper stood in front of her brother.

Calehan didn't speak.

"I'll wait all day, little brother."

"Xiomara is tied here, too. She would never move to Spain. Plus, Chief Thomas asked her to design a summer school. It's not a choice for her." Calehan finally looked up, meeting his twin's identical creamy brown orbs. "It means the end."

Juniper didn't speak. He knew that she wouldn't have an answer either. He had fucked up. Waiting this long had been a mistake and now he was at a dead end. Tell her now, it ends. Tell her later, it ends. The impending doom seized his heart and crushed it, his blood draining into the earth to keep him on Bunchberry forever. Juniper embraced Calehan, holding him in a hug tight enough to prevent his breathing.

Calehan stood in the hallway alone for enough time that his feet went numb. Finally leaving his hiding space, he searched the room for Xiomara. Panic rose in his chest the more and more he couldn't find her. Nearly ready to scream her name, he thought to check her newly finished office. Turning the gold knob, Calehan opened the door to find Xiomara behind her laptop, typing furiously. Her look of intense focus melted away when she saw him. Pink filled her cheeks.

"Why are hiding away in here?"

"Just taking some notes on the things people said." Xiomara stood behind her desk, rounding it to tuck into his arms.

"How are you doing?" Calehan smoothed her bangs.

"I'm happy." Her eyes were bright, despite the fatigue of the night.

Calehan toyed with the golden bird hanging against her exposed back. He leaned down and kissed her slowly, as though time had stopped just for them.

"I love you." He held her face in his palms, committing this moment to his eternal memory.

"I love you more." Xiomara rubbed her nose against his.

"Impossible." Calehan shook his head. He kissed her again, lifting her into his arms. He kissed down her neck, dragging his nose across her chest. "Convince me not to take you home right now."

"Only if I get to play devil's advocate." Seated on her desk, Xiomara hooked an ankle around his knees to pull him closer.

His face was buried in her chest when a knock rang out. The door opened seconds later, blue hair leaning through the crack.

"People are asking for you." Rosebud winked at the two of them, leaving the door ajar as she walked away.

Xiomara pecked Calehan on the lips fleetingly before sliding out of her office and back to the party. He watched her shake hands with a group of Elders.

Calehan waited behind, trying desperately and failing wholeheartedly to conceal her effect on him. Taking three deep breaths, he smoothed his braid and straightened his clothes. Relocating the evidence of their closeness, he stepped from the office and followed Xiomara.

"Any interest in designing some kind of archaeology summer camp?" A grey haired woman asked.

"I think Rosebud might be able to handle that." Xiomara directed the woman toward her friend. "She will be taking over once curation is complete."

"Has Calehan convinced you to stay forever yet?" A councilwoman with bright green eyes asked.

"The real question is if you're heading to Spain with him for three years or staying here to finish this museum like you promised," an older man grumbled, swallowing the remainder of his drink.

Calehan froze, grip tightening on her waist.

"I'm contracted until February with the possibility of extension." Xiomara smiled at the grumpy elder as though he hadn't just dropped a bomb in her lap. "I will not leave before the work is done and Rosebud is adequately prepared to transition to Director." She nudged Rosebud forward, hoping they would latch on to questioning her. Xiomara squeezed her arm and graced the Elders with a shining smile. "Please excuse me."

Calehan was still holding on to her waist as she beelined for the empty bar at the back of the room.

Ordering a glass of wine, her voice was cool, level, calm. Calehan's heart evaporated to dust inside his chest. Her eyes were cold, darker than a winter night, and narrow. Slivered in half, she looked at him in silence.

Calehan reached for her waist again. "I wanted to discuss it with you tonight."

"How long have you known?"

Calehan's mouth went dry.

"How long?" Her nails tapped on the wooden counter.

"Xo, please let's go home, and we can talk about this."

"You can't even give me the respect to answer my question?"

Calehan blinked, a voice shattering the tension around them.

"I can't find Joy," Nataani murmured, lips barely moving with the words.

"Go help him look for her." Xiomara dropped his hand and disappeared.

Xiomara walked quickly, circling the exhibits and chattering happily with a few guests before sneaking down the basement stairs. Hoping that no one had seen her, she teetered in her heels, pissed she hadn't stowed extra clothes down here.

Snow fell on her toes when she wrenched the emergency exit door open. It had started snowing again. Fuck. Xiomara hesitated, unsure if she could handle the walk while it was snowing. Maybe she could just hide here until the party was over.

Footsteps echoed through the basement, sending her running into the snow. Her anger was enough to keep her warm.

"Xiomara!"

Calehan caught up to her easily. He called her again.

Xiomara whirled on him, her face reddened with anger. "Spain?"

"I'm sorry. I never meant for you to find out this way. I was going to tell you tonight, after this."

"After you fucked me again, you mean?" Xiomara's voice cut like venom, stinging her lips upon exit.

"No!" Calehan threw his hands, disturbing the snow in front of him.

"You're leaving at the end of the year for the next three years." Xiomara was crying. "Why didn't you tell me?"

"Xo…" Calehan sighed, his dark eyes bloodshot and glossy. "I signed the contract months ago. I never imagined something like this would happen between us."

"You didn't think it was something important to mention before I fell *in love* with you?" Her anger bubbled, threatening to overtake her sadness.

"I had no idea what was going to happen between us. I didn't want to ruin what we had or could be." Calehan pleaded with her.

"Or could be?" Xiomara sniffed, trying to hold back the tears. "We aren't going to be anything except two people who used to fuck."

"Xiomara!" Calehan reached for her, wrapping his hands around hers and bringing them to his chest. "Xiomara, don't go. I love you; I want to be with you. I'm sorry, I'm so sorry."

"How, Calehan?" Xiomara ripped her hands from his, crossing them over her chest. "Are you going to buy out your contract? Abandon your career? Or are you going to fly to Mexico once a month to see me? You asked me to stay here, Calehan. And I wanted to!" Rage had scorched her tears, but numbness was setting in. "I care about myself too much to waste the next three years in a long-distance relationship with a man who couldn't even be upfront with me."

Xiomara made it two steps before Calehan called out to her again. "Did you know Mexican citizens can move to Spain?" Xiomara turned around to face him. "Come with me, Xo."

"Why? So you can keep me in the dark again? I won't even be done curating the museum when you leave. This whole thing…" Xiomara's breath fell heavily from her chest. "You and I, it was just a field fling. Happens to archaeologists all the time. Nothing to worry about." Xiomara tasted salt on her tongue as she turned toward the road. She could hear him calling out to her.

"Xiomara." Calehan walked closer again. "Please. Don't go. Let me explain."

"I do not want to hear your voice for the rest of the night." Her emotions weighed her tongue down, her words sounding heavier than he'd ever heard.

"Can I drive you home? Please. There's a storm coming."

"Driving me home is the least you can do." Xiomara spun around, heading toward his parked truck.

Calehan motioned to carry her, noticing her untied shoe. She batted his arms away from her and ripped off the heels, carrying them in her hand as she trudged through the snow. Calehan silently scooped her up, ignoring her protests and throwing her over his shoulder. His warm hands rubbed her feet as he walked, brushing the snow from her skin.

Opening the door to the truck, Calehan slid her down his body, depositing her in the seat without letting go of her feet. Calehan kneeled before her, brushing the snow from her chilled extremities. Xiomara let herself watch him, her silent tears mourning the man in front of her. She had told him her deepest fears, shared the most intimate parts of herself, and he couldn't even tell her about a job. The worst part was that she was so proud of him. She wanted to congratulate him, ask about his plans, watch him grow as an architect.

Xiomara jerked her feet from his hands and tucked them under herself. Arms crossed, she stared ahead, refusing to look at him.

Calehan closed the door for her, brushing his pants off before joining her in the cab. They sat silently beside each other.

Xiomara was out the door before he reached the driveway.

"Wait! Let me help you." Calehan threw the truck in park and ran to catch her.

"I can walk just fine, Calehan."

He let out a frustrated sigh and followed her to the front door. Xiomara didn't have a key on her. Calehan had been staying with her for a while now, driving her to and from work, so he kept her key on his ring. Right beside the truck key.

Xiomara turned around to face him. "I need my key."

"Xiomara." Calehan groveled. "Please, can we talk?"

"You should've told me." Xiomara turned then, facing him, and held out her hand for her key. "You're building an entire campus, Cal. It's incredible. I'm so proud of you." She huffed, the tears unstoppable. "You deserve it." Her bare feet slid through the snow on the stairs, finding solace on the warm mat in front of her door.

"Xo, we have time." Calehan gripped her hand and dropped to a knee, desperate to meet her eyes. "There's time. We can figure this out. I love you."

"There isn't anything to figure out." Xiomara gripped her own elbows, her hands tingling with his proximity. "I couldn't have ever imagined this." Her eyes stared out into the dark, blurred with tears.

"Whatever you want, I will do. We can work this out."

"Calehan, you lied to me. There is no *we*." Xiomara grabbed his hand then and stretched his fingers back to release her key from his palm.

She stepped through the door, shutting it quickly behind her.

"Xiomara." Calehan sighed, his face so close to the door Xiomara was sure she could feel his breath on her neck. "I'm sorry...about everything. Te quiero, mi vida."

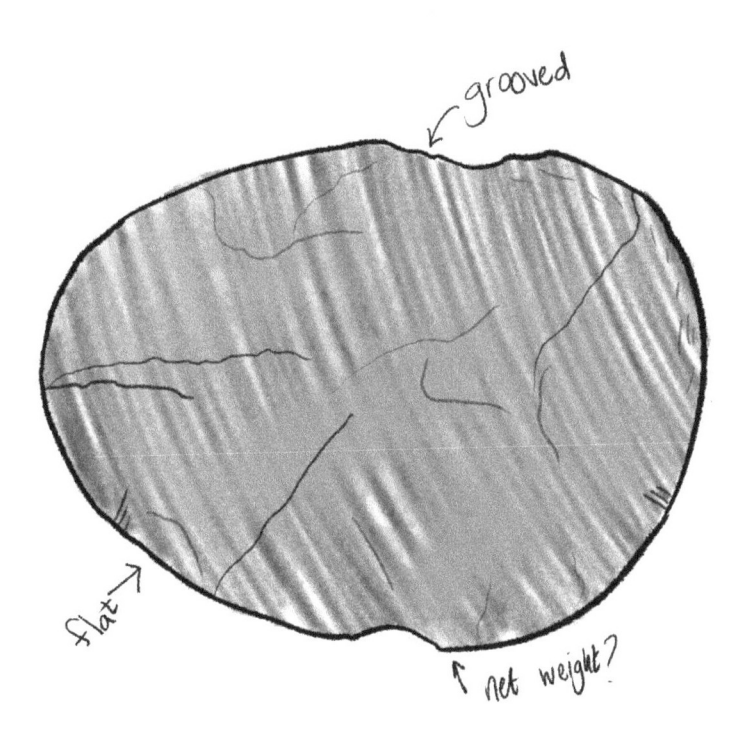

CHAPTER 20

Xiomara woke up with salt-stained cheeks and an entire house smelling of *him*. Anger bubbled in her stomach when her first thought was how much she missed him. She itched to steal heat from him and inhale his sweet grass smell.

Xiomara was alone.

She had been too gullible. Que tonta.

Calehan was just a fling. That's all. Male archaeologists slept with locals all the time. Why couldn't she? He could be just another name on the roster. The rappers did say to keep a booty call in every city. Xiomara was simply following directions.

She couldn't feel her limbs as she pulled herself out of bed. Her arms dragged along the sheets. The ice-cold floor should've made her shiver, but she couldn't feel it. All she felt was alone.

Xiomara closed her eyes, the dry scratch of every blink too painful to continue. Floating to the bathroom, she bumped her shoulder against the open door, hard enough to leave a bruise that she would deem a mystery after forgetting where she earned it.

Don't forget to salt tomorrow morning!!!!

Calehan must've left the sticky note on her mirror the night before. Xiomara ripped the blue paper, crumpling it between her fingers and tossing it behind her while she headed for her snow boots. She was pissed at him, but that didn't mean he was wrong.

Xiomara grabbed the salt, and opened her door, braced for the cold. She threw the salt at the ground with anger, scratching her palms against the jagged crystals. White crystals flew around her while she relished in the sting of her palms.

Tears formed as she dialed Lola's phone number.

Xiomara didn't even let Lola speak before she launched into a rant about how much she hated Calehan. Lola listened quietly, cursing him a few times as she learned the events of the night before. Tears mixed with steam, sorrow, and fury, making a home together in her chest.

"Hijo de puta, lo voy a matar," Lola muttered curses and threats into her phone.

Together they discussed what a piece of shit he was for lying to her, spewing curses back and forth. Xiomara attempted to change the subject.

"There were plenty of opportunities for him to ask me to come with him, and he never did." Xiomara was yelling now, her chest rising rapidly as she gulped for breath between her tears. "He told me he loved me, Lola."

Xiomara's voice was empty. Hollow.

"Why don't you come home for Christmas? I'll buy you a ticket." Lola did not have a way with words. Her preferred method of comfort was watching movies and crying together. "It's warm this winter. We can go to the beach."

"No." Xiomara sighed. "I want to stay here and work. The sooner I finish the museum, the sooner I can leave." She took the phone off speaker and lifted it to her ear. "I don't want to stay here longer than necessary."

"Xio..." Lola sounded defeated.

Xiomara was.

The snow came.

Rosebud came.

Then Juniper.

Calehan called her more than once, but she never answered. His texts went unanswered. He dropped off a bowl of her favorite hatch green chile stew. It was frozen on her porch a week later. Untouched.

Finally, Joy appeared, smacking a piece of gum as though she had better places to be.

"Hi." Xiomara cracked the door open, squinting into the white glare of the snow.

"Hi." Joy crossed her arms. "Can I come in?"

Xiomara nodded and opened the door wider, letting Anubis greet Joy as she stepped inside. Picking up her notebook again, Xiomara returned to the kitchen. Artifacts were spread out on her counter, white trays organizing them while she sorted.

"I heard my brother was an idiot."

Xiomara looked up, a jasper spearhead in her hands. She waited for Joy to continue.

"I'm sorry that he lied to you." Joy sat on the stool, picking up a chert core and inspecting it to avoid Xiomara's gaze. "I'm not here on his behalf or anything. I just..."

Joy trailed off while she watched Xiomara handle the pottery sherds in front of her. Holding them brought Xiomara peace. There was a relationship between

Xiomara and each artifact she touched, as though they could feel the honor that she gave them and thus they trusted her with each of their secrets.

"I wish he had told you." Joy sighed. "I thought you were going to be my sister by the end of the year, honestly."

Xiomara shook her head, a look of shock etched into her face.

Joy laughed. "Come on, you had to know he wanted to marry you."

Xiomara shook her head again.

"You really need to get your eyes checked." Joy flinched when Xiomara reached across to swat her arm in retaliation. "It was obvious to everyone else."

They let the declaration hang in the air between them. Xiomara had stilled her inspection of the artifacts. The jagged edges pressed into the skin of her palms, biting her to keep her present.

"Did he tell you I asked for you to be a tour guide?" Xiomara changed the subject.

"Yes."

"And?"

"I'll do it part-time." Joy flipped her hat around, settling it backward on her head. "I still have a ranch to take care of."

Xiomara hugged her at the door, realizing that Joy was wearing one of Calehan's hats. His sweetgrass scent infiltrated her nose, conjuring him in her mind's eye as if he was the one hugging her. Xiomara retreated quickly, waving goodbye.

She felt the flame of anger flicker to life in her belly again. Calehan had robbed her of an entire family. A new community, sisters and brothers and children. Another piece of her heart blackened and turned to dust in her chest.

Calehan appeared on her porch before every snow, salting the walkways and begging her to speak with him. She thanked the gods that if he had any feeling for her, it was respect, and he never cornered her at work.

He spoke to her through the glass, pleading for her. He begged to come inside and see her and Anubis, but he never forced the door open. Never even touched the handle.

Calehan simply came and cleaned her home of snow, begged for forgiveness, and left again. She saw tears on his face sometimes. Frozen to his cheeks, they caught the sunlight.

A man had never cried for her before.

NOVEMBER

Mothers can feel their child's pain, no matter the distance. She appeared when the snow reached their calves. Xiomara wasn't sure how many tears she shed in her mother's waiting arms.

They sat together on the couch, wrapped up in their own individual blankets. For a while, they said nothing, simply sharing each other's space. Breathing the same air as her mother, Xiomara felt the knot in her stomach loosen.

"How did you get here, Mami?" Xiomara boiled water in her tea kettle, pouring them each a cup of Abuelita.

"Calehan flew me out."

Xiomara almost dropped the hot liquid into her lap.

"Dime mija." Her mom smoothed the palm of her hand down the side of her face, cradling her cheek like she was still a baby. "Lola was panicked, dios mío, I thought she might die from her worries. I had to tell her about the trip to stop her from flying up here."

Xiomara smiled gratefully at her mother. Lola was the last person she wanted up here right now. She most certainly would beat Calehan on sight. Lola was too sturdy. She might actually be able to hold her own with him and Xiomara just couldn't take that risk. She didn't have enough bail money for both of them.

"Me estoy muriendo." She collapsed into her mother's lap, finally letting the Grand Canyon of tears fall from her broken heart.

"Mi cariño." Undoing her braid, she threaded her fingers through Xiomara's hair, massaging her scalp like her father used to. "I can feel it." Her fingers were firm against her scalp. "I am sorry, mija. To feel this pain twice in one life." Her mother held tears back. "It isn't fair."

Xiomara fell asleep, her head in the same lap that had always comforted her. After Javier, it had been years of therapy before she remembered who she had been before his death. Her mother's worry radiated and only intensified the fear in Xiomara that Calehan would also take years to recover from.

DECEMBER

Winter cut through to the bone. The cold came in a blink, packing the snow in layer after layer. Xiomara spent Christmas with her mother, assuring Rosebud and Juniper she just couldn't handle the crowd. In reality, she couldn't ask that Calehan be ostracized from his family for the day, but she couldn't stand to be near him. Living on the same reservation even miles apart felt too close.

Green painted the night sky when the weather treated them well, and Xiomara imagined riding that neon wave to a planet in another galaxy. It still didn't feel far enough. She could feel him everywhere, even in the brush of the grass and the breeze of the wind. The smell of fire conjured his face in the flames, her mind's eye expecting to see him at every turn.

It was torture.

The wind blew through this island with ferocity, dragging birds and flora from miles around. Snow built a curtain in the air, the thickness wavering in the headlights.

The moose appeared out of the white haze as though it had dropped in from some video game sky. Antlers cracked into her windshield, ripping through the glass and metal until they faced each other on opposite sides of the road.

It wasn't until the moose moved that Xiomara reached for her phone. Rosebud instructed her to cut the still running engine. Tears froze on her face, building little mountains on her cheeks while she watched the moose breathe through its pain.

She was near her breaking point when light shone through the trees. She would have recognized that truck anywhere. Calehan pulled close to the Jeep, bolting from the cab while the truck was still rolling.

"You shouldn't have come." She sniffled, letting him work her dented door open.

"Did you think Rosebud was going to take care of it?" His hand was bare as it wiped her tears, rubbing her frozen cheeks.

Calehan's eyes were glued to her figure, his hands ghosting over her back and face in search of injury.

"I don't need your help."

"Get in the truck," he said. Tilting his head to the side, he stood rooted to the spot as he watched her climb in through the driver's side.

The shot rang in her ears, despite covering them with her mittens. It had been foolish to hope the moose would survive, but she had hoped anyway.

"I'll pick up the Jeep tomorrow." Calehan turned toward town.

The only stoplight on Bunchberry Island was red although they were the only vehicle for miles. Sitting in silence, Xiomara didn't bother to mask the still-running tears on her face. She had taken a life tonight.

Finally reaching her cabin, Calehan took her hand and guided her out of the door behind him. Xiomara took a seat on the entry bench while he toed off his boots, scratching Anubis absentmindedly. Taking a knee before her, Calehan untied the laces of her boots. Sliding her foot out of the warm mukluk, he placed their snow-dusted shoes beside each other.

Taking her feet in his hands, Calehan rubbed them in earnest, bringing the blood back to her toes. Xiomara wrapped a chunk of his hair around her finger, twisting the strands in the low hall light. His hair was the warmest shade of brown, the same sunbaked shade of a desert mountain. She loved looking at him, admiring his features in new lighting and never-ending new expressions. Every surface on him added a shade to the color palette of her mind.

Calehan stood, her hands still in his. He pulled her up with him. She couldn't help the comfort that ebbed through her with his embrace. Instantly, she could breathe again.

He kissed her one last time. Feverish. That's how she felt against him, burning everywhere he touched. Calehan crushed her to his chest, never close enough. His hand fisted against her back, grabbing at her clothes and skin, lifting her from the floor and onto him.

Xiomara didn't open her eyes when she felt herself meet the earth again.

"Get in bed," Calehan whispered into her mouth, her lips turning to ice as he stepped from her. "I'll bring you some water."

In her bedroom, she helped herself to a pair of Calehan's boxers and one of his old powwow t-shirts he had left behind. Her skin ached where the fabric touched her, grating against her exposed nerves. The covers were under her chin when Calehan returned with water.

"Calito." Xiomara wasn't certain he heard her. "Quédate conmigo."

Calehan paused, summoning every ounce of courage he had. His knuckles whitened where they gripped the doorframe, the only thing keeping him from going to her. "Please."

She broke him.

Calehan climbed under the covers. Tucking himself in beside her, she let him hold her to his chest, their braids laying atop their arms. Wrapped together in their shared bubble of pain, they looked like a renaissance painting. An artist would've added gloss to her tears, coaxing the thick liquid to coat her face and neck in wet streaks. Calehan would've been captured with his tearful eyes still open, his broken heart laying on his arm beside their woven hair. Ripping out a strand of their own hair the artist would use it as a brush to show where Calehan's nose was buried in the hair at Xiomara's neck. Xiomara closed her eyes, silently wishing the artist would leave the creeping sunlight off the painting and allow them to remain permanently in their limbo of love and pain.

For the first time, she hated the light. Her hand scoured the sheets beside her, but she came up empty.

Calehan was gone.

Xiomara found him outside, standing in his shirt and jeans while Anubis and Ghost wrestled in the snow. White powder arced in the air above the dogs, the steam of their breath creating a blurry curtain around their tangled wrestling.

Xiomara retreated quietly, pulling on her boots and coat. She slipped silently out of the door behind him. She knew Calehan heard her but he didn't turn around. Nerves wound in her belly.

"Good morning." Her voice was quiet, a whisper through the cold.

Calehan nodded, eyes trained on Anubis. "How do you feel?"

She knew he was asking about the crash, if she had any injuries. The crash didn't hurt half as much as this. "Brokenhearted."

His head snapped to hers.

Xiomara took a deep breath, preparing herself to be completely honest for the first time in her life. "It's you." Cracking in the cold air, her voice broke. "I miss you so much. I can't breathe without you. It feels like I'm drowning, and the only person who can help me is holding me under."

"Xo, come inside." Calehan gripped her elbow, his eyes pleading.

"No." She shook her head. "You flew my mother out here?"

Calehan nodded. He'd known how much she was missing her mother. He knew her better than she knew herself.

Taking a deep breath, she looked him in the eye. "Calehan, you ruined me. And my mind—my mind made me feel like that feeling was going to burn me alive and leave nothing but dust. It was terrifying. And then Spain…you lied to me, Cal. That feeling was so much worse than the burning." The tip of her nose was dark red with the cold and her tears. "I was heartbroken and completely shocked. How was I supposed to believe anything you said after hiding something like that for so long?"

Calehan didn't know what to say.

Xiomara took a deep breath. "After losing Javier, I thought when love found me again it would feel like he made me feel. But you, Calehan Yellowbird, you ruined me." Tears cascaded down her red cheeks, blurring her vision. "I cannot come to Spain with you. I have to finish what I started. Here, in Bunchberry."

"Let me wait for you." Calehan reached for her, but she took a step back.

"No." Xiomara shook her head firmly. "I need time to forgive you. I can't just give myself to you again."

"I understand." He looked at his feet.

"It's not like I don't love you," she whispered, bringing herself into his space and touching the toes of her mukluks to his. "You should get home. You'll catch a cold out here dressed like this." Her voice was louder this time, the tears finally stopping. She stroked over his flannel shirt, the shiver of his skin unrelated to the cold.

Calehan wiped his face with the back of his sleeve. "Xo." He reached for her hand.

She went to him. Their kiss was messy, all teeth and squished noses, the salt of their tears reminding them this was not a reunion kiss. Calehan held her to him, squeezing the air from her lungs. He cradled the back of her head, holding her mouth against his. "I love you." His whisper slid over her tongue and settled into her spirit. Etching itself into her forever.

Xiomara broke the kiss first. Eyes closed, she rested her forehead against his. The wind blew, bringing a shiver through her as her teeth began to chatter. Calehan smiled, pressing a kiss of devotion to her forehead, tucking her beneath his chin to hold her close. Her nose was ice cold between the buttons of his shirt. Calehan kept her hand in his until they reached his truck. Kissing her palms, he held them close to his face. How was she going to survive being without him?

"You should really get warm." Xiomara eyed his pinking face.

"I will." Calehan nodded, but she knew he didn't hear her.

Xiomara willed herself to hold her tears, the car just barely starting to roll forward.

Don't cry. Don't cry. Don't cry.

The truck disappeared around the bend, sunlight flashing off the metal between trees until he was gone. A valley cracked through her heart when she let her sobs out, hoping he was far enough he couldn't hear it.

JANUARY

Muskwa found her on Calehan's porch, her face wet with tears. He didn't speak when he joined her, settling so gently onto the seat she almost couldn't feel him beside her. It was as though he floated above her shoulder, more like a visiting spirit than a living person.

"I'm too late."

"Daughter, you are right on time." Muskwa kept his eyes trained on the sky, peace etched into his face. Xiomara followed his eyeline to the tops of the trees.

Ravens.

Her favorite.

"My son will not love another the way he loves you." Muskwa watched the ravens fly in the winter sunshine, blue sky devoid of clouds. "He would wait for eternity if he knew you would be at the end."

Xiomara would've cried again if she hadn't been severely dehydrated.

"I had a fiancé." Her tongue was dry in her mouth. "He died."

Muskwa nodded, taking her hand in both of his.

"Do not wait for happiness in the afterlife." Muskwa looked at her then, Calehan's brown eyes staring back at her. "I had my happiness for twenty years, and I let her go." Xiomara was confused. Calehan's mom had died in childbirth. How had Muskwa let that happen?

"Hózhó was fearless, a force to be reckoned with." Hózhó. The beauty and balance of their family. "That's where my children get all their hardheadedness. She had more love to give than anyone in the world. It was her superpower. We lost a child once, before we had the twins." Muskwa kept his eyes trained on the ravens, watching while they painted the sky with purple black wings. "She spent thirteen years chasing that spirit, hoping she would feel them again in another child. I was blind to it; I saw her pain as love, and I wasn't the husband I should've been." Guilt swam in the brown pools of his eyes.

Xiomara had to look away. She joined him in watching the ravens.

"When Joy was born, they had offered to sterilize her. I thought she was angry on account of the history, you know. But now I know what it really was. Nataani was born during an eclipse, and she had been so certain that the spirit world would finally return our child to us." He breathed heavily, the pain evident in his voice. "After Nataani was born, she refused to deliver the placenta. I told you she was stubborn—more stubborn than anyone I've ever met. We tried everything, but eventually the doctors grew angry, wrote her off as another crazy Indian. I took her home, and she died in my arms." Muskwa's breath swirled in the air. "My wife's pain was so great that she left eight people behind in search of the one she had lost."

Xiomara looked at her feet.

"Don't make me watch you die, too." He squeezed her hand and stood. Kissing her forehead, he went down the stairs slowly, wary of the slip of fresh snow.

"You have a key to this house." Muskwa turned to look at her from the bottom of the stairs. "It's your house too."

Fresh tears found a way to form at his words.

Xiomara went to her borrowed car, fishing through her purse for a key ring. Xiomara never bothered to ask Calehan about the extra key, always distracted by other things. Her heartbeat rang in her ears as she inserted the key, half expecting the lock to no longer turn.

The door clicked open.

A deep breath filled her lungs in surprise. The scent of sweetgrass and tobacco overwhelmed her. More tears found their way to life. Xiomara squeezed her eyes shut, conjuring a memory of Calehan waiting for her in this same doorway, holding her to his chest. No one warned her the pain of walking away would physically hurt. It ached in her bones, scraped over her skin, and rang in her ears. His absence consumed her.

Forcing herself to the present, she stepped inside.

A new photo hung on the fridge, tucked between graduation photos and Frankie's regalia images. Xiomara gently removed the magnet holding the photo. She had never seen it before.

Xiomara was flat on the ground, teeth shining with laughter. Juniper was next to her, their arms wrapped around each other. Joy was between their hips, a genuine smile on her face, eyes closed with squished cheeks. Rosebud was upside down, her head on the other side of Xiomara, blue hair fanned out all around them, Kate wearing a lock over her head like bangs.

It was the sleepover they had all those months ago. Calehan's adoration for her was on his fridge, polaroids of her and Anubis across the magnetic surface.

She wanted to scream.

Giving up had been a mistake.

She should've asked him to wait. He offered to wait for her. Why had she denied him? Was it foolish to ask if he was still waiting for her?

Xiomara could feel Calehan here. His home wrapped her up in love, her clothes folded neatly in his bedroom dresser, her favorite comal tucked away on the back burner of his stove. Avocados were stuffed into his fridge, a lucky and pricey order he had negotiated with Ashley months ago. They had been delivered before.

Before she left him.

Crumbling to the floor in the center of his kitchen, Xiomara let herself cry.

deer bone →

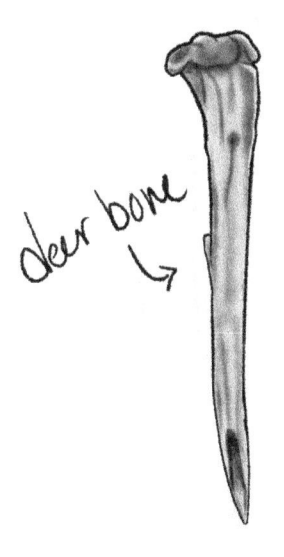

Chapter 21

"Good morning, prima." Chief Thomas peered brightly at Xiomara and set a steaming hot coffee on her desk. "How are we looking?"

"Pretty good." Xiomara smelled the coffee, noting the hint of cinnamon mixed in. "I've got a couple artifacts to bring up here, but other than that..." she trailed off, unsure how to end this statement. She stared out the window, the white buds of the cherry blossom tree moving in the spring breeze.

"And the field school?" Chief Thomas settled into the chair in front of her, relaxed as he sipped his coffee.

"I've been thinking about that, actually." Xiomara took a deep breath, hopeful that her confidence would be enough to sell him. "I'd like to design the curriculum remotely, and have David and Rosebud lead it here, on the ground. I would fly in quarterly, to check on things, of course. But I think this would be great for them. They're ready."

"Are you sure?" Chief Thomas raised an eyebrow at her. Since discovering their family connection, their relationship had settled easily into one of friendship and she found herself trusting him like she would a brother.

"One thousand percent."

Chief Thomas nodded. "When's your flight?"

"Saturday." Xiomara bit her lip to hold back her smile.

"Need a ride?"

Spain

The air was dry in Spain. It's one of his least favorite things about his new home. Calehan missed the humidity of Bunchberry—the kind that sank into his skin, keeping him hydrated even when he was working all day.

It was different here. He chugged water like a fish. Water was always bottled here, and he constantly forgot to purchase it, drinking from the tap even though he shouldn't.

Calehan had never hated the desert, but he hated this one. He hated how it reminded him constantly of his desert woman. His sun-holding lizard. His house of dawn. He yearned for her all day, every day with the dryness a constant pull of memories.

Shaking his head, he focused his eyes on the paperwork in his hands. Taking notes, he wove around the wooden studs, light flashing in and out of his eyes. A woman stood at the far end of the construction site, watching them work.

Calehan furrowed his brow. He had to be seeing things.

Weaving closer, Calehan reached the edge of the unfinished building. Between the studs and rebar, he thought he could see Xiomara standing off in the dirt, wearing a white hupile. He closed his eyes and rubbed his hands over his face, attempting to dislodge her figure from his mind. Calehan hadn't heard from her since that December morning. He was looking for sunglasses when one of his workers approached.

"Oye, jefe, ¿quién es la mujer?" Lucas gestured in front of them.

Calehan could feel his heart swelling in hope, threatening to break through his ribs and out of his chest, straight into Xiomara's hands. It couldn't be.

It couldn't be.

The woman waved at him, pink palm out.

It was.

Calehan strode as quickly as his long legs could carry him. His workers whistled as they watched him stalk over, standing proudly as she awaited him. Thumping through the dirt, his thick-soled work boots gave him a near two extra inches of height. Calehan towered over Xiomara as he reached her.

Calehan stopped centimeters from her chest, so close that he needed to peer straight down to look her in the eye. Xiomara took a step closer.

"Am I too late?"

His mouth was on hers before she was finished.

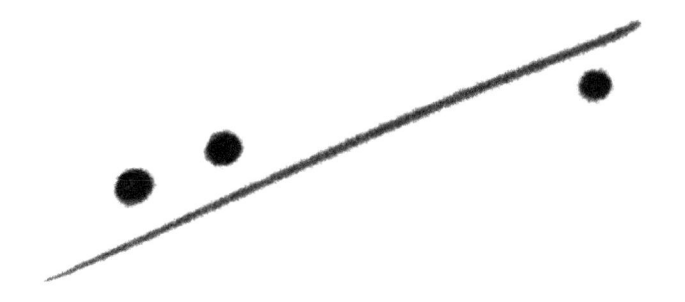

EPILOGUE

"Why didn't the Indians fight back harder?"

"What else could they have done?" Xiomara leaned against her desk.

"Raised an army or something."

"They did. But what good is an army against smallpox?" she continued. "What good is an army that is starving because the buffalo have been killed off? *56 million* Indigenous people gave their lives in the fight for our survival. How many more souls needed to be stolen?" Xiomara let the class sit in silence. She could feel the unease vibrating through the room. "Class dismissed. Don't forget about your AIM reports. They are due next week."

A lone seat remained filled, the hulking figure shrouded in the shadow of a back corner. The figure stood.

"Did you have a question?" Xiomara asked, crossing her ankles in front of the desk.

"Yes." He loomed over her, broad shoulders caging her into the desk. "Do I get extra credit for sleeping with the professor?"

Xiomara threw her head back and laughed, her chest quivering in time with each giggle. Calehan nuzzled into her neck, pushing the braid off her shoulder.

"I offer a multitude of extra credit opportunities," Xiomara breathed lowly in his ear. "Sleeping with the professor is certainly a viable independent study."

"God, I love you." Calehan stood tall and kissed her languidly.

They pushed through the double doors hand in hand, Calehan shouldering her weighty computer bag.

"Buffy said she finally booked a flight." Xiomara watched his serene face while the sky pinked around them.

"About time." Calehan scoffed. "Let's go home this way." Taking her hand in his, he guided her down a narrow street between two buildings.

The alley had a gentle incline as they walked farther from the ocean. Reaching the light at the end of the street, they came out into a small square at the back of three small buildings. Xiomara could smell it instantly. She turned wide eyes to Calehan.

"Is that?"

"It is."

Xiomara squealed and hugged Calehan, squeezing him with gratitude. She stole the breath from his chest with her embrace, nearly lifting him from his feet despite being half his size.

Calehan had improved his Spanish greatly over the last few months, but he still deferred to Xiomara for most conversations. In this case, he couldn't follow along with their rapid Mexican Spanish. The Castilian was easier even with the lisp, but for his Apache woman, Indigenous slang permeated their Spanish and kept it distant from the colonizer's language.

While they waited for their elotes, Calehan held her to his front. "Take me to Mexico, mi amor." He nosed the skin behind her ear. "Show me the land that gave me the greatest love of my life."

They finished their elotes talking story with the maker. Calehan watched with a smile as he saw refreshment from her community visibly sinking into her skin.

Calehan gazed at his berry-picker. Interrupted by a small crowd of international students, Calehan led her home. He brought her a glass of wine on the balcony, scratching Anubis along his sparsely haired chin.

Xiomara turned as she took the glass from him, facing him in the twilight city sky.

Stepping closer, Calehan slid his arms around her waist, crossing them on the railing behind her back. "You going to let me marry you yet?"

"I'm considering it."

"You wear the ring." Calehan nodded to the gold band clinking against her wine glass. "Sign the paper with me."

"I belong to you, Calehan Yellowbird." Xiomara traced his strong nose, trailing her fingers across his wide lips. "Regardless of what the paperwork says." Winding her arm around his neck, she let her lips linger against his while she spoke. "Haven't we done enough ceremony together to be bound in the old ways?"

Calehan threw his head back in a laugh. If only it were that simple. "Not in the slightest, my love." He took the wineglass from her hand, inspecting the gold ring on her finger. "I'll wait forever, if that's how long it takes." Calehan kissed the finger at the knuckle where her ring sat. "I'll marry you in the afterlife, where you can't escape it."

"How about the next snow?" Xiomara eyed him, waiting for his response.

"It's already snowing in Bunchberry." Calehan kissed her again, forgiving the unfortunately bad joke.

"Not that snow." Xiomara glared in jest. "When the mountains outside my home blanket in white, I want to marry you there. Where the two of us meet, the summer and the winter."

"Where the two of us meet." Calehan grinned, stretching his lips wider when Xiomara mirrored him.

Anubis fell asleep while his parents danced until morning, matching gold bands gleaming on their fingers in the red sunrise.

Acknowledgments

I wrote this book on a whim, out of a deep seated desire to read light and fluffy romances with characters like myself. I am still in shock that I finished the book, much less that I am here now writing the acknowledgements.

First, I have to give an enormous and monumental thank you to my friends and family who read the first, second, and eighth drafts. You are the only reason I finished this book. Thank you for being a constant cheerleader while meaningfully critiquing my work and pushing me to be better. Karime, Paz, Robin, Nancy, Lindsay and Tasha all read the first draft and had a hand in bringing *Lizards Hold the Sun* to the finished product we have today. Karime never pulled any punches or bit her tongue when it came to critiques. For that, I will be forever grateful. Robin finished the final draft while in labor and wrote my editing letter right before welcoming baby to our world. I consider both of you to be some of my harshest critics and I trust your opinion more than myself. I hope you had fun, because I'm going to need you both for the rest of my life. Nancy and Paz caught (most) of my Spanglish errors and kept me going with their excitement and willingness to be involved in every aspect of *Lizards* from start to finish. Tasha taught me about Canadian loonies, and provided a wonderful perspective different from all the rest of us. Your notes created some of the largest changes. Lindsay is my soulmate who graciously came up with the saving grace of Xiomara and Kenny being distant cousins. Thank you for listening to me ramble and reading all seven thousand texts I sent you at 3 a.m. A huge thank you to my husband, who constantly checked in on the book, talked through scenes or scenarios, and is a nonstop factory of story pitches. My mom and grandma cried reading the first draft and I knew *Lizards* was a story worth telling. I love you all.

Thank you to my editors who reminded me that we never really stop learning grammar.

Lastly, I thank my ancestors. Thank you, for raising me, for guiding me, for inspiring me and loving me. This book is my love letter to all who came before us and all who will come after.

We will remain.

When Stars Have Teeth

Chapter 1

These meetings were really starting to get on her nerves. It felt like she was on exhibition, *See Modern Indian Struggles Today*! No matter what Buffy said, pain won grants. Not success. Buffy hated it, but more money meant more programming. So, she sold pain.

It made her feel dirty.

Setting her bag on her desk, Buffy removed her high heels, switching to a pair of black leather moccasins. Freeing her red hair from the bun at the nape of her neck, she attempted to massage the tension from her muscles. Alcatraz Island loomed outside her window, a constant reminder of why she did this job.

Inhaling through her nose, Buffy forced the air out slowly through her mouth. The people needed this money. As many resources as the center offered, there was always a demand for more. The housing initiative was on the slaughtering line, and she was determined to keep it from being cut. The unhoused population in San Francisco continued to grow with rising rent prices and Natives needed places to fall back on. This program *had* to happen.

Pinching the bridge of her nose, she breathed deeply again.

Time to get yourself together, Buffy.

Everything would work out. She always got what she wanted. This grant would be no different.

"Are you ready?" Veronica poked her head inside Buffy's open office door. "Everyone's lined up."

Buffy sprang from her chair and followed Veronica down to the ground floor. The gathering room was the entire expanse of their building thanks to the knocked down walls from when they first opened a decade ago. Now, the room was wide, plenty of space for community activities and events.

Tonight was an Elder's dinner, free hot meals for all of the older Natives in the city. It was the only evening event Buffy worked religiously. She was worried that at their advanced age, an Elder might disappear between one week and the next. It was for the same reason that Msukwa received a call every Tuesday afternoon, while she shopped for fish at the wharf. Her excuse was that she needed his advice on fish, but they both knew she missed him.

Buffy noted multiple new faces in the crowd tonight. She washed her hands and pulled on a pair of white latex gloves. The ladle handle was warm in her palm. Stirring the venison and mushroom stew, she spooned it onto plate after plate. Along with acorn bread and crispy oven-baked sage leaves, the meal celebrated local Indigenous food while providing hearty and healthy meals for their aging population.

A young man came through the line, free of grey hairs and deep wrinkles. Buffy narrowed her eyes. She hadn't seen this man before. His ink black hair was cropped short to his ears, thicker than a forest on his head. His blue flannel shirt hugged tight to his lean body, dark brown skin peeking from his sleeve.

Buffy spooned the stew into a bowl and placed it on his tray, "This for you?"

"For her," he pointed to an old woman seated alone at one of the tables. A cane hung on the back of her chair, long grey hair wound into a braid in the center of her back.

"You're new," Buffy said, watching him gather utensils.

"Santiago," he extended a hand towards her, black ink peeking from under the sleeve.

"Buffy," she waved a gloved hand at him, watching while he pulled back.

"Nice to meet you, Buffy." Santiago nodded at her and turned back towards the old woman.

Buffy watched him from the corner of her eye while she served the long line. Soon the seats were full and she couldn't find the stranger in the sea of Elders and their family members. She put her curiosity to the side, there were plenty of regulars that deserved her full attention.

She started with Mr. Norman, an old Tlingit man from Alaska. He had taken a fishing job in the bay one summer and never left. His children vacated the island for cheaper cities but Mr. Norman remained. Buffy had been trying to convince him to join the Elder Drum Circle but he was obstinate. This was only his third Elder dinner and she still found him silent more often than not.

"How's the stew?" Buffy approached the men seated at the table with Mr. Norman.

She garnered only appreciative grunts and stuffed-mouth mumblings. Buffy brought them all fresh water bottles before pulling a chair up beside Mr. Norman.

He eyed her warily, offering only a grunt at her cheery greeting.

"The drum circle is having a beginner's class next Wednesday," Buffy said. "Can I sign you up?"

"Will you ever stop asking me to?" Mr. Normal grumbled around a bite of acorn bread.

"Nope." Buffy smiled wide, "I'm stubborn."

"Like a bull." Mr. Norman ignored her and continued eating. "Fine. Can you get me a ride voucher so I can skip the bus?"

"I'll see what I can do," Buffy kissed his cheek and moved on to her next victim.

Santiago watched as she moved around the room. Buffy was tall, strength evident in the roundness of her shoulders. Her figure was full and Santiago guessed she was an athlete of some kind. She moved through the packed room easily, twisting and turning herself through open spaces between people and tables. Her smile stole the breath from his chest and he watched her intently, hoping for her to do it again.

"Santiago," his grandmother's voice pulled him from his thoughts. "Can you get me a tea?"

When he found the table again, the redheaded enigma was in his seat. Chatting animatedly with his grandmother, that big smile was hinged wide on her open mouth. Someone was blessing him today.

Santiago set the tea in front of his grandmother, grasping the back of her chair.

"Did you get a plate?" Buffy turned umber brown eyes on him, concern in her gaze.

"No," he shook his head, staring straight back at her.

"Family members are welcome once Elders are fed," she pointed back towards the food table. "You should get a plate."

"I don't need any," Santiago tried to dismiss her offer.

"We usually have leftovers," she narrowed her eyes at him. "It's your first visit, humor me and get a plate. Promise I'll be out of your seat by the time you come back."

"You're welcome to keep it," Santiago dragged his eyes over her seated figure, moccasins up to her dyed red eyebrows. She didn't grace him with a second glance, bringing his grandmother back into conversation again.

By the time he returned with a full plate, Buffy was gone.

"Abuela," Santiago took his seat, offering his plate to her. "Quieres mas?"

"No, estoy llena mijo," she patted his hand and watched as he devoured the food. "Te gusta?"

"Yeah," Santiago swallowed another bite of the venison stew, mushrooms catching on the roof of his mouth. "It's different, but good."

"The young lady was telling me about all of the events they have here," his grandmother's eyes were bright, her voice excited. "They even have a shuttle, so that I could come here during the day."

"Que bueno, aubelita," Santiago squeezed her hand, relief finally settling into his heart.

Santiago worried for his grandmother in her old age. Entering her eighties, his father had found her frail and malnourished last summer. With no family in the area and living in a rapidly gentrifying neighborhood, his grandmother had fallen into a depression. The demons pulled her into the darkness and withered away at her body, stealing her sun and energy.

Abuela Paulina was strong but stubborn as an ox. She had refused for months to see a doctor or even consider an antidepressant. It wasn't until Santiago quit his job and booked a flight that she was finally willing to see a professional. Santiago spent the first three months of his new life in San Francisco taking his grandmother to a myriad of appointments, watching as she blossomed once again.

Finding this Chicano Indian Center was the cherry on top. If Santiago was ever going to be able to move back to Colorado, he needed to find her a community. Surround her with a family that would keep her in the sunlight and remind her how much she could glow.

"There is a quilting session tomorrow night," Abuela turned wide brown eyes on him. "Can you drive me?"

"Por supuesto."

About the Author

Dani Trujillo is a fiction storyteller born of Pueblo and Mexican descent. The desert is her happy place and serves as inspiration for many of her works. She holds a Bachelor of Anthropology from the University of Hawai'i and a Master of Forensic Behavioral Science from Alliant International University. She currently resides on the East Coast with her husband, two spooky black cats, an elder chihuahua named after jeans, and the plethora of ghosts inhabiting her 1949 home.

Follow her on Instagram for a look behind the scenes: @dh.tujillo

Sign up to the monthly newsletter for early releases and bonus content: https://www.danihtrujillo.com/